Focus on Special Educational Needs

Oxford Key Concepts for the Language Classroom series

Focus on Assessment
Eunice Eunhee Jang

Focus on Content-Based Language Teaching
Patsy M. Lightbown

Focus on Grammar and Meaning
Luciana C. de Oliveira and Mary J. Schleppegrell

Focus on Learning Technologies
Nicky Hockly

Focus on Literacy
Danling Fu and Marylou M. Matoush

Focus on Oral Interaction
Rhonda Oliver and Jenefer Philp

Focus on Reading
Esther Geva and Gloria Ramírez

Focus on Special Educational Needs
Cristina Sánchez-López and Theresa Young

Focus on Special Educational Needs

Cristina Sánchez-López and Theresa Young

OXFORD
UNIVERSITY PRESS

OXFORD
UNIVERSITY PRESS

Great Clarendon Street, Oxford, OX2 6DP, United Kingdom

Oxford University Press is a department of the University of Oxford.
It furthers the University's objective of excellence in research, scholarship,
and education by publishing worldwide. Oxford is a registered trade
mark of Oxford University Press in the UK and in certain other countries

© Oxford University Press 2018

The moral rights of the author have been asserted

First published in 2018

2022 2021 2020 2019 2018

10 9 8 7 6 5 4 3 2 1

ISBN: 978 0 19 400087 1

Printed in China

This book is printed on paper from certified and well-managed sources

ACKNOWLEDGEMENTS

*The authors and publisher are grateful to those who have given permission to reproduce
the following extracts and adaptations of copyright material*: pp.14–15 Collaborative
Conversation by Cristina Youtsey. Reproduced by permission. p.17 'Sensory,
Graphic and Interactive Supports chart' from *Understanding the WIDA English
Language Proficiency Standards: A Resource Guide (2007)* www.wida.us. Reproduced
by permission. p.39 Figure 2.1 created by Angel Ardon. pp.120–122 'Improving
Science Vocabulary of High School English Language Learners With Reading
Disabilities' by Amanda L Helman, Mary Beth Calhoon and Lee Kern, *Learning
Disability Quarterly*, 38(1), 40–52, Sage Publications. pp.123–124 'Modified
Guided Reading: Gateway to English as a Second Language and Literacy
Learning' by Mary A Avalos, Alina Plasencia, Celina Chavez and Josefa Rascón,
The Reading Teacher, 61 (4) pp.318–329, DOI 1598/RT 61 4 4, John Wiley & Sons.
pp.85–88, 155–156 'Instructional conversations: Promoting comprehension
through discussion' by Claude Goldenberg, *The Reading Teacher*, 46(4), 316–326.
December 1992/January 1993. Republished with permission of John Wiley
& Sons Inc; permission conveyed through Copyright Clearance Center, Inc.
pp.79–80 'Becoming a reader and writer in a bilingual special education
classroom' by Nadeen T. Ruiz, Eleanor Vargas, Angélica Beltrán, *Language Arts*,
79, 297–309. Copyright © 2002 by the National Council of Teachers of English.
All rights reserved. Reproduced by permission.

*Although every effort has been made to trace and contact copyright holders before
publication, this has not been possible in some cases. We apologize for any apparent
infringement of copyright and if notified, the publisher will be pleased to rectify any
errors or omissions at the earliest opportunity.*

To our dear families who have supported us in so many ways during this process: Angel, Kirsten, Pop, Butch, and Mom. We love you!

Acknowledgments

In deep appreciation of all the children we have been blessed to know and work with—language learners, those experiencing challenges, and DLLsSEN, along with their amazing families—for all they have shared and taught us through our experiences with them over the years. Our students continue to instruct and inspire us!

We would like to thank the teachers and school administrators for the privilege of being invited into your classrooms and schools, and for your dedication to the students and families you serve. We appreciate partnering with colleagues who join us in embracing the diversity of all our students and their families—with all their complexity, creativity, and learning strengths and potential.

Thank you, Janette Klingner, for your commitment to educators and for all your contributions to the field and to the lives of so many students, families, teachers, and researchers. The world lost you too soon.

Thank you to our family and friends, who have adjusted their lives to accommodate our multi-year writing project. We could not have completed this work without your love, support, and understanding.

We are grateful for the skilled editing and clear guidance from our esteemed editors, Nina Spada and Patsy Lightbown, along with the editorial team at OUP, especially Sophie Rogers, Alexandra Paramour, and Sarah Finch, who have crafted and improved our work. Thanks also to Kim Scannell, who has supported our writing through her skilled sleuthing and sharing of research articles and books.

It was an honor to write this book together. May you find inspiration from our collaboration in your work with your students!

Contents

Series Editors' Preface

The Oxford Key Concepts for the Language Classroom series is designed to provide accessible information about research on topics that are important to second language teachers. Each volume focuses on a particular area of second/foreign language learning and teaching, covering both background research and classroom-based studies. The emphasis is on how knowing about this research can guide teachers in their instructional planning, pedagogical activities, and assessment of learners' progress.

The idea for the series was inspired by the book *How Languages are Learned*. Many colleagues have told us that they appreciate the way that book can be used either as part of a university teacher education program or in a professional development course for experienced teachers. They have commented on the value of publications that show teachers and future teachers how knowing about research on language learning and teaching can help them think about their own teaching principles and practices.

This series is oriented to the educational needs and abilities of school-aged children (5–18 years old), with distinct chapters focusing on research that is specific to primary- and secondary-level learners. The volumes are written for second language teachers, whether their students are minority language speakers learning the majority language or students learning a foreign language in a classroom far from the communities where the language is spoken. Some of the volumes will be useful to 'mainstream' teachers who have second language learners among their students, but have limited training in second/foreign language teaching. Some of the volumes will also be primarily for teachers of English, whereas others will be of interest to teachers of other languages as well.

The series includes volumes on topics that are key for second language teachers of school-age children, and each volume is written by authors whose research and teaching experience have focused on learners and teachers in this age group. While much has been written about some of these topics, most publications are either 'how to' methodology texts with no explicit link to research, or academic works that are designed for researchers and postgraduate students who require a thorough scholarly treatment of the research, rather than an overview and interpretation for classroom practice. Instructors in programs for teachers often find that the methodology texts lack the academic background appropriate for a university course and that the scholarly works are too long, too difficult, or not sufficiently classroom-oriented for the needs of teachers and future teachers. The volumes in this series are intended to bridge that gap.

The books are enriched by the inclusion of *Spotlight Studies* that represent important research and *Classroom Snapshots* that provide concrete examples of teaching/learning events in the second language classroom. In addition, through a variety of activities, readers will be able to integrate this information with their own experiences of learning and teaching.

Introduction

In this book, we will summarize theory, research, and evidence-based practices that pertain to **dual language learners (DLLs)** with **special educational needs (SEN)**. Our goal is to help teachers—for example, classroom, ESL, bilingual, special education, and reading specialists, along with instructional assistants—understand the unique needs of these children and adolescents so that they can design instruction to support their linguistic and academic development, address their specific learning strengths and needs, and affirm their identities as multicultural individuals. Related practitioners—for example, social workers, school counselors, speech-language pathologists, occupational therapists, and psychologists—may also find this volume relevant in engaging with these students, supporting their teachers, and participating with school teams.

Throughout the book, we will use the term 'dual language learners' (DLLs) to refer to a wide range of students who are in the process of developing two or more languages. We are aware that readers, particularly in North America, may be more familiar with the term '**English language learners**' (**ELLs**), also known as 'English learners' (ELs). Other terms that may be familiar include 'English as an additional language' (EAL) and 'limited English proficient' (LEP). '**English as a second language**' (**ESL**) has been used to refer to students, as well as educators, and to the language programs and services designed for them in an English context. We prefer the term 'DLLs' to acknowledge that all linguistic resources, not just English, are valuable in learning and life. We will use the term 'language of instruction' to refer to the language in which students primarily receive their education and/ or the language spoken in the larger community. In many of the examples presented in this volume, the language of instruction is English. However, we understand that in different classrooms, programs, and communities, this will not be the case. Another language may be the primary language of schools and public life in many countries and regions; and in many parts of the world, multiple languages are used regularly in daily life, education, and commerce. Although most of the classroom-based studies we include focus on students who are developing two languages, we will make note when the studies relate to multilingual students.

A key premise of this book is that the wide range of special educational needs that are observed among monolingual students are also found among DLLs. At the same time, it is important to note that SEN are conceptualized and described in a variety of ways around the world. In some settings, it is required that students are formally diagnosed as having disabilities to qualify for specialized services; in others, students can receive support as soon as difficulties arise. With the more recent trends towards supporting students in the general classroom, some school systems provide students with additional assistance without formal diagnosis as part of early intervention while discerning their learning needs.

This volume explores a growing body of classroom-based research pertaining to DLLsSEN who are diagnosed as having **learning disabilities (LD)**, **specific language impairment (SLI)**, and **reading disabilities**. Other terms to describe learning challenges that may be familiar include **specific learning disabilities (SLD)**, **primary language impairment (PLI)**, and **dyslexia**. In some contexts, students who have disabilities are also referred to as having **specific learning differences (SpLD)** (Kormos & Smith, 2012). We will endeavor to use the terminology that the educators, practitioners, and researchers have employed to describe the nature of the students' learning characteristics in the studies included in this volume. The heterogeneity found among students in terms of their wide-ranging strengths and learning needs will also be explored.

Educators who support DLLs with SEN (**DLLsSEN**) work in a variety of environments. Some teachers work alone in their classrooms, while others work collaboratively with other educators and professionals from various disciplines. In some settings, schools provide time to coordinate and plan instruction so that educators can co-teach to address the multifaceted needs of their students. In other settings, DLLsSEN are instructed in the same way as monolingual students with SEN, without consideration for their unique linguistic and cultural characteristics.

The foundational perspectives in this book are grounded in **culturally and linguistically responsive** theory, research, and practice that create accessible, relevant, and meaningful **learning environments**. 'Learning environments' include elements of the physical environment, methods, and strategies used to deliver instruction, and the culture and social-emotional climate, including attitudes and the nature of interactions, as well as the human and material resources that are present. Educators who work with DLLs need to deliver academic content in ways that make it comprehensible for them in the multiple learning contexts they participate in throughout their school day. Teachers are called upon to **differentiate** instruction for students who are at varying stages of developing English or other languages of instruction. A solid understanding of how students acquire additional languages allows educators to plan lessons and units of study that satisfy the academic language and literacy demands pertaining to different grades and content areas. Understanding and addressing these multiple dimensions of instruction for DLLs is complex. When DLLs also have SEN, planning instruction becomes even more complex. Further refinement is required to attend to the learning characteristics of individual students that are related to their special educational needs. Teachers serving DLLs who also have SEN need to learn about and strategically address each student's particular profile of strengths and needs.

Providing appropriate instruction and intervention for DLLsSEN is multifaceted. This is where the accumulating research that specifically focuses on DLLsSEN is critical to improving instructional practices that optimize their educational experience. The research, practices, examples, and resources highlighted in this book are classroom- and school-based and therefore directed primarily at classroom teachers, bilingual teachers, ESL teachers, reading specialists, and special education teachers for students aged 5 to 18. By reviewing intervention studies with individual students and small groups, this book also aims to inform practices that can support DLLsSEN across all learning environments and assist teachers in their conversations and collaboration with other school practitioners. We advocate for progressive approaches to special education that are based on theory and accumulating research as well as on insights from our own combined experience with classroom-based instruction and school-based intervention. We encourage educators to build upon their students' resources and assets in instruction and intervention. This is especially important for students who regularly experience challenges in school. Such a view urges us to reconceptualize DLLsSEN as learners whose linguistic and cultural experiences are advantages—educationally, socially, academically, and vocationally. Taking an **asset** or **strengths-based orientation**, educators focus on what students with SEN are able do, what they have accomplished, and the strategies they bring to the learning process, in order to support them as capable but different learners. The experiences and interests of DLLsSEN, like those of all learners, provide opportunities for engagement in instruction that can be leveraged to assist them with their areas of particular difficulty and to prepare them to capitalize on their strengths throughout their lives.

Another critical aspect of reconceptualizing the education of DLLsSEN is to view **second language** (**L2**) learning as a developmental process. When we look at language acquisition as a 'work in progress', as we naturally do for young monolingual **first language** (**L1**) learners, we notice and celebrate what children can do at each stage of their development. Likewise, for DLLs and DLLsSEN, when growth is perceived and acknowledged in positive ways, students are affirmed as they move through the natural evolution of language learning. In schools, however, children in the process of learning the language of instruction are often viewed as somehow 'problematic' until they become fully proficient in that language. This underlying but pervasive view of DLLs as having deficits until they function comparably to monolingual students can negatively influence all our interactions with them. To align with current understanding, we must challenge ourselves as professionals to revise our thinking and change our language to embody an asset-oriented, developmental perspective in our interactions with students, their families, and our colleagues.

1
Educating Language Learners with Special Educational Needs

Preview

In this chapter, we will describe the unique place that **dual language learners (DLLs)** who also have **special educational needs (SEN)** hold in schools. Their instructional and social-emotional needs must be understood and addressed by professionals from multiple perspectives. The fields of bilingualism, biliteracy, and multicultural education, as well as special education, can inform educators' practice (Baca, Baca, & de Valenzuela, 2004). There needs to be an overlapping space where professionals from each field can meet to blend their expertise and practices to educate dual language learners with special educational needs (**DLLsSEN**). Unfortunately, instruction and intervention from these different fields of specialization in education have not always merged to provide balanced, coordinated, cohesive, and comprehensive approaches that fully serve DLLsSEN. We will consider some historical challenges faced in educating DLLsSEN so that we can build upon the lessons of the past. We will provide opportunities for educators and practitioners to reflect on their current understanding and practices, and then summarize theory and research that offer guidance in optimizing **learning environments** for DLLsSEN.

Special Education and Dual Language Learners

Students, their families, and teachers may have strong affective responses to the concept of 'special education', based on a wide range of personal, familial, or professional experiences. Some may have had the positive personal experiences of benefiting from special educational services or witnessing growth in students who received support. Others may have had memorable teachers who met their instructional needs, resulting in engaging and successful school experiences. Teachers feel a strong attachment to students with whom they have developed positive relationships or whose special educational needs have been instructive to them professionally. They may have connections with students whose learning needs were especially challenging to meet in the context of limited resources and/or an unresponsive educational system.

Reactions to special education can also carry negative emotions based on personal experiences with learning challenges in school. Responses may be related to the stigma associated with receiving special educational services or supports. Students and their families may bear the weight of these negative perceptions and experiences long after the students have completed their schooling. Parents (and other caregivers) themselves may have received or been denied access to special educational services in an earlier era. Navigating complex support systems to obtain services or to ensure that services are meeting their children's needs across the grades can become discouraging, and they may experience frustration when they attend meetings where the school staff focus on what their children cannot do without acknowledging their strengths, unique gifts, or abilities. Families can feel alienated when the professional terminology that is used to share information is not explained or translated.

Educators practicing in **culturally and linguistically responsive** systems focus on each student as a unique learner, bringing forward students' strengths to uncover their learning potential in their areas of need. Culturally and linguistically responsive practitioners partner with students and their families in interactions that start with an **asset** or **strengths-based orientation** and the mutual expectation that they will learn from one another as they work together. Cultural reciprocity in special education refers to a process by which educators and other service providers recognize, examine, and explain their own cultural perspectives, taking time also to listen to and value the perspectives of the students and families they serve. School personnel need to work collaboratively with families to provide services that explore, acknowledge, and respect families' value systems, knowledge, and experiences (Kalyanpur & Harry, 2012).

Unfortunately, DLLs' experience with special education has been fraught with a troubling history of misidentification and ineffective services. Artiles, Trent, and Palmer (2004), Harry and Klingner (2006, 2007), and Valencia (2010) provide thorough reviews of the complex historical, social, and cultural factors that have contributed to the development of special educational systems for DLLs in North America. Special education emerged in the US as school populations were becoming increasingly diverse. It evolved as a subsystem within the larger educational system to provide different programs and services in separate classrooms for students who did not appear to learn in the same ways as the larger group. Diverse learners, including DLLs, were compared to the monolingual monocultural English-speaking students perceived as 'the norm'. When differences in performance were found, these were assumed to be due to disabilities inherent in the child. Learning environments, resources, books, and teaching approaches had been designed with monolingual monocultural English-speaking students in mind. Tests and assessments were also based on this model of homogeneous learners, and the process of identification based on standardized measures did not account for the possibility that the challenges experienced by students were caused by the lack of **opportunity to learn** (Gee, 2008) rather than by disabilities. When instruction did not consider the needs of students who were acquiring a new language while also learning content, DLLs did not have full access to the curriculum. The difficulties were typically attributed to the students having an intrinsic deficit of some sort. It was seldom considered that learning differences were related to educational systems that failed to adapt instruction to learners who were in the process of learning a new language. Although content was being delivered, these students were often unsuccessful when instruction did not also take their stage of language development into account. Nor was it always recognized that the learning challenges experienced by many DLLs could be related to mismatches between the existing monolingual monocultural curriculum and the different life experiences of linguistically and culturally diverse students.

When DLLs experience difficulties in school, discussions among educators often begin with a dichotomy: 'Are the student's difficulties related to learning another language or to a disability?' 'Is it a language or a learning issue?' Consequently, students are often viewed from only one of these perspectives, as either DLLs or students with SEN, without acknowledgment that these learning characteristics can coexist within individuals. The organization of school systems and funding that compartmentalizes programs and services further contributes to this either/or thinking, as educators seek to qualify students for the most effective program to meet their needs. We strongly advocate for reframing these initial questions as: 'Does this student who is experiencing challenges and in the process of learning two languages also demonstrate behaviors or characteristics that indicate the presence of a disability?' This acknowledges that DLLs continue to develop their language skills and require instructional support, even when they are also found to have a disability (Sánchez-López & Young, 2008; Young & Sánchez-López, 2017).

Before we look in more depth at how schools can best meet the needs of DLLsSEN, take a moment to reflect on what you think about the education of DLLsSEN in Activity 1.1.

Activity 1.1

The statements below represent views that some people hold about the education of DLLsSEN. Read each statement and check one of the columns to indicate how much you agree or disagree with it.

SA = Strongly Agree   A = Agree   D = Disagree   SD = Strongly Disagree

	SA	A	D	SD
1 It is important to start with the students' strengths in planning and implementing instruction and intervention for DLLsSEN.				
2 Once a DLL has been diagnosed with a SEN, it would be better to focus on learning one language.				
3 DLLsSEN benefit from instruction and intervention that build on their cultural backgrounds as resources.				
4 If DLLs are experiencing academic challenges, then special education is the most direct avenue to addressing their needs.				
5 Instruction and interventions developed for monolingual students are effective for DLLsSEN.				
6 Instructional approaches that focus primarily on mastering discrete skills are optimal for DLLsSEN.				
7 The development of oral language is integral to learning for DLLsSEN.				
8 Emphasizing comprehension during reading instruction beginning in the early grades benefits DLLsSEN.				
9 Educators and practitioners can support the **home languages** of DLLsSEN, even when they do not speak these languages.				
10 DLLsSEN benefit from instruction provided by educators who understand DLL pedagogy and have knowledge of special educational practices.				

Reflecting the complexity of instructing DLLsSEN, the statements listed above represent issues that frequently arise in discussions among educators on this topic. While considering these statements, you may have thought to yourself: 'Well, that's what I've heard'; 'It depends, doesn't it?'; 'I wonder what other teachers and schools do'; 'That has been my experience'; 'I'm not sure'; or 'I hadn't thought about this'. These are all reasonable responses and a good basis for exploring the challenges of providing the best educational opportunities for DLLsSEN. After reflecting on your own responses, discuss these statements with other educators. Ask colleagues from different professional backgrounds what they think. The discussions that arise may form the beginning of further collaborative conversations that can be instrumental in developing instruction and intervention for DLLsSEN. In the chapters that follow, we will present theory and research addressing each of these statements, before returning to them in Chapter 5.

Collaborating to Meet the Needs of DLLsSEN

As mentioned earlier in the chapter, collaboration is key to meeting the needs of DLLsSEN. Professionals in **English as a second language** (ESL) or bilingual education need to come together with those in special education and related services to support the education of DLLsSEN (Baca et al., 2004). To address students' learning strengths and needs in a comprehensive way, the pedagogy and practices of each field need to be merged to inform the other. One perspective cannot override or exclude another. It is imperative that special education teachers and practitioners refer to the research base on **second language** (L2) instruction and intervention for DLLs. This contrasts with the frequent assumption that the evidence base for monolingual students with disabilities provides entirely sufficient and effective guidance for teaching DLLsSEN (Ruiz, 2012). It is also vital that ESL/bilingual educators coordinate and collaborate with their colleagues in special education to understand the specific and unique ways that SEN manifest for individual students. Instructional approaches need to be informed and guided by the knowledge, skills, and perspectives of educators and practitioners that represent the learning characteristics of both dual language learning and special educational needs. The goal of providing effective and comprehensive education for DLLsSEN is achievable when services are derived from these multiple perspectives and coordinated, with the central focus on the learner.

Collaborative practice among educators from both ESL/bilingual and special education can comprehensively address the instructional needs of DLLsSEN. Without this coordination of programming, students are often pulled in different directions such that their needs are not wholly met in any one academic setting. This leaves students with daily instruction and programming that is often compartmentalized, fragmented, and disjointed (Delgado, 2010; Harry & Klingner, 2006). When professionals work collaboratively to plan and implement culturally and linguistically responsive approaches, DLLsSEN benefit from more integrated, cohesive, and comprehensive pedagogy. By coming together from the outset, educators can address students' linguistic, literacy, and content area objectives, as well as their individual learning characteristics, throughout all their school learning environments.

Classroom Snapshot 1.1 features a conversation between an ESL teacher and a special education teacher who were asked to work together to support the DLLs with SEN on their grade-level team. The school provided a time and place for the two teachers to learn about the students and each other in order to collaboratively plan units of study that they would implement throughout the school year. The sixth-grade team had approximately 85 students. Thirty-four students were DLLs and of those students, eight were DLLsSEN. There were five teachers in total on the team: three were monolingual English speakers and two were bilingual Spanish–English educators, one with specialized training and experience in teaching students with special educational needs. All five teachers worked together to include and teach all the students.

The classroom teachers, ESL teachers, and special education teachers began by planning their units of study together, with the mutual goal of making the instruction accessible and interesting for all their students. They reviewed the curriculum maps for science, history, language arts, and mathematics, as well as the academic and language development standards used in their school district. It was important to the teachers that all their students received equitable access to the grade-level content, skills, and academic language. They developed their units of study by taking special care to anchor instruction in contexts they believed would be meaningful and relevant to their students. For example, they included the early civilizations of the Americas in a history unit on ancient civilizations since many of their students' ancestors were from Central and South America. In science, the teachers studied ancient recipes for dye-making during a chemistry unit after learning that some students' families had used these natural dyes when they wove tapestries in their villages. The teachers developed a good professional relationship as they interacted to develop culturally and linguistically responsive instruction for all their students.

Classroom Snapshot 1.1

This conversation is adapted from an interaction that took place between the ESL and special education (SE) teachers as they planned a lesson.

SE teacher: I think I'll do a preview with my students using this visual before we do the whole-group activity.

ESL teacher: [puzzled] I'll be doing a whole-group preview using the visual prompt we'd already agreed on. I'll present it in Spanish. Is that your concern? Would you like to lead that activity? I don't mind.

SE teacher: We agreed you'd lead the introductory activity. It's OK. I still want to do preview activities with a small group related to the content before you present the lesson for the larger group.

ESL teacher: What specifically do the students need that I could support in the larger group? What are their specific learning needs?

SE teacher: All the students are enjoying the lessons we've planned for them! What's different is that students with disabilities find it challenging to immediately apply something they've just learned. What I've noticed in our lessons is that our typically developing bilingual students are able to understand new content in this very visual and engaging way—right away, it seems. The bilingual students with disabilities also benefit from all the visuals and **scaffolds** that we both use but need more opportunities to practice.

ESL teacher: I see what you're saying. I'd noticed that in the last lesson. Plus, the small group and one-on-one activities you're doing connect to the lesson but will show different examples.

SE teacher: That's right! It's important to provide our students who have disabilities with more opportunities to talk through and interact with different examples before extending what they've learned to new material. I should have said something before, but these are things I think about so automatically for students with disabilities. I hadn't ever had the opportunity to talk so specifically with a colleague about their needs before.

ESL teacher: Are there more things like this you can share? I really need to learn more about what's especially challenging for our students with disabilities. ◼

In this conversation, the teachers discussed how some of the DLLsSEN had significant challenges comprehending auditory information in both of their languages. Such challenges contributed to difficulties that these students experienced in fully understanding lessons and immediately applying new information or skills. The special education teacher built in additional opportunities for students to interact orally with the content in a small-group setting before the larger group did a concept-based preview activity together. The teacher with special education training readily incorporated learning strategies based on language learning pedagogy into her instructional approach—for example, visual prompts, graphic organizers, oral language practice, modeling, and shared writing. As the unique learning needs of the DLLsSEN became more apparent, she intensified the use of the strategies, first in a smaller group and even individually when needed. This also served to provide ample practice in multiple contexts for the students. This teacher further mediated by scaffolding individual students' systematic use of graphic organizers before reading, during reading, and in preparation for writing. Students with SEN often require additional modeling and extended opportunities for shared and guided practice as they build and maximize their independence in applying new learning. Doing so offers DLLsSEN added experience with the concepts and learning strategies in both languages. Enhancing the students' use and understanding of strategies in smaller groups may help to build confidence and reduce stress during the subsequent lesson with the whole class. As these teachers continued to collaborate, they integrated additional scaffolds, supports, examples, varied and fluid groupings, and other components into their units for the wide range of learners in their classrooms, including DLLsSEN.

In Classroom Snapshot 1.1, the educators demonstrated a commitment to sharing responsibility for the education of DLLsSEN (García & Ortiz, 2006; Hunt, Hirose-Hatae, Doering, Karasoff, & Goetz, 2000). The school administration made it a priority for educators to systematically consult with their colleagues across various disciplines by creating time and space in their schedules for collaboration (Delgado, 2010; Hoover, Eppolito, Klingner, & Baca, 2012; Zehler, Fleischman, Hopstock, Pendzick, & Stephenson, 2003). With regularly scheduled opportunities, teachers can share specific knowledge about strategies that have been effective for individual students. Time to attend professional development that reaches beyond their areas of specialization facilitates cross-disciplinary knowledge and insights while extending and refining instructional approaches (Delgado, 2010; Hickman, 2004).

Activity 1.2

Reflect on the following questions:

- What professional learning communities are you currently participating in?
- Who in your school or district could you collaborate with that represents a different professional perspective?
- What online learning communities could you join to collaborate with colleagues from different professional backgrounds?
- Where have you been able to share your professional perspective on DLLsSEN with others?

Generate a list of questions that you have about DLLsSEN from your own perspective. Begin a collaborative conversation with an educator or colleague from another professional background or area of specialization. Explore possible answers together, using your own experience and what you learned during professional learning opportunities.

 the

:

Culturally and Linguistically Responsive Practice

Becoming culturally and linguistically responsive means that educators integrate learners' languages, backgrounds, experiences, and **funds of knowledge** (González, Moll, & Amanti, 2006; Moll, Amanti, Neff, & González, 1992) into the curriculum, instruction, and assessment (Klingner, Boelé, Linan-Thompson, & Rodriguez, 2014). Characteristics of culturally and linguistically responsive teaching include: positive perspectives towards students' families; communication of high expectations; learning within the context of culture; student-centered instruction; a reshaping of the curriculum; and teacher as facilitator (Trumbull & Pacheco, 2005).

From this perspective, all learners are cultural beings and diversity among students is a valued asset in the classroom (Klingner & Edwards, 2006). It is vital that students see themselves throughout their experiences at school—in the stories and literature that are studied, the way classrooms are organized, the images that are shown. In culturally and linguistically responsive inclusive learning environments, students' strengths, talents, gifts, and abilities are acknowledged, explored, celebrated, and employed in learning. Educators and administrators invest time in learning about their students' languages, life experiences, and family stories. Incorporating this knowledge and these perspectives into a supportive learning environment affirms students' multilingual and multicultural identities and makes learning more engaging, relevant, and meaningful to them (Banks, 2005; Cummins, 1994; Gay, 2000; Ladson-Billings, 2006).

Classroom Snapshot 1.2 provides an example of culturally and linguistically responsive lesson planning. An instructional coach was invited to model a lesson for teachers on how to make English language arts content more comprehensible to DLLs in a diverse sixth-grade inclusive classroom. The teachers had specifically mentioned how difficult it was for their students to make inferences when reading English texts, so the coach chose this topic as the focus of the lesson. Another goal the teachers were focusing on was how to reflect their students' experiences and backgrounds to make lessons more relevant for them.

The students in this classroom all spoke English as an L2; they came from a variety of home language backgrounds and were at different stages of English development. There were typically developing DLLs in the class, as well as students with **language impairment** and **reading disabilities**, and one student with a significant behavioral disorder. This student was accommodated by being seated by the door in case he felt the need to step out or go to see the school social worker.

To plan the model lesson, the coach asked the teachers to tell her about their students. The next day, she received a list of test scores and other academic achievement information for each student. The coach realized that she had not communicated precisely what kind of information she sought. She wrote back, apologized for not being clear, and asked the teachers to describe their students' languages, interests, hobbies, travel experiences, talents, and any other relevant and unique information. That same day, the teachers responded with a very well-organized document detailing each student's hobbies, travel experiences, interests, and frequent topics of conversation. The teachers apologized for not sending this document initially, explaining that they had never been asked for this kind of descriptive information about their students. Clearly, these teachers had invested time in getting to know their students and were happy to share this experiential and personal information with the coach. The coach would model the lesson in one teacher's classroom while the others observed.

For the lesson, the coach gathered images, photographs, and graphics that allowed her to introduce the idea of making inferences conceptually. This made the content more readily comprehensible to DLLs than might have been the case if instruction had started with a lecture and been followed by students reading an English text. The coach made certain to select images that reflected the students' experiences, interests, and hobbies.

Classroom Snapshot 1.2

The classroom teacher thought about how she would strategically partner the students for the lesson. She told the coach that she wanted students who had similar English proficiency levels and shared the same interests to work together, so the desks were arranged in pairs throughout the room.

On the day of the lesson, the coach began by explaining to the students that an inference is an educated guess based on evidence combined with a **schema**—what a person already knows. She had made a poster with a photograph of students working at a computer together. Under the photograph, she had written the following 'formula':

evidence + schema (what you already know) = inference

The students (and the teachers sitting in on the lesson) learned how to say the words 'guess' and 'infer' in English and in all of the students' languages, as well as practicing orally with sentence starters, which were also written on the poster:

The evidence shows that _____ . I already know _____ .
Therefore, I can infer _____ .

The coach explained that they were first going to practice making inferences using photographs, before applying this skill to English texts.

The coach projected a large photograph of two students—of similar cultural background and age to those in the class—working on a computer together. She asked the students to talk with their partners in their home languages about what they saw in the photograph, i.e. evidence. The students then shared their observations and the coach listed their answers on a chart in the 'Evidence' column: 'two students', 'students sitting close to the computers and smiling', 'desks', 'a computer', etc.

Then the students were asked what they already knew about this evidence, i.e. their schema. They said that since the students in the photograph were dressed the same, they might be wearing school uniforms. They also said that they knew young people liked working with computers and that the kinds of desks in the photograph were often found in schools and libraries. These answers were listed in the 'Schema' column of the chart. Finally, the students were asked to talk with one another about what they could infer based on the evidence and their schema. They shared very reasonable inferences, such as: 'students are working on a school project'; 'they are working on social media'; 'students are playing a game together'.

The next step was for students to practice the same process more independently in pairs, with a photograph assigned to them. The teacher had marked the back of all the photographs with the initials of the student pairs so that they would correspond to their interests and experiences. Each pair completed a chart for their photograph, listing evidence, schema, and inferences. Then they had to write down their thoughts and practice reading their sentences out to one another. The teachers observed how engaged all their students were in understanding the concept of making inferences using the photographs that reflected their backgrounds and interests.

One group especially impressed the teachers. The boy who experienced difficulties with his behavior was partnered with a very calm and shy student. When they got to the schema part, the shy student began to talk in depth about what he knew about the topic in the photograph. The other student turned to him and replied, 'Dude, how do you know so much about fighting fires? 'The shy student turned to him and replied, 'That's what I do every summer with my uncles. We travel to Guatemala and volunteer to fight fires in mountains, just like these guys in the picture!' Both appeared very interested in the topic.

The final part of the lesson required the students to apply their 'formula' with short texts that the coach projected onto the large screen. They worked together with their partners to look for the evidence in the short passages, talk about what they already knew, and then make inferences. At the end of the lesson, they completed a piece of shared writing with the coach to describe the process they had followed to make inferences, before adding this summary to their learning logs. The coach had extra photographs and other pieces of homework at the end of the lesson and asked if anyone wanted to take them home to complete over the weekend. All the students raised their hands! ■

Classroom Snapshot 1.2 illustrates how engaged all the students were when their experiential knowledge and interests as well as their languages were integrated into the lesson. The teachers had already invested time in learning about their students and they were excited to talk about how this information could be incorporated directly into various lessons across content areas and other units of study. They noted how culturally and linguistically responsive instruction benefited all their DLLs. The teachers noticed that the DLLsSEN with language impairment and reading disabilities, as well as the student with behavioral challenges, were engaged when the activity started with an image rather than text. Throughout the lesson, DLLsSEN remained engaged as they saw themselves reflected in many of the images and topics selected as the vehicle for developing the concept of inferencing. Instead of a generic lesson, this was a lesson created for them that was about them. The teachers noted all the supports and scaffolds that were built into the lesson to allow their students opportunities to understand the content and participate in the activities. Working with partners gave students the opportunity to discuss and refine their ideas before sharing them with the whole class. This was especially important for two of the students who had difficulties with expressive language. As part of their reflection, the teachers and coach made an inventory of all the strategies, scaffolds, and supports that were embedded into the lesson to make the language accessible for the students. These are listed in Figure 1.1.

Linguistic	• language objectives • sentence frames • time for oral practice • use of home languages throughout lesson
Interactive	• partners • teacher modeling • whole-group guided practice • cooperative groups
Graphic	• visual inference 'formula' chart • shared writing • graphic organizers
Sensory	• photos and pictures • diagrams • think and plan time • physical movement

Figure 1.1 Inventory of Supports and Strategies (adapted from WIDA Consortium, 2012, p. 11)

Next, the teachers and coach had a conversation specifically about what explicit teaching strategies were employed that allowed DLLsSEN to engage and experience success during the lesson. These are presented in Figure 1.2.

- Developing student interest survey to inform instruction
- Connecting lesson directly to students' experiences
- Partnering based on language proficiency and shared interests
- Welcoming and integrating students' home languages into instruction
- Providing time for students to use their home languages and English for thinking, processing information, planning, responding, and problem-solving
- Scaffolding oral practice and writing through sentence frames
- Incorporating photographs of students' interests

Figure 1.2 Culturally and Linguistically Responsive Practices (adapted from WIDA Consortium, 2012, p. 11)

The teachers noted that the DLLsSEN were actively engaged because they were connecting to what they knew through personally meaningful material. Because **recurrency** was built into the instructional design, students observed multiple concrete applications of the concepts, tasks, and expectations throughout the lesson. They had repeated opportunities to interact by talking through their ideas, confirming their conjectures, and discovering new understandings as they co-constructed meaningful responses in variable groupings across a range of topics. The lesson also provided opportunities for focused practice of skills, including 'thinking aloud' strategies modeled for the whole group and shared practice structured by visual references. The teachers guided the students as needed during these extended opportunities to apply what they were learning as they worked toward independent use of strategies.

Activity 1.3

Following the example of the classroom teachers in Classroom Snapshot 1.2, create an interest survey for the students you serve. You can let them know that you are interested in getting to know them better.

- Decide what categories you will use—for example, hobbies, favorite conversation topics, travel experiences, interests, home languages, gifts, etc.
- Interview your students to gather information for each of the categories. Having individual conversations with students is one way of gathering these data. In what other ways could you gather information for your survey?

The Heterogeneous Nature of DLLs

The recognition that DLLs are a heterogeneous group who have already had a wide range of linguistic and cultural experiences before we meet them in school is a core principle in our interactions with students and families. They are a diverse group, considering the wide variation in their ethnicities, nationalities, socioeconomic levels, and immigration histories. An understanding of the diversity that exists among DLLs is essential when comparing the progress or performance of these students with that of their peers.

Some DLLs may have begun to develop English alongside another language from a very early age. These DLLs are **simultaneous bilinguals** who are learning two languages in parallel. Other DLLs may have been exposed to English for the first time when they entered school. They would be regarded as **sequential bilinguals**, acquiring one language after another. Some DLLs may have been exposed to a language other than English at home from birth but then, early on, spent a great deal of time in a predominantly English environment, such as day care, preschool, or school. They are often referred to as **heritage speakers**. Other DLLs may experience loss of their home language as schooling in monolingual environments proceeds. Sadly, these students gradually lose expressive abilities in their home language and may even develop difficulties understanding it. They may become disconnected from their families and communities linguistically (Wong-Fillmore, 1991). These students are DLLs as well because they have had experiences developing early language and thinking in their home languages. Schools and community organizations may offer language programs to help heritage speakers and students who have experienced language loss to revive their home and community languages.

Some DLLs have experienced limited or interrupted formal schooling due to a refugee experience or other disruptive events. Others immigrate to another country as adolescents after having had a great deal of formal schooling in their home language. Children who are adopted internationally at any age are also viewed as DLLs because of their early language experiences, even if they lose contact with their **first language** (L1).

Once DLLs begin school, the type of instruction they receive— bilingual, multilingual, or English-only—will contribute further to the heterogeneity of this group of students. Learning environments can have an **additive** or **subtractive** influence on students' bilingual development. Some schools and school systems actively value and integrate students' languages into their program of instruction for all students. Others have policies that actively discourage students and educators from using and developing multiple languages. García and Kleifgen (2010) describe a model of dynamic bilingualism in which individuals 'develop different language practices to use in varying degrees to interact with increasingly multilingual communities' (p. 42). Dynamic bilingualism refers to the simultaneous use of more than one language to communicate (sometimes referred to as **translanguaging**). It promotes fluid language practices that enable individuals to make meaning and communicate in multicultural settings (García, 2009). The dynamic use and development of languages is contrasted with an additive conceptualization of bilingualism that views one set of language skills as being added to another as separate entities in a linear manner. The dynamic bilingualism model builds on the ever-changing, complex, and creative ways that students use all their languages in school, at home, online, and in their various communities.

Bialystok and Hakuta (1994) affirm that the conditions in which second languages are learned are often more heterogeneous than those in which home languages are typically acquired. Recognizing and planning for this tremendous diversity of characteristics and experiences among DLLs is crucial when creating systems and processes for assessment, instruction, and intervention. Kohnert (2013) summarizes key elements related to DLLs' heterogeneity for practitioners to consider when gathering student histories to assist in planning for assessment and intervention. One aspect of heterogeneity among DLLs pertains to their relative proficiency in each of their languages. This proficiency is dynamic, changing over time. Early bilingual development is shaped by the age at which children are exposed to consistent input in each language and the variety of communication partners who speak each language—for example, parents, teachers, and peers. Other influential features include the places where the languages are spoken—for example, home, school, or childcare—and the purposes for which the languages are used—for example, social interaction, instruction, or literacy. Other factors that affect early bilingual development include the social prestige of and community support for each language and the amount and nature of exposure to literacy in the home and in the community.

Educational systems can address the heterogeneous nature of DLLs and keep pace with instructional approaches and resources by considering the changing characteristics and evolving demographics of the student populations in their school communities. The frequent mismatch between the design of educational systems and the diversity of the student populations they serve is the central impetus for developing culturally and linguistically responsive inclusive systems of education. School districts can design and reorganize their systems to address diversity as the norm rather than continually facing the need to adapt, modify, and accommodate systems that were not created with DLLs in mind (Miramontes, Nadeau, & Commins, 2011). When school practices and initiatives systematically incorporate L2 learning and culturally responsive pedagogy from the start, they are better equipped to proactively support the academic progress of DLLs, including those with SEN (Hamayan, Marler, Sánchez-López, & Damico, 2013).

In our view, the educational challenges and difficulties that DLLs experience in school can be the result of several interacting factors. These are conceptualized as extending across a continuum, as shown in Figure 1.3.

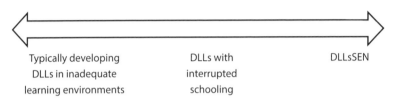

Typically developing	DLLs with	DLLsSEN
DLLs in inadequate	interrupted	
learning environments	schooling	

Figure 1.3 A Continuum of DLLs Experiencing Challenges at School

At one end of the continuum, there are typically developing DLLs who face challenges because they are receiving all their instruction based on a monolingual understanding of education without regard for them as dual language learners. Appropriate evidence-based instruction for typically developing DLLs includes culturally and linguistically relevant resources, materials, and pedagogy that are infused into all their learning environments (Gay, 2000; Hill & Miller, 2013). Without these types of learning experiences, DLLs will not have consistent or sufficient access to the grade-level curriculum, and will likely have difficulty making linguistic and academic progress.

Further along the continuum are DLLs who, for a variety of reasons, have experienced interrupted formal schooling that has limited their opportunity to learn (Gee, 2008). With intensive, culturally, and linguistically appropriate instruction, these students will make progress.

Towards the other end of the continuum are DLLsSEN who have psychologically or biologically based challenges that significantly impact their learning across contexts and languages. DLLsSEN are students who are in the process of learning a new language and who also require specialized and intensified instruction and support to address their particular learning challenges. The substantial difficulties that students at this end of the continuum experience are present across all their languages and communication contexts (Carroll, 1993; Cummins, 1994; Kohnert, 2013). When DLLs experience difficulties in only one language or in only one context, these challenges are attributable to the learning environment rather than to any intrinsic condition. In contrast, DLLs with disabilities related to short-term memory or expressive language impairment, for example, will demonstrate some form of these difficulties when using each of their languages—in social as well as academic settings (Gottlieb & Sánchez-López, 2008). When DLLsSEN receive instruction that is aimed at their current stage of **language proficiency** and combined with interventions designed for their specific profile of strengths and needs, they can be expected to make progress. Although DLLsSEN may require ongoing adaptations and tools, with a comprehensive approach they can develop skills to the level of their individual capabilities.

In using this continuum to understand the range of challenges that DLLs experience in school, it is important to recognize that multiple overlapping factors may contribute to students' challenges. While DLLsSEN appear here at one end of the continuum, they may also have experienced interrupted schooling or encountered inadequate learning environments.

The Heterogeneous Nature of SEN

In addition to the heterogeneous nature of DLLs, it is important to understand the very heterogeneous nature of SEN. This section will begin with a description of some of the disabilities that can be identified among your students. Next, it will offer examples of how disabilities manifest both across different individuals and within an individual at different stages of development. A look at factors that can impact the way an individual experiences disability will follow, and we will conclude with a discussion of how definitions of special educational needs can vary from one context to another.

A Wide Variety of SEN

SEN that impact participation in the classroom can result from a wide range of physical, social-emotional, behavioral, intellectual, language, learning, or reading impairments. Affected areas may present singly or overlap to different degrees within individuals. For example, intrinsic language learning challenges can manifest as the predominant area affected, as with specific or primary language impairment (Kohnert, 2013; Leonard, 1998; Prelock, Hutchins, & Glascoe, 2008). Alternatively, they may occur as part of other conditions, as exemplified by the social communication challenges experienced by people with **autism spectrum disorder (ASD)** (Geurts & Embrechts, 2008; Williams, Botting, & Boucher, 2008). Both language and speech impairments may exist with cleft lip and palate (Kuehn & Moller, 2000) and **Down syndrome** profiles (Feltmate & Kay-Raining Bird, 2008). Language impairment has also been found to co-occur with **attention deficit hyperactivity disorder** (**ADHD**) (Westby & Watson, 2004). Language difficulties often manifest with intellectual disabilities of various origins, including developmental delays (Goldstein, 2006) as well as acquired brain injuries resulting from head trauma (Ylvisaker, Hanks, & Johnson-Green, 2002).

Disabilities may also present differently across developmental stages. Early identified language impairments evidenced in auditory comprehension (listening) and/or oral expression (speaking) are often later recognized to be part of a learning disability or **reading impairment**. These oral language abilities are related to comprehension and/or decoding of text and expressive written language, as well as speaking (McArthur, Hogben, Edwards, Heath, & Mengler, 2000).

Individual Manifestations of SEN

Language and learning disabilities are due to factors intrinsic to the learner, and each is characterized by wide-ranging variation in the degree and nature of their manifestation within individuals. Professionals use terms such as 'mild', 'moderate', and 'severe' to describe the degree of impairment in functioning. These terms are also generally taken to reflect the extent of the impact of a disability on a person's daily life. Definitions of disabilities are often framed by exclusionary criteria; that is, by what areas are not affected. For instance, children with specific language impairment (SLI) exhibit typical social-emotional development, hearing, motor-speech abilities, and overall intellectual functioning but have language abilities significantly below age expectations when compared to like peers (Leonard, 1998).

Although individuals who are diagnosed with the same disability will tend to share central characteristics, each person will exhibit a different combination of these to a differing extent. For example, children with SLI can experience difficulties in one or multiple aspects of their receptive and/or expressive language functioning to varying degrees. They may find it challenging to understand and/or use the structural components of language, including **phonology**, **syntax**, and **morphology**. This can be evidenced in the classroom when the student exhibits difficulties following syntactically complex directions or clearly formulating sentences to effectively communicate what they know in response to questions—whether they are speaking their home language or the language of instruction.

Alternatively, difficulties may center on the **semantics** of language—how meaning is relayed or understood. These challenges can be evidenced with frequent use of non-specific words or loosely related vocabulary in all of the student's languages. With expressive vocabulary difficulties, students may frequently use words such as 'thing' or 'stuff', or use related terms but not be able to zero in on the precise word. A student might describe the word by saying, for instance, 'cross' instead of 'plus' when adding during a mathematics lesson. They may frequently pause or reformulate as they search for the words to communicate their intent. With expressive vocabulary challenges or word-finding difficulties such as these, listeners may fail to wholly understand the student's message. Difficulties with receptive vocabulary can also hinder full understanding of directions, questions, or the content of classroom lessons. Misunderstandings of multiple meanings of words or of figurative expressions in print materials or in the context used by the teacher during instruction can be a frequent occurrence. Although students with SLI may understand concrete, fact-based information when they listen to lessons or read text, they can have difficulty grasping implied meanings, making abstract connections, and/or performing complex reasoning.

Pragmatics is another aspect of language that may pose subtle challenges while sometimes having profound effects in interactions with peers and educators. Also referred to as 'social communication', pragmatics concerns how we use language to interact with others. This includes understanding and navigating the unspoken rules of conversational exchanges for social purposes. Especially relevant to students are the embedded rules of how language is used in classrooms to guide learning activities and academic exchanges. Examples include expected ways to respond to or pose questions, relate personal events, or explain information. These rules can vary across subject areas, classrooms, or teachers. For students with ASD, lack of understanding of implicit classroom expectations when entering a new setting may lead to increased anxiety that can overflow into unexpected behaviors. For other types of SEN, challenges with pragmatics can be much subtler and more difficult to discern in the classroom. Some students may withdraw in response to their uncertainty about the frequently implicit social expectations or interact awkwardly in social situations at school and beyond.

For DLLsSEN, the difficulties described would be present in their home languages as well as in English. Difficulties with any of these components of language can co-occur and interact in ways that affect participation across social, recreational, academic, and eventually employment contexts. To exemplify, difficulties with understanding and using grammatical structures may impact how students understand the content of lessons or make it difficult for them to explain or write about what they do understand. Challenges with comprehending subtle aspects of meaning can lead to misunderstandings in social settings where individuals need to discern implied messages, idiomatic expressions, or humor. Both language and cognitive abilities that impact social functioning can affect interactions during the school years and eventually in the workplace.

How disabilities manifest is deeply influenced by multiple factors, including personality traits and life experiences. Extrinsic factors that affect the impact of a disability include age and accuracy of diagnosis, the quality and extent to which intervention services and resources are accessible, and the nature of instructional approaches in school. For DLLs, the availability of cultural and linguistic resources and the extent to which professionals use culturally and linguistically responsive practices with students' families can also influence outcomes for each DLL (Klingner & Eppolito, 2014; Klingner et al., 2014). Viewing disability from a social-cultural perspective offers insights into the importance of interactions between individuals and their environments and acknowledges how social, economic, environmental, and cultural factors interact and influence an individual's experience of disability.

Perspectives on 'Disability'

Interpretations of what constitutes normal behavior varies across cultures. For example, in the languages of some Northwestern Native Americans, there are no words for the concept of stuttering. It is theorized that although disfluencies in speech patterns likely occur in the same ways across all languages, these behaviors have not been experienced as impairments or viewed as disabling across all groups (Bloodstein & Bernstein-Ratner, 2008).

The use of terminology also influences how disabilities are generally perceived in society. Corbett (1992) points out that, throughout history, the language and conceptualization of disabilities demonstrate deference to professionals, especially medical and psychological practitioners. This tends to disempower those with disabilities, characterizing them as dependent and passive recipients of services. Intervention approaches often focus on deficits with the goal of fixing or eradicating the difficulties, as if they were separate from the person, their life experiences, and their identities. Corbett contends that, rather than identify people with disabilities solely by their deficits and limitations, we need to acknowledge them as agents of change who have strengths and differences.

How disabilities are conceptualized influences our approach to instructing students with learning challenges. For example, viewed from a sociolinguistic perspective, dyslexia or reading impairments are described as an individual's 'ineffective use and/or coordination of strategies for constructing meaning' (Weaver, 1998, p. 320). This understanding promotes proactive pedagogy with an emphasis on meaning-based interventions in using authentic reading (Damico & Nelson, 2010; Weaver, 1998). This approach contrasts with more traditional views of dyslexia that are often based in deficit perspectives and focus on developing decoding skills at word level or on skill-building, often without an emphasis on meaning.

In some settings, students with SEN are referred to as having **specific learning differences (SpLD)** in efforts to shift away from deficit views and use of negative terminology (Kormos & Smith, 2012). Referring to students as **exceptional learners**, rather than as disabled, is another change in terminology that acknowledges students' strengths, assets, abilities, and gifts rather than defining them by focusing on their challenges. Students who experience difficulties in learning—as well as those who learn more easily than their peers and are not sufficiently challenged by general education instruction—can be referred to as exceptional learners. Modifications to curricula and instruction are necessary to support both sets of students in fulfilling their potential. The term 'exceptional learner' is used by some school districts to describe programs designed to support these learners.

There are people among the Deaf community who also view what is broadly perceived as a disability in the larger community as a unique and valued way of life. They see their differences from a cultural perspective and view American Sign Language (ASL), with its distinct syntax and morphology, as their home language. Another example of a strengths-based perspective has evolved among individuals diagnosed with ASD who share similar views about their life experiences with a 'disability'. While acknowledging their challenges, some have used their strengths to carve out satisfying lives and careers. They have clearly articulated how not being neuro-typical is a valued aspect of their identities.

The experience of Temple Grandin exemplifies a profound change in perspective toward people perceived as having disabilities. Her insights into sensory integration and thinking in pictures were garnered from her life experience with ASD. Drawing on her abilities and different perspectives, she introduced a major redesign of livestock processing facilities for the more humane and efficient handling of animals. Her experience as a 'neuro-atypical' thinker, widely viewed as having a deficit in school and life, was the source of the unorthodox perspectives that guided her innovative adaptations of this industry. Her story captures a critical conceptual change in the view of disabilities that leads us to embrace all differences as potential strengths. Grandin's (2012) book *Different ... Not Less: Inspiring Stories of Achievement and Successful Employment from Adults with Autism, Asperger's and ADHD* provides more in-depth stories from this perspective.

A historical account of how professional understanding and treatment of ASD has evolved, along with insights from people who live with what is commonly perceived as a disability, is shared in *NeuroTribes: The Legacy of Autism and the Future of Neurodiversity* (2015) by Steve Silberman. Another book about the changing views on disability is entitled *Uniquely Human: A Different Way of Seeing Autism* (Prizant & Fields-Meyer, 2015). These authors also challenge popular thinking about deficit perspectives of disabilities, with insights from Prizant, a researcher, clinician, and educator, as well as from Fields-Meyer's experience as the parent of a child diagnosed with ASD.

We view the use of labels with caution, given the history and complexity of obtaining accurate diagnoses, especially for DLLs. Indeed, in our experience of collaborating with school teams, we have found that using diagnostic labels to describe a student's disability is not the most informative way of learning about the student. Although diagnoses are relevant, discussions that center on how individual students' disabilities manifest in the classroom and in their lives yield much richer, more informative, and more useful data for interacting with and instructing those students. At the same time, there is wide agreement that DLLs exhibit the same range of disabilities with the same frequency as monolinguals, and it is imperative to understand that language learning does not 'cause' disabilities among DLLs, nor does eliminating one language from a child's environment remedy an existing disability.

Special Education Categorization and Services

Special education has been created in many cases to provide instruction and additional services for students whose needs are not adequately met with typical classroom instruction. To coordinate and deliver these specialized educational services for students with wide-ranging needs, categorization systems of disabilities have been developed. However, special education terminology and categories are not defined consistently across educational systems, and conceptualizations of what constitutes a disability continue to evolve. Consequently, when students move across school districts, regions, and countries, their identifying labels and the categories applied to qualify them for services may vary. Their identification as a student with SEN can be changed, removed, or added, even though the nature of their learning profile essentially remains the same.

Systems of special education have evolved in different ways over time, influenced by our developing understanding of disabilities as well as by changing funding models. From early on, categorization systems have relied on medical diagnoses of physical disabilities such as blindness and deafness. Categorization systems built upon these medical views of disabilities have continued to change in order to provide specialized education and treatment for an increasing range of disabilities. *The Diagnostic and Statistical Manual of Mental Disorders* (American Psychiatric Association, 2013) and the International Classification of Functioning, Disability and Health (ICF) published by the World Health Organization (WHO) (2001) are examples of categorization systems based on medical perspectives that are widely referenced for diagnosis. However, the WHO's ICF system has evolved to include both medical and social models in defining how disability is experienced. This recognizes that individual strengths and needs interact with social factors, such as environmental and attitudinal barriers, to shape each person's life experiences. To improve the daily lives of individuals, actions to address both social and environmental barriers are called for as components of intervention.

For conditions with observable, measurable biological characteristics, such as sensory or physical disabilities, medical diagnosis has been useful in identifying students for specialized services. However, when this medical view has been extended to the dimensions of learning, diagnosis and identification have not been as clear-cut and this has been especially problematic when applied to bilingual students.

As discussed earlier in this chapter, cognitive and language characteristics are less directly observable and more complex, interconnected, and multifaceted. As a result, the task of delineating what constitutes a disability is much more complicated. Standardized, norm-referenced tools that have typically been employed often rely on comparisons to monolingual speakers of the **majority language**. DLLs have typically been assessed in the language of instruction that they are in the process of developing. Their performance—on standardized tests and in the classroom—has often been compared to that of monolingual speakers matched for age while their unequal level of language development is overlooked. Given what we are learning about how DLLs develop language, attempting to equate their performance to that of speakers of only one language does not result in a valid comparison. Tests often focus on subskills and lack accuracy and precision for assessing the complex nature of dynamic language use, and this is especially true for bilingual or multilingual students.

Identifying language or learning disabilities in DLLs is especially challenging because characteristics of *second language learning* and those of *language or learning disabilities* may present similarly when observed superficially in the language being acquired (Hamayan et al., 2013; Paradis, Genesee, & Crago, 2011). This has led to confusion and misunderstanding in discerning the source of DLLs' difficulties in schools.

Special educational programs and services have changed over time, based on educators' and professionals' evolving understanding of disabilities, and ways of providing support for students with SEN vary significantly across school systems. Students may be served in inclusive education classrooms; they may go to a resource room for blocks of instruction during the day; or they may be placed in specially designed self-contained classrooms. Schools may offer one or a combination of these models. Some jurisdictions have designed specialized schools for students with specific types of disabilities. A current trend is that of increasing integration into inclusive settings (UNESCO, 1994) to provide instruction for students with SEN alongside their grade-level peers to the extent possible. Additionally, instructional assistants who work with one or more students may support their learning in the classroom context. Other students may leave their classroom individually or in small groups for additional support or special educational services.

In the North American setting, school or district teams typically identify and recommend placement for students according to their needs. The personnel responsible for assessing and educating students with SEN may include general education teachers, reading specialists, special educators, and ESL/bilingual teachers, along with paraprofessionals. A variety of related practitioners, such as psychologists, social workers, speech-language pathologists, and occupational therapists, can also be involved, depending on the nature of the students' learning challenges. It is important that these teams look to the students' families to play a vital role throughout this process, as they can share a wealth of information about their children's lives outside of school—their strengths, interests, and daily challenges. While school personnel can make recommendations, it is critical that students' families are engaged and informed to make decisions about their educational options.

Creating an Inclusive Learning Environment

With the shift toward providing instruction in more inclusive learning environments, classroom teachers may feel daunted by the complexity of teaching DLLsSEN while delivering a curriculum to address the already wide-ranging skill levels typical of any classroom. Often, teachers have not received extensive professional development pertaining to instruction for DLLs or DLLsSEN. They may also lack administrative support or scheduling that enables them to collaboratively plan and implement instruction in partnership with colleagues who have special education or ESL/bilingual training. These are examples of systemic changes that are needed to support educators in meeting the complex needs of DLLsSEN. When time to collaborate is regularly built into schedules, educators and practitioners can participate as members of a team that shares responsibility for implementing and coordinating instruction and intervention for students. It is important to engage multiple perspectives, including those of parents, in developing **Individualized Educational Programs** or **Individual Education Plans** (**IEPs**) for students who are identified as having SEN.

Another challenge in responding to the needs of DLLsSEN is that educators and allied professionals often come with ideas about special education from their experiences of instructing monolingual English students. While it is important to learn about the research that exists for monolingual English-speaking students with SEN, we must not assume that the same practices can be implemented without adaptation for DLLsSEN (Ruiz, 2012). Although there may be common aspects, wholesale use of monolingual approaches is not sufficient for instruction and intervention for DLLs (August & Shanahan, 2006) with or without SEN, nor is it culturally or linguistically responsive (Artiles & Ortiz, 2002; García & Tyler, 2010; Harry & Klingner, 2006; Orosco & O'Connor, 2014).

Prior to considering a disability to be the source of DLLs' observed difficulties in the classroom, it is essential to systematically examine the effectiveness of the instructional environment to determine whether DLLs have fully benefited from instruction that has enabled them to learn (Hamayan & Damico, 1991; Hamayan et al., 2013). The opportunities to learn needs to be examined beyond the immediate time and place where DLLs currently receive bilingual or L2 instruction. Throughout the school day, their instruction needs to be comprehensible and accessible. In addition, the extent to which their instruction has aligned with L2 pedagogy in previous grades also warrants consideration in determining if DLLs have experienced adequate opportunities to learn.

Unfortunately, for many years, educational thinking and practice has not kept pace with changing student demographics. The early work of Jim Cummins (1984) shed much light on several significant problems with diagnostic assessment practices for DLLs. In a landmark study, Cummins' post hoc analysis of 400 psychological assessments uncovered factors that contributed to frequent misdiagnosis of DLLs as having intellectual and learning disabilities. Psychological assessments employed standardized tests for monolingual English speakers to assess the cognitive and academic skills of DLLs. Cummins pointed to the pervasive practice of comparing DLLs' scores in English, the language they were in the process of learning, to the performance of same-age native English speakers. He argued that this was an invalid comparison and often resulted in misdiagnosis and inappropriate identification of DLLs as having disabilities that required special educational services. The normative populations for standardized tests did not include a valid comparison group of DLL peers who were from similar language, cultural, and experiential backgrounds. Furthermore, it is problematic to assess DLLs' intellectual abilities using psychological tests in English while they are in the process of developing academic English, as these tests are essentially assessing their stage of English proficiency rather than their academic or cognitive abilities.

Because the presence of a disability is diagnosed with reference to 'the norm'—i.e. expected performance among peers—it is critical to compare DLLs with their true peers. These are DLLs who share similar cultural experiences, language background, and level of language proficiency, as well as length and nature of exposure to each language.

Furthermore, at the time of Cummins' study, practitioners often assumed that DLLs' conversational English reflected their overall proficiency. Subsequent research has shown that even when their conversational language seems to be similar to that of their peers, students often need several additional years to develop age-appropriate academic language abilities (Cummins, 1981, 2008; Thomas & Collier, 2002). Unfortunately, when DLLs experienced academic challenges, the difference between their perceived English language abilities—based on informal conversational language—and their academic performance was often assumed to be due to an intrinsic deficit. Extrinsic variables, such as a mismatch between the instructional language of the classroom and the students' level of English development or a lack of culturally and linguistically responsive instructional practices, were seldom considered. As a result, DLLs were often placed inappropriately into programs designed for students with cognitive delays or learning disabilities and this further impeded their access to the type of instruction they needed to develop their academic and language abilities, with consequences for their overall social-emotional well-being.

Cummins' work challenged educators and allied professionals to gain a deeper understanding of L2 acquisition and to implement valid diagnostic assessment practices for DLLs. Assessing DLLs in both of their languages and observing them as they communicate for a variety of purposes with multiple communication partners better captures the richness and complexity of DLLs' full range of linguistic skills. Providing DLLsSEN with instruction and intervention in both languages gives us further insights into their capacities to learn, by accessing their full suite of linguistic and cognitive resources.

Challenges with creating valid assessment procedures for DLLs have contributed to disproportional representation of these students in special education. Disproportional representation encompasses both over- and underrepresentation of any group of students. This concept is often used in North America to refer to unequal proportions of linguistic and ethnic minorities in special educational programs (Artiles & Ortiz, 2002; Donovan & Cross, 2002; Harry, 2014; Klingner, Hoover, & Baca, 2008). Native English-speaking students who have disabilities are often used as a comparison group, on the assumption that the same percentage of students of other linguistic and ethnic groups would be identified with disabilities in any special educational category. For example, if disabilities occur in seven percent of the general population, then it would be expected that seven percent of any subgroup would also have disabilities. However, in some special educational categories, DLLs are identified at much higher rates, and in others at much lower rates (Donovan & Cross, 2002).

Categories used by special education that rely on clinical judgment to determine if a student qualifies are often the ones in which DLLs are overrepresented (Klingner, Artiles, & Méndez Barletta, 2006). When clinical judgements are made by comparing the performance of DLLs to that of monolingual students, DLLs are often misidentified. Categories in which DLLs are frequently overidentified include intellectual, emotional, behavioral, language, and learning disabilities. While a variety of methods exist to calculate proportional representation in special education, looking closely at the representation of DLLs in these programs can be a helpful tool for educational systems to reflect upon the accuracy of their current identification processes and prompt change for equitable access to appropriate services.

Classroom Snapshot 1.3 presents a team of educators working together to address the needs of two third-grade DLLsSEN who were both described as having difficulties with reading comprehension. This multiperspective team included teachers with special education expertise and ESL/bilingual teachers as well as a reading specialist and a school administrator. To discern how each student's reading comprehension difficulties were manifested, the team collaboratively gathered information about what individual students could do and how each demonstrated understanding in the classroom. From this conversation, two very distinct learner profiles began to emerge.

Classroom Snapshot 1.3

Through their extensive conversations about each student, the team noticed that the descriptions of the students' needs on each IEP did not provide sufficient information to plan instruction. Their discussions about the students' performance in class led to a deeper understanding of what each could do and illustrated how the nature of their disabilities impacted the two students' learning quite differently.

The first student seemed to understand best when she was offered more opportunities for small-group or individual instruction, with specific scaffolds and practice to support comprehension of texts in both languages. The team created sets of visual manipulatives that reflected exactly the images and characters in the fiction books they would be reading. The pictures and the book were sent home so that the student's family could read and talk about the story in their home language throughout the week before the lesson. A teacher would work with her in a small group and then individually as needed to preview the characters and events orally using the visuals. The student was asked to describe what she thought the story would be about in order to work on predicting and inferring orally.

While the classroom teacher read the story with the entire class, the student had opportunities to participate successfully as she was familiar with the characters and had developed background information about events in the story. She was also able to compare what she had predicted about the story to what happened. The team saw that the student's comprehension of text was deepening with her ability to predict, compare, contrast, and answer concrete and inferential questions. When these types of support were offered to her consistently throughout her instructional day, she began to make progress.

The team agreed that the second student's difficulties with comprehension seemed to go deeper than understanding print in either language. This student appeared to comprehend language best in activities that related directly to him. If the intervention was too removed from him, he had difficulty understanding or retaining that information. The team worked with his parents to photograph him engaged in various home- and school-related activities—laughing, talking, eating, thinking, reading, jumping, helping, etc. Using these digital photographs, the teachers and the student's parents helped him build oral language and comprehension related to those photographs. He would dictate stories about the photographs and these stories became his texts to read with teachers, peers, and family. As the year progressed, the team used photographs of the student interacting in more content-related activities with his peers to continue to build comprehension of oral language and literacy. Starting with photographs, this student gradually expanded his scope of understanding that supported his comprehension of text. ■

These distinct profiles of two DLLsSEN illustrate how students described as having learning disabilities may manifest learning challenges in distinct ways that require highly individualized approaches to instruction and intervention to meet their specific needs. This example clearly shows that, alongside systems of diagnosis and categorization, educators and practitioners must take the time to discover together how individual DLLsSEN can learn best.

What Teachers Need to Know

Information about what constitutes culturally and linguistically responsive instruction and intervention for DLLs with special educational needs is emerging from the growing research base for DLLs. Teachers need to know that established instructional principles for typical DLLs, combined with current research findings for DLLsSEN, provide the evidence base to guide classroom instruction and intervention.

It is important to note that there is no one method, approach, or strategy that will address every need a student may have or the learning needs of all DLLs. Therefore, educators need to critically examine any programs, strategies, or approaches that are marketed as panaceas. We must go beyond the 'evidenced-based' marketing labels to fully explore the research base that was used in developing instruction or intervention materials. It is imperative to know who conducted and sponsored the research and how it was done, and to make certain that DLLsSEN were included in the sample. If the studies do include DLLsSEN, then it is important to examine the language proficiency levels, cultural backgrounds, socioeconomic status, and school experiences of the participants. To consider how the interventions can benefit DLLs, it is crucial to look for studies that disaggregate data, i.e. separate out the results for learners according to the characteristics above (Klingner & Edwards, 2006).

Implementing approaches that promote culturally and linguistically responsive practices and perspectives can proactively address specific challenges that may arise for DLLs (Artiles & Ortiz, 2002; Baca et al., 2004; Hamayan et al., 2013; Klingner et al., 2005; Ortiz & Wilkinson,

1991). We advocate for bringing professionals with multiple perspectives together in anticipation of the challenges that DLLs may experience in their educational settings. This multiperspective team can learn about the different DLLs attending their school and seek to create culturally and linguistically responsive general education learning environments for all DLLs (Hamayan et al., 2013; Commins & Miramontes, 2006; Miramontes et al., 2011). While making changes at the school level, the team can also address the needs of specific DLLs who may be experiencing greater-than-expected challenges. Considering DLLs as typical language learners before assuming their difficulties are due to disabilities is a recommended first step toward learning more about them and improving their learning environment (Hamayan & Damico, 1981; Hamayan et al., 2013; Sánchez-López & Young, 2008; Young & Sánchez-López, 2017).

Viewing DLLs first and foremost as language learners is a core component of culturally and linguistically responsive practice and can counter the tendency of school teams to consider special education programming too soon when DLLs experience difficulties. Multiperspective teams can deepen their understanding of their DLLs' strengths and needs as language learners and recommend culturally and linguistically appropriate pedagogy for these students across instructional settings. The students' responses to this instruction can be used to guide the diagnostic process. Should students not, after sufficient time has passed, demonstrate expected growth compared to other DLLs with similar linguistic and cultural backgrounds and experiences, multiperspective teams can begin to consider possible explanations from an 'exceptional learner' perspective. Investing time in ensuring that instruction provides DLLs with ample opportunities to learn within linguistically and culturally appropriate learning environments lays a strong DLL foundation should the team progress to consideration of the student as an exceptional learner whose needs may also warrant special educational services (Hamayan et al., 2013; Sánchez-López & Young, 2008; Young & Sánchez-López, 2017).

Summary

In this chapter, we have introduced important contexts and conditions to help explain some of the challenges that DLLs can experience in school. Throughout the chapter, we highlighted the multifaceted nature of serving DLLs who may or may not have special educational needs. Educating DLLsSEN requires that teachers and practitioners who serve these students take the time to get to know them and work collaboratively to achieve deeper understanding in order to fully address their learning characteristics as DLLs. All our students are multidimensional and wonderful. They are full of potential, strengths, and gifts. When we create culturally and linguistically responsive inclusive learning environments for DLLsSEN, they can develop their talents and interests, reveal their creativity and determination, and reach their personal, academic, vocational, and professional goals.

In the next chapter, we provide an overview of theoretical frameworks and foundational research relevant to the education of DLLsSEN. The chapter begins with a discussion of all learners as meaning-makers and shows how sociocultural theory underpins our work with DLLs. Specific considerations for DLLsSEN are described within this framework. We will explore research and theory on how bilingualism and biculturalism can be both personal and academic assets for DLLs with and without special educational needs. The chapter expands on the importance of culturally and linguistically responsive inclusive educational systems to support DLLsSEN.

Chapters 3 and 4 elaborate on classroom and clinically based studies of instruction and intervention that have been effective in supporting DLLsSEN. Chapter 3 pertains to young DLLsSEN from preschool age to about 10 years old. Chapter 4 will focus on adolescent DLLsSEN in middle school and high school. Some studies include only DLLs with special educational needs; other studies were conducted in inclusive classrooms and included typically developing DLLs as well as monolingual English-speaking students with and without SEN. While many studies have addressed DLLs who are described as 'at risk' educationally, in our review of research we have concentrated on those studies that shed light on DLLsSEN already diagnosed as having disabilities.

Selected research in Chapters 2, 3, and 4 will be highlighted as Spotlight Studies, providing details of particularly important and relevant research. These studies offer guidance for educators in implementing effective instruction and intervention for DLLsSEN. In Chapter 5, we will return to the statements about the education of DLLsSEN in Activity 1.1. For each statement, we will provide a response based on the theory and research presented throughout the book.

2

Theoretical Foundations for the Education of Language Learners with Special Educational Needs

Preview

In Chapter 1, we saw that creating optimal learning experiences for dual language learners with special educational needs requires strategic and systematic collaboration among educators who come with a variety of professional backgrounds, experiences, and expertise. In this chapter, we present theory and research that are relevant to the academic growth and emotional well-being of DLLsSEN. This work is influenced by cognitive and sociocultural theories that are foundational to the framework we have developed for creating culturally and linguistically responsive inclusive learning environments for DLLsSEN.

Like typically developing DLLs, students with SEN face the challenges of learning an additional language while acquiring academic content and skills, often in the new language. Additionally, the educational experiences of DLLsSEN are shaped by their individual set of strengths and needs related to their learning disabilities. The instructional complexity involved in addressing the combination of these learning characteristics may be daunting, but new approaches to their education can lead to successful outcomes for DLLsSEN.

The UNESCO Framework for Action on Special Needs Education states that 'every child has a fundamental right to education, and must be given the opportunity to achieve and maintain an acceptable level of learning' (UNESCO, 1994, p. viii). This statement challenges us to recognize the unique characteristics, interests, abilities, and learning needs of each child. It tasks us with designing and implementing systems and programs that respond to the wide diversity found among our students. Schools with this inclusive orientation are viewed as 'the most effective means of combating discriminatory attitudes, creating welcoming communities, building an inclusive society, and achieving education for all' (UNESCO, 1994, p. ix). This statement clearly encapsulates what we believe the goals of our educational systems need to be with respect to DLLsSEN. Inspired by the work of the UNESCO group, we encourage educators and administrators to create culturally and linguistically responsive inclusive learning environments for DLLsSEN, using the framework illustrated in Figure 2.1. The elements listed within each component of this framework are supported by the theory, research, and examples outlined in this volume. The framework captures vital characteristics of the learning environment as a guide to designing instruction that maximizes learning for DLLsSEN. Additionally, we have included features critical to both school climate and system-wide practices that enhance the learning experience for DLLsSEN.

Before we describe this framework for **inclusion**, it is important to recognize that some student groups have been excluded from full participation in general education classrooms (Slee, 2011). In addition to students with disabilities, students from **minority language** backgrounds have experienced barriers excluding them from full access to their education. Disproportionately high numbers of these students have been placed in special education programs (Waitoller, Artiles, & Cheney, 2010). In the US, students from minority groups who have been identified as having SEN are less likely than other students to be instructed in general education classrooms and less frequently receive language development services. They are also less likely than other students with SEN to go on to higher education (Waitoller & Artiles, 2013). Even when minority students with SEN are placed in general education classrooms, there are linguistic, cultural, socioeconomic, and other barriers that must be addressed so that all students can access the curriculum. By acknowledging and then systematically working to remove barriers, school systems can create culturally and linguistically responsive learning environments that are truly inclusive for all students.

Culturally and Linguistically Responsive Inclusive Learning Environments for DLLsSEN

Figure 2.1 illustrates the components of culturally and linguistically responsive inclusive learning environments that are vital to the education and social-emotional well-being of DLLsSEN. It is important to envision the central components as nesting within and being supported by the surrounding components. Thus, the learners, as meaning-makers, are influenced and shaped by their learning environment, which is designed to be responsive to their learning characteristics. The components are also conceptualized as dynamic and interacting with one another. We will now describe each component of the framework in depth.

Instruction
- is embedded in meaningful and relevant contexts
- develops conceptual understanding and oral communication
- affirms students' multilingualism and multiculturalism
- addresses language, literacy, and content.

Learners
- are meaning-makers
- are creative and full of potential
- have unique profiles of strengths and challenges.

Interventions
- are strategic, coordinated, cohesive, and comprehensive
- are embedded within and across inclusive learning environments.

Culturally and linguistically responsive inclusive educational systems support educators and practitioners to
- take an asset orientation in interactions with students and families
- value and integrate family and community resources.

Figure 2.1 Culturally and Linguistically Responsive Inclusive Learning Environments for DLLsSEN

The framework situates individual learners as meaning-makers at the center (Vygotsky, 1978; Wells, 1986). Surrounding the learners is relevant and affirming instruction that focuses on developing their knowledge and skills in meaningful contexts while supporting their social-emotional well-being (Cloud, Genesee, & Hamayan, 2009; Gay, 2000; Gee, 2008; Klingner et al., 2005; Klingner et al., 2014; Ladson-Billings, 1995; Nieto, 1999). To optimize learning for DLLsSEN, culturally and linguistically responsive educators and practitioners need to collaboratively plan, coordinate, and integrate instruction, intervention, and support across instructional settings (Baca et al., 2004; Harry & Klingner, 2006; Klingner et al., 2014). Collaborative practice is essential both within schools and across the educational system. Enriched and cohesive instruction for DLLsSEN is embedded in culturally and linguistically responsive inclusive educational systems. These build upon students' sociocultural backgrounds by designing schools for diverse student populations from the outset (Commins & Miramontes, 2006; Harry & Klingner, 2006).

The cultural and linguistic resources and life experiences that students bring with them from their homes and communities influence their learning and interactions in school (González, Moll, & Amanti, 2006; Kalyanpur & Harry, 2012; Moll et al., 1992; Wong-Fillmore, 2000). Culturally and linguistically responsive educators honor and incorporate these resources into the curriculum and across instructional settings. This facilitates and enriches learning experiences for all students, especially DLLsSEN.

Before delving deeper into the research and theory supporting each component of the framework, we would like you to meet Melissa, a DLL with SEN whose school experience is described in Spotlight Study 2.1.

Spotlight Study 2.1

This case study by Delgado (2010) provides rich insight into the school experience of one DLL with SEN from the perspective of her bilingual fourth-grade teacher, Mrs Carrillo. Melissa, a Spanish-speaking student who was identified as having a learning disability in second grade, had attended first grade in an all-English classroom. The difficulties Melissa experienced during that year resulted in repetition of first grade, this time in a bilingual classroom. In third grade, in addition to her core instruction in a bilingual classroom, Melissa was provided with some home language support from a special education resource teacher. At the time of this study, she was in a fourth-grade bilingual class and receiving English special education support in a resource room setting. Mrs Carrillo noted that Melissa spent very little time in the bilingual class—her core instructional environment—and that, due to scheduling for the special education support, she was also missing the ESL instruction.

As Melissa's bilingual teacher, Mrs Carillo acknowledged that she did not feel adequately prepared to work with students with SEN. Although she had actively sought professional development opportunities, the training she received only addressed how to develop IEPs and failed to zero in on how to help students in the classroom. Few opportunities were provided for her to attend professional development that focused on instructional strategies for students with SEN. Nor was time available for her to observe special education teaching or consult with the special education teacher about individual students. The teachers were never afforded an occasion to share specific strategies that could be used in the bilingual classroom to extend the supports Melissa was getting in special education to her bilingual setting. To the extent that there was coordination between bilingual and special education programs, the focus was on legal requirements rather than instructional strategies or approaches.

Based on interviews with the bilingual teacher, the researcher found that neither the special education nor the bilingual setting fully provided for all aspects of Melissa's educational needs. The special education teacher was not planning for Melissa's L2 needs during intervention. Likewise, the bilingual education teacher acknowledged that she was not modifying her instruction to meet Melissa's disability-related instructional needs. As a result, Melissa experienced instruction that fulfilled only some of her learning needs throughout her school day. Her bilingual teacher referenced Nieto (1999) to describe Melissa as 'losing the sparkle in her eyes', observing that she gradually withdrew from active participation in the bilingual classroom as she split more of her time between the two programs. ■

Activity 2.1

Reflect on the following questions:

1 What factors appear to have contributed to Melissa's learning and well-being?
2 From the teachers' perspectives, what is not currently working?
3 What would you suggest or do differently 1) as the bilingual/ESL teacher and 2) as the special education teacher?

Make note of your reflections. We will revisit these in Spotlight Study 2.4.

The Role of Meaning-Making in Theories of Learning

As we return to the discussion of specific components of the framework, we begin with the understanding that learners are meaning-makers. This notion is central to the classroom-based research, examples, and discussions presented in this volume. As meaning-makers, all individuals are active participants in making sense of the world through their experiences within it. For educators who support DLLsSEN, it is important to understand the meaning-making process and to advocate for instructional environments and practices that engage students in learning. In this section, we will examine the role of meaning-making in theories of learning.

Behaviorism

Prominent during the 1940s and 1950s, behavioral psychology focused primarily on observable behaviors. Researchers extended their findings from laboratory experiments with animals to humans and proposed that human learning resulted from the shaping of behaviors and the formation of habits through stimulus, response, and reinforcement. However, behaviorist explanations could not fully account for the complexity of human learning.

Nevertheless, the influences of behaviorist perspectives remain evident in some methods and materials currently used in instruction.

Approaches to special education based on this perspective focus on deconstructing learning tasks, reducing them to isolated components, ranging from simple to complex. With **reductionist** approaches like these, activities are often simplified and may subsequently become divorced from a meaningful context for learners (Damico & Ball, 2010; Shuell, 1986). As a result, what seems simple to teachers can become more demanding for learners when they cannot make sense of it. Without meaningful connections, learners resort to memorization, which may not result in long-lasting retention or deep understanding (Smith, 1998). Students with SEN benefit more from practicing skills and applying newly learned concepts in the complex but real contexts in which they use them. For example, think about asking DLLsSEN to read and memorize lists of words pertaining to botany and gardening. Then compare this to all the reading, writing, talking, and negotiating with peers that would be involved in learning to grow plants in the school's community garden as part of a science unit.

Gersten and Woodward (1994) caution against reductionist approaches in instruction for DLLs, for reasons that also apply to the use of such approaches for students with SEN. They argue that focusing on systematic skill-building outside of meaningful contexts inhibits language development for DLLs. Furthermore, overall cognitive development can be hindered when meaning and enjoyment are taken out of learning, with student engagement reduced in the process. Reading materials that control vocabulary in order to introduce prescribed sequences of phonics were found to limit language development for DLLs (Tharp & Gallimore, 1988). Instruction that systematically focused on practicing specific language forms, morphology, syntax, and definitions without a communicative purpose did not advance L2 acquisition (Speidel, 1987). Approaches that centered on groups of students completing a prescribed progression of skills—without consideration of each learner's specific profile of learning strengths and needs and with little attention to L2 learning pedagogy—were not found to promote language development for DLLsSEN (Ruiz, 2012). Given that reductionist approaches have not been found to promote language or cognitive development for DLLs, they are not recommended for DLLsSEN. In the next section, we will explore **cognitive theories** of learning that frame instructional practices which do support learning for DLLsSEN.

Cognitivism

The concept of meaning-making is derived from theories that define learning as an active process that depends primarily on the mental activities of the learner. Cognitive psychologist Jean Piaget (1951) proposed that knowledge gained through our experiences is organized into schemata—interconnected maps that change and grow as new information is added. Through interactions with the environment, all learners build on prior knowledge and experiences, using strategies to identify, organize, and integrate new information into internal networks of associations (Shuell, 1986). In this view, the focus of learning is on modifying one's internal system in ways that improve understanding and interactions going forward. Piaget's focus was on the development of cognition, and he viewed language as a system of symbols for the expression of thought.

More recent usage-based linguistic theories also suggest that language and cognition develop together and are based on children's experience of creating internal networks connecting meaning to language (Ellis, 2002; Lieven & Tomasello, 2008). From this perspective, the development of language structure is driven by what we need to support understanding and express ourselves as we interact in the world. Usage-based views of language learning support the use of functional **authentic** learning activities to guide the instruction of language form and structure for DLLs.

In schools, the cognitive development of DLLs has often been assessed in English, but DLLs typically have more knowledge than they can express or understand in their developing language. This can result in underestimation of their intellectual abilities and contribute to deficit perspectives, as assessments only in the language of instruction fail to adequately measure the knowledge they have acquired through their home language and their previous educational and life experiences (Cummins, 1984, 1994). For sequential or simultaneous bilingual learners, assessing their abilities in only one language and comparing their performance to that of monolingual speakers of that language does not access the full complement of their linguistic or cognitive abilities.

Sociocultural Theory

Lev Vygotsky's (1978) sociocultural theory is derived from social constructivist perspectives on cognitivism. Vygotsky proposed that knowledge is developed through social interaction which is mediated by cultural understandings and experiences. As young children interact socially with more skilled others in their home and communities, their daily experiences shape their understanding of the world around them

(Orosco, 2010). Cultural practices embedded in their social relationships are derived from these everyday interactions and form the basis for cognitive development (Gutiérrez & Rogoff, 2003). These culturally and socially constructed understandings are what children use to organize their thinking and make meaning (Bransford, Brown, & Cocking, 2000). This explains why learning can be facilitated when cultural perspectives, knowledge, and skills are incorporated into instruction. As disabilities may render meaning-making more challenging for DLLsSEN, it is especially important that educators access and build upon students' cultural understandings and assets.

This social constructivist perspective of cognitivism highlights the social component of learning that occurs as people interact with one another and with their environment to make meaning. In this view, language becomes a tool that learners use to construct knowledge as well as to express their understanding as they interact with one another, their teachers, and instructional materials in the classroom.

For DLLsSEN who may experience specific challenges in understanding and using language, instructional approaches must be strategically scaffolded as the students continue to develop their languages and use them for learning. Furthermore, the use of language to make meaning has significant implications for DLLs, especially in the early stages of acquiring the language of instruction. Their development of knowledge may be inhibited in classrooms where they are restricted to only the language of instruction, which they are in the process of learning. This can restrict students' interactions with others to construct understandings, confirm or disprove hypotheses, and refine their thinking about concepts. Promoting home language use in the classroom is therefore an essential component of instruction for DLLs and DLLsSEN. This will be explored later in this chapter, together with the importance of affirming the multicultural and multilingual identities of DLLsSEN.

Instructional language used by educators must be adapted to match the DLLs' level of proficiency to make concepts and knowledge comprehensible and accessible to them during lessons and throughout their day. Social constructivism sees all learners, including those with SEN, as active participants in meaning-making as they interpret information and develop understandings and strategies based on their life experiences. Vygotsky recognized that learning occurs in sociocultural contexts and that background knowledge based on accumulated life experiences is integral to the learning process.

The framework presented in Figure 2.1 is grounded in sociocultural theory, which is central to current views of learning for all learners and is especially relevant in the education of DLLsSEN. For students with SEN, perceptions and experiences that support meaning-making are filtered through their unique physical, sensory, linguistic, and cognitive characteristics as shaped by their disability. The challenge for educators is to discern individual students' unique characteristics of learning in terms of what they can do in the classroom and what they are still in the process of learning.

An important concept contributed by Vygotsky that is particularly relevant to instruction for DLLsSEN is the **zone of proximal development** (**ZPD**). This is described as the difference between what individuals can do independently and what they are able to do with support from another individual. It is conceived as a dynamic space where educators mediate learning by providing scaffolds to support a student's progress toward independent use of new skills and knowledge. **Mediation** is a collaborative activity in the negotiation of meaning. It involves the use of language facilitation and learning strategies in authentic communication contexts for real purposes by a more skilled speaker, reader, or writer to guide the development of a less experienced speaker, reader, or writer. Mediation includes familiar teaching practices, such as modeling and scaffolding. For DLLsSEN, mediation needs to be specifically tailored to address each student's characteristics as a learner of both knowledge and language. In Chapters 3 and 4, we will discuss research and examples of how to mediate for the individual learning profiles of DLLsSEN.

Peers can also co-construct meaning and facilitate skill and strategy development as they scaffold for each other through their actions and verbal exchanges. Oliver and Philp (2014) discuss how oral interaction functions in this way in language acquisition, with young children supporting each other in language learning. Learning environments designed from a social constructivist perspective reflect the natural complexity of authentic learning and promote communities of learners who participate together in purposeful activities.

In addition to interacting with their peers and with adults, learners also co-construct meaning by interacting with elements of their environment. Although learners with SEN can respond strategically in the context of challenges they experience, they may not always choose the most effective or efficient ways of learning (Damico & Nelson, 2005; Perkins, 2005). Classroom Snapshot 2.1 illustrates how a DLL with SEN in an early elementary classroom refined her thinking and adopted a more efficient strategy after having the opportunity to interact with interesting mathematical materials and talk with peers. In this example, the teacher created a learning environment with activities that illustrated Vygotsky's sociocultural theory in practice. All the students in this class had opportunities to show their thinking, try out their hypotheses, talk with one another, and communicate in authentic and purposeful ways.

Classroom Snapshot 2.1

The teacher asked students to 'make 20' with their connecting cubes. How they chose to group their cubes to make their 20 varied. As the teacher walked around, she could observe the students' number sense, their mathematical reasoning at that moment, and how their thinking changed after conversing with peers.

Initially, some students, including DLLsSEN, counted out 20 individual cubes. Other students connected four groups of five cubes together, and a few students connected two rows of ten cubes. Next, everyone was asked to walk around and look at each other's cube models, ask each other questions, and converse with their peers about what they did to represent 20. The following is an example:

Student A: What did you do?
Student B: I counted 20. What did you do?
Student A: I made fives.
Student B: Oh!

Students were then asked to go back to their own cubes and rearrange them in a new way to represent 20. Most students used one of the ways they had observed and learned about from their peers. One DLL with SEN who had initially counted out 20 individual cubes decided to connect ten groups of two cubes. As the teacher listened to the student count the cubes while putting them together, she noticed that the student began from the number one each time; that is, the student put two cubes together and counted 'one, two' and then connected two more cubes and counted 'one, two, three, four', then connected another two cubes and counted 'one, two, three, four, five, six', and so on. ∎

In Classroom Snapshot 2.1, the DLL with SEN showed progress in her mathematical reasoning, using a more efficient model than the one she had started with, and yet she likely needed more time, examples, scaffolds, and opportunities in this process of using more effective strategies and more advanced mathematical reasoning. Watching her progress to more efficient methods provided the teacher with insights into this student's strategies for making meaning. By observing that she began counting from the number one each time—rather than counting in twos or fives, or being able to count up from a given number—the teacher found a good starting point for scaffolding and supporting the student's mathematical reasoning within her ZPD. This example illustrates how students with SEN do develop strategies for learning, even if they may not be the most efficient approaches. When this is the case, students will likely need individualized scaffolding with additional opportunities to practice (Damico & Damico, 1993) in order to make progress toward more efficient strategies and independence. Adopting a sociocultural view of learning compels educators to engage DLLsSEN by designing learning experiences that will build on their knowledge and are interesting to them, while creating opportunities for them to interact with others to co-construct and refine meaning.

The significance of creating learning experiences that are interesting to students is underscored by research demonstrating that engagement in literacy is a significant predictor of literacy achievement (Cummins, 2017; Cummins & Persad, 2014). Engagement in reading has been measured in terms of time spent reading various materials, use of various learning strategies, and enjoyment of reading. In studies of 15-year-olds across several countries by the Organisation for Economic Co-operation and Development (OECD), reading engagement was found to be better at predicting reading outcomes than socioeconomic status (OECD, 2004, 2010). In Canadian studies, data on the performance of students on the Ontario Secondary School Literacy Test (OSSLT) have been disaggregated to gain insight into the influence of literacy engagement for these adolescent DLLs. Findings have been consistent with the international results (Cheng, Klinger, & Zheng, 2009; Zheng, 2005). Zheng (2005) measured the reading engagement of 4,311 DLLs by looking at both the number of hours and types of literacy activities that students engaged in after school—i.e. digital, non-fiction, newspaper, and magazine reading. Among the DLLs, literacy engagement was found to positively predict their literacy performance. Cheng et al. (2009) used the same data to compare DLLs and monolingual secondary students who either passed or failed this secondary literacy test. The DLLs who passed the OSSLT demonstrated higher engagement in reading than the two groups of students who failed. Of those who did not pass this test, both the DLLs and the English speakers reported much less outside-of-school reading. How do we, as educators, generate students' interest and engagement with literacy in ways that influence their choice of activities beyond school and enhance their academic outcomes as adolescents? Capturing and building upon students' interests, making connections to their experiences, and involving them in talking, writing, and reading about their lives are practices that engage learners, including DLLs and DLLsSEN. The concept of engagement will be touched upon throughout this volume as central to how culturally and linguistically responsive educators support DLLs and DLLsSEN.

In this section, we have described theories that have contributed to viewing learners as meaning-makers. It is important for educators to understand how these theories have influenced and continue to guide instructional approaches for DLLsSEN. We turn now to a growing body of research that continues to demonstrate that DLLs with a variety of disabilities are not disadvantaged by the development of two or more languages.

Bilingualism and Children with Disabilities

A frequently asked question is whether children who are diagnosed with disabilities are hindered by learning more than one language. This question is posed more frequently in contexts where monolingualism is common than in multilingual settings. To date, most research on this topic has included children with language impairments, Down syndrome, and autism spectrum disorder. It indicates that bilingualism does not negatively impact the nature or severity of students' disabilities. This is especially the case in additive language learning environments and when exposure to each language is relatively balanced (Kay-Raining Bird, Genesee, & Verhoeven, 2016). Researchers have consistently reported that the language and cognitive profiles of DLLs with disabilities are comparable to those of monolingual speakers with the same diagnosis (Drysdale, van der Meer, & Kagohara, 2015; Uljarević, Katsos, Hudry, & Gibson, 2016). Bilingualism benefits children with disabilities by extending their range of possible communication partners for social interaction, caregiving, and service provision (Kohnert, 2013; Paradis et al., 2011; Pesco et al., 2016).

Specific Language Impairment

Studies of children diagnosed with specific language impairment (SLI) have reported comparable language abilities for bilingual and monolingual speakers (Paradis, 2010). In Canadian studies of 7-year-old French–English bilingual children with SLI, researchers found that they used the same patterns of morphology and syntax as monolingual children with SLI (Paradis, Crago, & Genesee, 2005/2006; Paradis, Crago, Genesee, & Rice, 2003). These studies explored the children's use of grammatical structures in their spoken language. Both bilingual and monolingual children with SLI experience challenges with grammar for longer than their typically developing peers. The authors examined the use of ten morphological structures—for example, third-person singular -s and past -ed in English—in spontaneous speech samples. These included morphemes that distinguish children with language impairments from their typically developing peers in both English and French. These simultaneous bilingual children were found to make the same types of errors with the same frequency in each language as their monolingual peers with SLI. A study in the US of monolingual and bilingual 4- to 5-year-old children with SLI showed the same pattern and frequency of errors among the more proficient language of Spanish–English bilingual children compared to their monolingual counterparts (Gutiérrez-Clellen, Simon-Cereijido, & Wagner, 2008). Another study with Spanish–English bilingual children with SLI revealed strengths in their effective use of both languages to code-mix in ways that were comparable to their typically developing bilingual peers (Gutiérrez-Clellen, Simon-Cereijido, & Leone, 2009). **Code-mixing** involves the expressive use of two languages in grammatically appropriate ways to communicate with others who speak the same languages (Genesee, 2009). Some observers in the past assumed that switching between languages was a symptom of a disorder or a lack of linguistic knowledge, but code-mixing is now understood to be a skillful use of languages that is shared by typically developing DLLs and those with SLI. Like their unaffected peers, these DLLsSEN could draw on vocabulary, concepts, and expressions in both languages to effectively relay their ideas to other bilingual speakers.

Bialystok (2001) has identified other linguistic and cognitive benefits experienced by DLLs who achieve proficiency in more than one language. Bilingual children have demonstrated advanced metalinguistic awareness— the ability to think about, discuss, and analyze features of language— which is purported to relate to literacy development and academic success. Continuing to actively use both languages has also been found to enhance cognitive flexibility, with lifelong benefits that delay the onset of dementia symptoms (Bialystok, Craik, & Freedman, 2007). These researchers found that among the people who acquired dementia, bilinguals developed symptoms on average four years later than monolinguals. Superior executive functions have also been reported among typical active bilingual speakers across the lifespan (Bialystok, 2011; Poulin-Dubois, Blaye, Coutya, & Bialystok, 2011). Collectively, studies of bilingual adults confirm that speakers who continue to interact in both languages can experience lifelong advantages. In a detailed review of this research, Paradis (2010) proposes that such advantages may exist early on and support DLLs with SLI in compensatory ways that counter the limitations on processing abilities that are characteristic of individuals with SLI.

When DLLsSEN are diagnosed with more pervasive disabilities that extend beyond the language realm, the same question often arises: how does speaking more than one language affect children who have cognitive disabilities? Researchers have found that it has often been assumed that children diagnosed with ASD, for example, should focus on *only one language*. However, in studies to date, the same positive pattern of results has been reported for children with ASD and Down syndrome as for those with language impairment (de Oliveira, 2015; Kay-Raining Bird, Lamond, & Holden, 2012). Current evidence affirms that disabilities are not exacerbated by bilingualism, with some studies suggesting that bilingual learning experiences can benefit language development and learning for DLLsSEN. These benefits are in addition to the social-emotional advantages of remaining connected linguistically to one's family and community.

Down Syndrome

In one study, Kay-Raining Bird, Cleave, Trudeau, Thordardottir, and Thorpe (2005) compared monolingual and bilingual children with Down syndrome. All the participants were in the early stages of language development, with the bilinguals experiencing early, ongoing, consistent exposure to both languages. The bilingual children all spoke English, along with one of the following languages: French, Cree, Lebanese, Portuguese, or Italian. Assessment of children's language abilities included standardized measures and oral language samples. These were collected while the children interacted with familiar adults and played with toys designed to elicit nouns and verbs. The parents completed language history questionnaires and surveys of their children's vocabulary knowledge in each language. They also worked with the researchers to collect receptive vocabulary data, using adapted protocols of existing tools when standardized measures were not available in the home language.

Whether monolingual or bilingual, the linguistic profiles of the children with Down syndrome were characterized by receptive vocabulary strengths and expressive grammatical difficulties. The bilingual children with Down syndrome were found to be developing English skills as well as the monolingual English-speaking children with Down syndrome. While acknowledging small sample sizes, the researchers found no evidence of a detrimental effect of bilingualism for the children with Down syndrome.

A subsequent study examined the language performance of the French–English children with Down syndrome in greater detail, comparing it to that of matched monolingual English-speaking peers with and without Down synrome (Feltmate & Kay-Raining Bird, 2008). The researchers concluded that children with Down syndrome do become bilingual and that their bilingual experience does not hinder their acquisition of English; on the contrary, bilingualism brings many advantages, including the maintenance of the children's relationships with family and increased potential for communication partners.

Autism Spectrum Disorder (ASD)

Research is beginning to accumulate that can guide families and practitioners about exposure to multiple languages for children with ASD. This condition can vary dramatically in the way it manifests for each individual. Each student with ASD has a unique combination of strengths and varying degrees of challenges with communicative, cognitive, and sensory capabilities. Information from a database created for a Canada-wide longitudinal research project, Pathways in Autism Spectrum Disorder (n.d.), has been used to compare the language characteristics of recently diagnosed bilingual and monolingual children with ASD. In one study, Ohashi et al. (2012) focused on 2- to 4-year-olds who grew up as simultaneous DLLs in homes where English or French was spoken, as well as another language—Mi'kmaq, French, English, Croatian, Cantonese, Greek, Urdu, Arabic, Italian, Spanish, Mandarin, Japanese, or Berber. As the 20 bilingually exposed children began to use spoken language, their early language development was found to be analogous to that of 40 monolingual children with ASD. Similarities included the age at which they spoke their first words and phrases, together with their performance on receptive, expressive, and functional communication measures.

In the US, Valicenti-McDermott et al. (2012) performed a retrospective study with 1- to 2-year-old Spanish–English children diagnosed with ASD. On the basis of speech and language assessments, the characteristics of the 40 bilingual children were compared to those of 40 matched English-speaking peers. Assessments included standardized measures, along with parental reports and clinical observations of home language use. The researchers found that the early language skills of the two groups of young children with ASD were very similar. There were no significant differences in their expressive language in terms of vocalization, babbling, or the number of words and combinations. The researchers also reported similar cognitive functioning and autistic characteristics across the groups. The differences that researchers found between monolingual and bilingual children with ASD included advantages for the latter group. The bilingual toddlers with ASD used cooing vocalizations, engaged in pretend play, and employed gestures to point and lead people to objects more often than their monolingual English peers. The team of researchers concluded that dual language exposure did not create additional vulnerability for these young children with ASD in the early stages of language development. Moreover, contrary to popular belief, the bilingual environments appeared, in some ways, to facilitate the children's early use of communication.

In another study of Canadian children with ASD, Hambly and Fombonne (2012) assessed social and linguistic abilities of those who had bilingual and trilingual language experience. The 75 children who participated ranged in age from 3 to 6 years and spoke French, English, Chinese, Farsi, Hebrew, Italian, Romanian, Spanish, and/or Tamil. Comparing outcomes in the children's most proficient languages, the researchers found no differences between those with simultaneous language development and those who had learned their additional language(s) sequentially. In all comparisons to monolingual children with ASD, those with multilingual exposure were found to be equally capable based on these social and linguistic measures.

In a smaller Canadian study, Petersen, Marinova-Todd, and Mirenda (2012) compared the vocabulary development of 14 Chinese–English children with ASD to that of 14 monolingual English children with ASD. All of these 3- to 7-year-old children were assessed with a combination of standardized measures of vocabulary, along with non-verbal visual and motor scales. No differences were found on any of these measures between the groups of children with ASD who were studied. The number of words they understood and the size of their spoken vocabularies were comparable for all the participants, whether English-only or bilingual speakers. Also, the bilingual speakers demonstrated equivalent vocabulary performance in both languages on these measures.

Collectively, these comparative studies confirm that bilingualism is attainable for children with disabilities. It is important to note that these results are contrary to pervasive misconceptions. The research affirms the decision of parents (and other caregivers) who have persevered in using multiple languages with their children with diagnosed disabilities, despite professional recommendations to do otherwise. Educators and practitioners who have persisted in promoting the multilingual capabilities of DLLsSEN in the face of pressure to succumb to the status quo of monolingual systemic practices can also take heart. As educators and practitioners, our roles include advocacy for the use and development of multiple languages in all learning environments for students with disabilities and for collaboration with parents to support the bilingual aspirations they have for their children.

In the following section, we will describe characteristics of instruction for DLLsSEN. These characteristics are relevant to all DLLs, and, in fact, to all learners, but they are particularly important in our work with DLLsSEN.

Characteristics of Instruction for DLLsSEN

Teachers who serve DLLsSEN know first-hand that students' learning profiles are all unique and that the potential of these students continuously shows itself during rich classroom experiences. Educators endeavor to create learning opportunities for all students and are prepared to support each learner in activities, lessons, or units of study. By working within the ZPD of individual students, educators can see when learners are engaged— when things seem to *click* as they make sense. Students may even lose track of time when learning is fun, purposeful, and full of meaning. DLLsSEN benefit from special education pedagogy, such as strategic instruction, and specific and extended scaffolding tailored to address their SEN. Likewise, they benefit from DLL pedagogy that has the characteristics of instruction that are optimal for all DLLs. The framework in Figure 2.1 for culturally and linguistically responsive inclusive learning environments helps us to examine this pedagogy in more detail.

Embedding Learning in Meaningful Contexts

As indicated in Figure 2.1, learning experiences that are engaging and interesting for DLLs must be embedded in meaningful and relevant contexts. From a social constructivist view, new information, vocabulary, skills, or ideas become meaningful for students when they are related to previous learning and experiences and are also connected to a larger theme or topic. Another way of describing this is to contrast instruction that goes from whole to part with lessons that go from part to whole. **Whole-to-part** instruction exemplifies social constructivism in that it begins with a meaningful context that focuses on building schemata about the lesson content. Additionally, it engages students in co-constructing meaning through shared hands-on experiences with visual input and verbal exchange. The skills and knowledge that are being addressed are embedded into the larger instructional context. In contrast, **part-to-whole** instruction reflects more behaviorist perspectives in that it begins with smaller units, such as a skill, fact, or strategy, and then works through a series of steps toward mastering a larger skill set or concept.

In an example of a whole-to-part reading lesson about the topic of urban and rural communities, the teacher begins by showing photographs or posters of two different types of communities. Students talk in their home languages as well as in English about what they see on each photograph/poster. They may also discuss with a partner how the communities depicted are similar to or different from what they are used to seeing. In a larger group, the students share their ideas about what they observed.

The teacher then writes their ideas and utterances on the board or on large chart paper. During this pre-reading activity, the teacher takes the opportunity to highlight the grammatical structures the students used in their brainstorming, categorizing what was shared orally into two columns:

The boys	run
Girls	ride (their bikes)
People	buy (food)
The man	helps (the lady cross the street)
The teacher	walks (with her students)
The bus driver	drives (the bus)

The teacher asks the students to discuss what they notice about the two categories. After having some time to think and then converse with their peers, the students recognize that the first is a listing of different people and the second tells us what the people were doing. The teacher may prompt further discussion about the features of nouns and verbs at this point, labeling the concepts that the students are developing and understanding intuitively. As an introduction to a shared reading (Damico & Nelson, 2010; Enguidanos & Ruiz, 2008) about communities, she may return to the bigger picture related to the different things people who live in urban and rural communities might see and do, and then compare the two. This is an example of a whole-to-part approach to instruction because the lesson is primarily about the features of rural and urban life, as part of a social studies curriculum. The materials are selected to feature interesting people and activities that happen in different kinds of communities, and the lesson simultaneously provides a meaningful context for a focused mini-lesson on nouns and verbs (Cloud et al., 2009).

In contrast, in a lesson with a part-to-whole orientation, the teacher may start by focusing on nouns and verbs. She might introduce nouns and verbs, define what they are, and then have students generate lists of random nouns and verbs that they know, asking 'What nouns do you know?' or 'What are some verbs that you know?' The students could provide some examples— such as 'trees', 'balloons', 'sandwich', 'running', 'falling', 'crying'—and then perhaps compose oral or written sentences. The students may then build sentences about rural and urban communities, and the teacher could follow this by reading a book about communities.

While part-to-whole may seem like a logical way to organize instruction, for DLLs the beginning of the lesson would be mostly incomprehensible. Without a theme or organizing topic, there is little that is meaningful to help students make connections. If instruction begins with the smallest component, without a meaningful context, it is not surprising that DLLs may appear uninterested or find it difficult to focus throughout the lesson. If the beginning of the lesson is not **comprehensible** (Krashen, 1982) for DLLs, it will be difficult for students to stay engaged to develop their understanding of the larger theme or topic (Echevarria, Vogt, & Short, 2004). Providing context and meaning within thematic units of study becomes even more critical for DLLsSEN who, like typically developing DLLs, are in the process of learning the language of instruction and who may also have difficulties related to language, reading, or cognition.

Another aspect of effective instruction for DLLs pertains to the use of content and materials that are personally relevant (Gay, 2000; Ladson-Billings, 1995). In the lesson about urban and rural communities, the inclusion of images and references to students' current community immediately makes the topic more engaging and meaningful for them. Using images from the students' or their families' countries of origin could also personalize the lesson. The teacher can include all the questions, comparisons, descriptions, reading, writing, and conversations she had planned for the unit, but with images, contexts, and points of view that are more familiar to the students in the class. By taking this multiperspective approach, students are more likely to find personal connections with the content while also being stretched to see other perspectives (Banks, 2005). In the following section, we will explore instruction that focuses on teaching for understanding.

Developing Conceptual Understanding

In addition to embedding learning in meaningful and relevant contexts, we need to provide students with the means to develop a deep conceptual understanding of the content they are learning (see Figure 2.1). Bransford et al. (2000) convened a group that looked at the science behind human learning and what is needed for optimal learning to take place. Donovan and Bransford (2005) followed up the original work by looking at how the findings applied to classroom practice across different content areas and grade levels. They identified three principles that optimize education for all learners. These principles can help educators to design instruction that promotes deep conceptual understanding for DLLsSEN.

The first principle is that new learning must *engage students' prior understandings*. Like all learners, DLLsSEN must have the opportunity to bring all their linguistic, cultural, and experiential resources, as well as school knowledge, skills, and understandings, to their present learning (Piaget, 1951; Moll et al., 1992). In this asset-based approach to instruction, it is important to recognize that all learners develop their own understandings of concepts and related ideas, which continue to be refined throughout their lives. Classroom teachers can create shared experiences such as experiments, simulations, projects, and investigations to encourage their students to question and develop their understandings. Students can also dispel myths or misconceptions along the way as their knowledge of academic concepts and content grows more sophisticated.

The second principle highlights the importance of *integrating factual knowledge into conceptual frameworks to build deep understanding.* Facts and skills that are taught randomly and out of context are more difficult for learners to retain and access later. From a cognitive perspective, when information is organized into a conceptual framework, or schema, as suggested by Piaget (1951), students gain deeper understanding and can better recall and apply the information in new contexts. For example, in a unit on butterflies, students may learn the parts of a butterfly and then receive a diagram of the butterfly that they label. This reflects the part-to-whole approach described earlier. A whole-to-part approach to this same content would have students participate in a unit of study on the life cycle of butterflies. The teacher could collect the leaves of a milkweed plant that have butterfly eggs and place them in a glass tank with milkweed, sticks, leaves, and a mesh covering. Over time, the students would discuss, measure, question, describe, read, and write about the insect as it transforms from egg to larva, pupa, and then adult butterfly. Through such multisensory experiences and opportunities to see, hear, and use concepts, students develop schematic networks with multiple connections that can facilitate application of these concepts to new learning. In this case, students develop a deep understanding of vocabulary related to butterflies which enables them to apply the concepts of metamorphosis and the life cycle in new contexts. This principle can be particularly helpful for DLLsSEN in developing the depth and breadth of their understanding, which, in turn, assists them in applying learning from one context to another.

The third principle regards providing learners with the opportunity to *self-regulate, monitor, and direct their own learning.* Instructional environments that support this principle give students choices of topics and reading materials, and they incorporate methods and projects that allow students to demonstrate their learning. Students are guided to set learning goals, reflect on their understanding of concepts or principles, and strategize on how to achieve their goals. As they acquire awareness of their learning process, i.e. **metacognition**, they become more aware of personal strategies that they use to understand ideas, principles, and concepts and to remember information. Teachers can model and expand their students' utterances to provide feedback about their understanding of content and their spoken language. These strategies are frequently used in both L2 instruction and special education to help students reflect on their ideas and on how to communicate them to others. Recognizing that DLLsSEN often need explicit support and extended practice, educators can systematically 'think aloud' with them to reflect on how they are learning throughout instruction and intervention. DLLsSEN have the advantage of being able to share their thinking in both of their languages with teachers, paraprofessionals, and peers as they build metacognitive awareness of their learning.

These principles derived from research on learning provide a solid foundation for educators who understand the far-reaching impact of teaching for understanding (Gardner, 2011; Commins, 2011). Teachers can optimize understanding for DLLsSEN by consistently engaging their prior knowledge and experiences; always integrating concepts, facts, and skills into organizing frameworks; and systematically fostering the students' metacognitive awareness of how they learn best.

Developing Oral Communication

Oral communication includes comprehension of incoming auditory messages as well as speaking to communicate information and thoughts for a range of purposes with a variety of audiences. It plays an essential role both in acquiring language and in learning content in the classroom. At every stage of developing their new language, DLLs benefit from authentic and purposeful oral interactions with communication partners to advance their understanding and to revise and refine their spoken language. Educators need to give DLLs regular opportunities to interact with peers so that they continue to develop oral communication in all their languages.

Oral communication skills can be an area of particular challenge for students with SEN, who require more frequent opportunities for extended periods to develop these skills to their optimal level. For example, students with SLI typically experience difficulties with spoken language, which for some occur in combination with auditory comprehension challenges (Kohnert, 2013; Leonard, 1998; Prelock et al., 2008). Students with autism often have difficulty understanding the nuances of meaning in social interactions and/or effectively using these subtle features of oral communication when speaking with others (Geurts & Embrechts, 2008; Williams et al., 2008). While students who have learning disabilities may primarily experience challenges with reading and writing, they too may have underlying difficulties with auditory comprehension or in clearly expressing their ideas in spoken language (McArthur et al., 2000).

For DLLsSEN with oral communication disabilities, their difficulties will manifest in all of their languages. In addition to understanding the challenges that DLLsSEN experience with oral communication, it is important for educators to gather information about the students' linguistic strengths so that these can be employed as resources to mediate learning. Students' strengths can be used as scaffolds to address specific areas of difficulty in instruction and intervention. This is exemplified by the educators in Spotlight Study 2.4 (see page 79), who were able to engage a student whose verbal or written output in the classroom was very limited by starting with his talents and linguistic resources. Through the use of interactive journaling, combined with his artistic ability, the student began to draw. With very gradual and careful scaffolding by educators, he eventually spoke and began to write in Spanish. The educators' willingness to identify and incorporate the student's unique strengths optimized his access to instruction. Given that the different language modalities of listening, speaking, reading, and writing are linked conceptually and inform one another (Fu & Matoush, 2015), selected modalities can be utilized strategically to support the development of others. For example, a student's strengths in oral expression may be employed to develop written language using speech-to-text software; and auditory comprehension strengths can be used in developing reading comprehension skills.

Students' multiple languages are also conceptually connected and influence each other, and can therefore be activated to scaffold learning across languages. Strong receptive skills in the home language can support understanding of concepts and provide a bridge toward developing speaking or writing skills in the language of instruction. Speech-language pathologists Kohnert, Yim, Nett, Kan, and Duran (2005) recommend that intervention address oral language development in both languages for DLLs with SLI. Given that these students' overall pace of language learning is slower, their language abilities are typically less developed than those of their DLL age peers. Consequently, instruction and intervention that emphasize English only make these DLLs with SLI especially vulnerable to loss of their home languages. Kohnert et al. (2005) assert that access to both home and school languages is fundamental to the social, emotional, cognitive, academic, and vocational success of DLLs. Therefore, when DLLs also have SLI, intervention needs to develop oral communication skills in both languages. Chapters 3 and 4 will include classroom and clinical examples of how we can support all the languages of DLLsSEN, even when we do not speak or understand those languages ourselves.

Affirming Students' Multilingualism and Multiculturalism

Schools that create learning communities where DLLs feel welcome and included are filled with conversations, thinking, reading, writing, and artistic works that reflect their languages and cultures. As discussed in Chapter 1, culturally and linguistically responsive teaching ensures that students see themselves reflected in the lessons, materials, and classrooms throughout the school environment. DLLs, including DLLsSEN, who know that their teachers are keen to learn about them, their languages, and their cultures become more invested in their own learning (Klingner & Eppolito, 2014). When educators incorporate students' languages and cultural experiences into instruction, multilingual multicultural students are affirmed and receive a clear message that they need not leave any part of who they are at home when they come to school (Cummins et al., 2005).

Returning to Donovan and Bransford's principle of engaging students' prior understandings in order to optimize learning (see page 55), it is important to acknowledge that in addition to what they are learning at school, DLLsSEN will also have acquired experiences, knowledge, skills, and resources at home with their families and in their communities. Because cognitive understanding and schemata can be encoded in students' home languages and developed through their cultural perspectives, incorporating these into instruction facilitates access to background knowledge in ways that promote learning (Cummins, 2009). If, however, DLLs and DLLsSEN are limited to using only the language of instruction to share their thoughts, conjectures, and opinions, then a great deal of their thinking and understanding may not be fully accessed or shared in the classroom. This is especially the case for students in the early stages of developing proficiency in the language of instruction. Similarly, for DLLsSEN, using only English to learn may further limit what they can comprehend and express in the classroom. However, when the students' languages and cultural perspectives are actively integrated into units of study, DLLs, including those with SEN, can access more of their cognitive and linguistic resources to build understanding and demonstrate what they know. While it would be challenging to instruct all students bilingually in highly diverse classrooms, teachers can implement strategies that 'encourage students to use their L1 as a cognitive tool and feel proud of their multilingual abilities' (Cummins, Mirza, & Stille, 2012, p. 29).

The smallest shift in this direction can produce significant changes in the sociocultural environment of our schools and classrooms. When daily practices encourage students to talk and write in their home languages, the message is clear that what DLLs know and can communicate in their languages is valued (Cummins, 1994). When school libraries invest in dual-language books that reflect the linguistic diversity of their communities, students' multilingual identities are affirmed. Increases in verbal participation and engagement are reported in classroom-based studies where teachers incorporate instructional strategies that employ home languages. Some of these studies will be explored in Chapters 3 and 4. Activity 2.2 provides a starting point for educators to welcome students from all linguistic backgrounds into their classrooms at the beginning of the school year.

Activity 2.2

Gather information about the languages represented in your classroom from your students, their families, or intake information. With students and/or colleagues, create a visually appealing display about these languages.

You could create a 'Welcome to Our Classroom' sign for your door, with the word 'welcome' or 'hello' translated into the languages of your students. During history class, you could map the languages onto a globe and title it 'The Languages of Our Classroom'. In mathematics class, students could create a bar graph representing the number of students who speak each language, including English, with DLLs appearing more than once for all the languages they know.

Discuss these questions with students and/or colleagues:

- What message would students receive in a classroom where all their languages are prominently acknowledged and displayed?
- How might families feel when they come to school and see their languages displayed along with English in the school?
- How might you extend these activities to connect to different content areas?
- What are other ways of showcasing students' languages at the beginning of the school year?

Teachers who actively invite students' languages into the classroom create a more inclusive environment for their DLLs and DLLsSEN. These teachers recognize that students are in the process of acquiring the language of instruction as well as learning concepts and content. Students can think, process information, and participate in lessons more readily when all their languages are employed in instruction.

At the program design level, the use of home languages to instruct DLLs has been shown to be beneficial for language development and academic outcomes. A study by Thomas and Collier (2002) followed the academic performance of DLLs from five different US school districts from 1996 to

2001. These researchers gathered information on the school climate as well as academic achievement data from the districts' standardized tests. Comparing the performance of students in various program models, they found that DLLs who were instructed bilingually for four to seven years in all subject areas outperformed DLLs receiving monolingual English instruction. Analysis also revealed better long-term achievement among DLLs in schools with supportive sociocultural learning environments.

DLLs who experience learning challenges in school can develop bilingualism and have been found to perform as well in bilingual programs as similar DLLs attending monolingual programs (Genesee, Lindholm-Leary, Saunders, & Christian, 2005, 2006; Myers, 2009). It is important to consider, however, that how and when home languages are incorporated into instruction can vary widely across bilingual programs for DLLsSEN. One study of a group of DLLsSEN who received home language and culturally relevant instruction in their special education classrooms over three years reported higher levels of English language proficiency than that achieved by similar students receiving monolingual special education (Maldonado, 1994). In another study, even when the program had bilingual special educators, use of the home language was not maximized. Across the classrooms studied, English instruction predominated and Spanish was used mostly for clarification and giving directions rather than as a resource for learning content (Paneque & Rodriguez, 2009).

In addition to promoting students' multilingualism, we encourage educators to look at students' language and literacy practices in their daily lives at school and in their homes and communities. Below, we explore the pedagogy of multiliteracies that can provide more avenues to engage DLLs and DLLsSEN in meaningful and relevant instruction.

Adopting a Multiliteracies Approach

Taking a multiliteracies approach to literacy instruction is a way to move beyond monolingual approaches and embrace the cultural and linguistic diversity of our students. Such an approach uses multiple languages, modalities, and technologies to make and express meaning through projects that are personally relevant to students. It acknowledges the diversity of literacies that students encounter and often engage in beyond the classroom. The framework for teaching literacy that emerged from the New London Multiliteracies Group challenged educators to rethink traditional methods, materials, and programs that were based on a monolingual English perspective (Cazden, Cope, Fairclough, & Gee, 1996; Cummins et al., 2005). This pedagogical framework put forth the idea that educators can build classroom experiences and units of study by integrating students' linguistic and cultural resources into instruction to advance their literacy and thinking. The four major components of this pedagogical approach are *situated practice, overt instruction, critical framing*, and *transformed practice* (Cazden et al., 1996).

In *situated practice*, educators build meaning-making literacy experiences based on different domains of students' lives—for example, social, public, school, home, and community. With *overt instruction*, educators create a learning environment where students feel comfortable and safe sharing their thoughts. In these supportive environments, all students develop ways to talk about their meaning-making strategies and thinking processes. Given the opportunity to enter *critical framing*, students and teachers take the time to examine the deeper meanings of texts and other media. Educators specifically plan instruction so that students have the tools and opportunities to recognize and analyze issues of power, social justice, oppression, and other themes during literacy instruction. Engaging students in *transformed practice* encourages them to become creators and designers of new knowledge, products, literary works, multimedia projects, and performances. When students become critical consumers and creators of texts—for example, digital texts, film, websites, multimedia, visual texts, or paper texts—they will be able to distinguish what is meant to provoke, persuade, oppress, convince, educate, or inform.

One application of the multiliteracies approach has focused on developing multilingual **identity texts** (Cummins & Early, 2011). Identity texts actively engage students in using home languages and personal experiences through the creation of dual-language stories (Chow & Cummins, 2003; Schecter & Cummins, 2003; Cummins & Early, 2011). These are student-created projects and literary works that incorporate learners' languages, cultures, life experiences, and interests. They can also integrate DLLs' diverse perspectives on global and local issues. The essence of identity texts is that learners see themselves reflected in the works they create.

Identity texts can take many forms. Young students can write a story in both of their languages about a cultural practice from their home or community. Students in secondary settings can create dual-language science picture books in biology class to give to elementary students. Elementary students can record podcasts of their own dual-language books and post these on the school website. Preschool teachers can engage their students' families in helping to develop dual-language concept books about many topics.

Students can create identity texts that incorporate their cultural funds of knowledge as well as build on their community and family experiences.

The creation of identity texts invites the participation of families, community members, elders, and siblings, as well as bilingual peers, all of whom may provide culturally relevant content for these texts or help with translations and with word processing in the home languages (Schecter & Cummins, 2003). Literacy instruction that includes identity texts invites students to discuss, analyze, write, and read about historical events, literary works, shared experiences, scientific inquiry, etc. in their own voices, in their own languages, and from their own perspectives.

Building upon the languages of DLLs as assets, this orientation challenges educators to extend the traditional classroom focus beyond print literacy in the instructional language to multiple modes of meaning-making and communication—for example, audio, visual, linguistic, spatial, and performative (Ntelioglou, Fannin, Montanera, & Cummins, 2014; Toohey, Dagenais, & Schulze, 2012). Throughout this volume, we will delve deeper into research and examples of the benefits of supporting students' bilingualism and multilingualism at all ages.

Strategically Addressing Language, Literacy, and Content

As shown in Figure 2.1, instruction that supports DLLs and DLLsSEN must simultaneously address language development, literacy, and academic content. Instruction must be **differentiated** to meet the needs of students at varying levels of proficiency in the language of instruction as well as to incorporate the specific academic language and literacy skills inherent in the subject matter.

This multifaceted instruction can be facilitated through collaborative planning among ESL/bilingual specialists and classroom teachers. The process can be fruitful when colleagues co-plan (Honigsfeld & Dove, 2010) to ensure that the needs of DLLs are met. Adding the expertise of the special educator to this collaboration when working with DLLsSEN, teachers can provide students with the support they need across all their learning environments in an integrated and cohesive manner. Content area classroom teachers can embed strategies that make important concepts more comprehensible to students by incorporating visuals, manipulatives, diagrams, and shared experiences throughout their units and lessons. Language teachers can share strategies for integrating academic language and literacy instruction into the content area lessons. Together they can coordinate language instruction with content area topics (Commins & Miramontes, 2006).

Effective classroom instruction for DLLs provides many opportunities for students to use their academic English for authentic communication, both orally and in print. Research pertaining to effective classroom instruction for DLLs points to the importance of integrating the development of listening, speaking, reading, and writing into meaningful content, with focused instruction on language form (de Oliveira & Schleppegrell, 2016; Lightbown & Spada, 2013). For DLLsSEN, it is especially important that special educational approaches are shaped by current L2 learning pedagogy while addressing the students' individual strengths and needs.

Ensuring Strategic, Coordinated, Cohesive, and Comprehensive Interventions

In some school settings, instructional planning for DLLsSEN occurs in 'silos'; that is, in a compartmentalized manner. Especially in the later grades, teachers and other practitioners who support DLLsSEN each plan in ways that address their departments' requirements and goals for the students. The ESL/bilingual teachers incorporate culturally responsive language and literacy in their lessons. Teachers with a special education background refer to each student's IEP to address the goals listed in that document. The general classroom teachers look to the subject area standards, content, and skills to guide the development of units of study and individual lessons. When instruction is not coordinated and cohesive, the student is pulled in different directions and the instructional day can become fragmented (Harry & Klingner, 2006). Spotlight Study 2.1 illustrated an example of the kind of unfortunate experience that can emerge for DLLsSEN when instruction does not address the full range of their needs in any setting due to educators working in isolation.

All the educators involved with DLLsSEN need regular opportunities to coordinate their efforts and build instructional units of study and lessons with strategic scaffolds that seamlessly incorporate the components of the framework in Figure 2.1. Learning can be optimized when teachers and practitioners come together to implement comprehensive, cohesive, and responsive instruction and intervention across all settings (Baca et al., 2004; Harry & Klingner, 2006; Ruiz, 1995). In this way, the linguistic, cultural, literacy, social-emotional, and academic needs of DLLsSEN can be addressed in each setting during their instructional day.

In Classroom Snapshot 2.2, we visit a school with an intervention team that assessed students' learning environments to better support those who were experiencing difficulties.

Classroom Snapshot 2.2

An instructional coach responsible for meeting with and supporting teachers started seeing a pattern emerge in her school. She noticed that the students who had the greatest need for additional support and resources were being pulled in many directions. The teacher talked with the principal and proposed that she would accompany one student through a typical day. After identifying a fifth-grade student who was having difficulty, the principal contacted the family to get their permission and informed the student's teachers of the plan.

The student had an intermediate level of English proficiency and was comfortable with the instructional coach as she had modeled lessons in her class on various occasions. The coach followed the student throughout a day while documenting her observations to share with the principal and the teachers. She noted that there was a problem in the way instruction for this student was organized. The student was being pulled from the general classroom to work with different people throughout the day on the various skills that had been identified through assessment. While the student seemed to be receiving a great deal of support and intervention, these were delivered by various adults in different settings. Each educator worked on different and separate goals with various sets of materials that were unrelated to the instruction in the classroom.

At the end of the day, the coach interviewed the student to ask her how she felt about school. The student said she felt that a lot of people cared about her and that people were nice to her. When asked what she was learning about in the different settings throughout the day, she could not say. She did not feel she understood what everything was about or how it was connected. ▪

The team realized that the organization of their additional interventions and supports led to fragmentation of the instructional day. Students with disabilities, who had the greatest challenges, were being asked to make connections across well-intentioned but disjointed programming (Harry & Klingner, 2006; Herrera, Perez, & Escamilla, 2010).

Subsequently, the school leadership team discussed ways to coordinate their support for students. The team recognized that all teachers shared responsibility for the students and appreciated the flexible time the principal had created for grade-level teams to work together. They decided to align instruction and intervention as closely as possible to the content of each student's main classroom. In this case, the classroom teacher was working on a unit about the Solar System in science. The school interventionist, who was focusing on providing the student with extra support in vocabulary development, used instructional strategies that aligned with ELL pedagogy to preview, build, or review understanding of the academic vocabulary from the Solar System unit. The reading specialist who supported the student used the material in the same unit during her intervention. These strategies were shared for use throughout the day in different content areas across instructional settings. They included recurrent and consistent use of the same graphic organizers, reading comprehension strategies, writing prompts, and technology—for example, use of the same dictionary app for academic vocabulary and speech-to-text software.

Creating Culturally and Linguistically Responsive Inclusive Educational Systems

The next component of the framework in Figure 2.1 speaks to the importance of systematically addressing the diversity of the student population in our schools. This system-wide component wraps around and contributes to the other components in the framework. Reorganizing educational systems so that they immediately acknowledge and attend to diversity as a resource is essential (Miramontes et al., 2011). If we do not plan for diversity from the outset, teaching and learning, leadership, decision-making, pedagogy, curriculum development, materials purchases, and other critical processes will continue to operate from a monolingual monocultural rather than a multilingual multicultural perspective. Using a monolingual lens disadvantages a student population with diverse learning profiles, language and cultural backgrounds, abilities, interests, learning strengths and challenges, socioeconomic backgrounds, and life experiences—in short, most of the students in our schools. A culturally and linguistically responsive inclusive educational system shifts away from the prevalent deficit perspective of learners, their families, and their communities toward an asset orientation. Educational systems that are designed to anticipate rather than react to wide-ranging diversity of learners create learning environments that are inclusive, responsive, and effective for more students (Commins & Miramontes, 2006; Hamayan et al., 2013; Ortiz, 2001; Ortiz & Wilkinson, 1991).

The reauthorization in the US of the Individuals with Disabilities Education Improvement Act (IDEIA) in 2004 allowed states to develop criteria for early intervention and **Multi-Tiered Systems of Support (MTSS)** to proactively support student achievement. Central goals of this law are to address academic or behavioral difficulties, while reducing the disproportionate representation of cultural, ethnic, and racial minority students in special education. As we saw in Chapter 1, the use of standardized assessments designed for monolingual students contributed to the significantly disproportionate representation of students from linguistic and cultural minority backgrounds in special education. By the time students were tested, they had often struggled academically and experienced failure in school for months or years. This was especially the case for DLLs, as school teams were often misguidedly waiting for students to become proficient enough to use English tests that still compared them to monolingual norms (Cummins, 1984).

Many states in the US have designed models for MTSS with the intent of better meeting the needs of their student populations. Using MTSS offers options for early intervention to support academic achievement and for reducing the misplacement of DLLs into special education (González & Artiles, 2015; Klingner & Edwards, 2006; Orosco, 2010). Culturally and linguistically responsive MTSS is a framework for continuous systemic improvement in which data-based problem-solving and decision-making is practiced across all levels within school systems for supporting the diverse range of students. It is intended to utilize high-quality, evidence-based instruction, intervention, and assessment practices, starting in general education classrooms. MTSS guides schools and districts to organize resources for these purposes. When implemented effectively and sustained over time, MTSS is meant to accelerate the performance of every student to achieve or exceed expected proficiency.

Although the federal legislation did not specify the approach or number of tiers of support, many states have adopted **Response to Instruction and Intervention** (**RTI**). An RTI framework consists of multiple levels of increasingly intensive instruction known as Tiers.

Districts can choose to employ standard protocols or a problem-solving approach to design interventions (Fuchs, Mock, Morgan, & Young, 2003). The standard protocol approach or standard treatment protocol can be used in the context of MTSS/RTI to address the needs of students who are struggling academically. School-based teams recommend and implement an intervention—treatment or program—that will be employed systematically with a group of students. In contrast, school systems that take a problem-solving approach within MTSS engage school-based teams that identify the challenges or difficulties that students are experiencing to hypothesize possible causes. These collaborative teams develop an instructional plan based on their hypothesis to address the specific learning challenge(s). This process guides teachers and practitioners in implementing evidence-based strategies and techniques, in assessing the plan's effectiveness, and in beginning the process again to refine and/or change the plan as needed.

In Tier I, the focus is on improving the quality of universal or core instruction that all students receive in the classroom. Tier II represents additional targeted or supplemental interventions provided to a small group of students. Tier III provides the most intensive and strategic interventions that a smaller group or individual students would receive.

Frequent assessment is used to monitor student progress (National Center on Response to Intervention, 2010). In 2004, the reauthorization of special education in the US allowed school districts to use part of their special education funding to develop and implement these coordinated early intervention services for students who need additional academic or behavioral support to be successful in general education classrooms. MTSS/RTI approaches have potential for all DLLs if school systems shift the focus from discerning the nature of educational deficits assumed to be within the student to an asset-based instructional approach that starts by making changes to the learning environment (Klingner & Edwards, 2006; Orosco, 2010). Of significance for all DLLs, including DLLsSEN, this approach allows resources—for example, human resources or time—to be used by school systems to make core instructional learning environments more culturally and linguistically responsive.

Spotlight Study 2.2 was conducted by the US Department of Education's Institute of Education Sciences (IES) in 2015 to examine the effectiveness of early implementation of RTI. They explored 1) the extent to which schools implemented various RTI practices; 2) how effectively they identified the students who required supplemental reading intervention services; and 3) how the interventions impacted reading outcomes for the students who received these additional services.

Spotlight Study 2.2

This large-scale study by the US Department of Education (Balu et al., 2015) included more than 140 schools in 45 districts and 13 states representing students across socioeconomic groups in first through third grades. Along with monolingual students, the study included DLLs (6–13 percent) and students with SEN (10–12 percent). However, the study did not report on DLLsSEN; nor were the data disaggregated for any of the subgroups in this study. Participating schools had all been implementing an RTI system to support students for a minimum of two to three years. The findings for the three areas of focus were as follows:

- At the school level, there was extensive implementation of the various components of RTI. Schools screened all their students, with the majority receiving Tier I core reading instruction. A smaller number of students were identified as needing Tier II intervention services, and a still smaller number received additional Tier III intensive supplemental reading interventions.
- At the reading group level, most schools were providing intervention services through specialized staff—rather than instructional aides—to the students who were reading below grade level. The supplemental Tier II and Tier III interventions consisted primarily of phonics instruction for all students. Most schools provided these services in addition to the core reading block.

However, some were providing them not only to students reading below grade level but also to students reading at or above grade level. Furthermore, some schools provided the interventions during rather than in addition to the 90-minute core instructional block.

- At the student level, the outcomes were disappointing for those children reading just below and significantly below grade level who were chosen to receive small-group Tier II or individual Tier III interventions. In first grade, negative impacts were found on a general measure of reading and decoding fluency for all students receiving the intervention. This equated to losing one-tenth of a year of learning. In second and third grades, there was no statistically significant positive change in reading for students receiving these supplemental reading interventions (Balu et al., 2015). ■

In Spotlight Study 2.2, we see that the schools involved in this evaluation implemented the RTI interventions as prescribed, using one system to identify students for intervention services in reading. However, the outcomes for students were not positive and in some cases the students lost ground. This calls into question the extent to which the prescribed instruction actually addressed the specific learning needs of the selected students. There was no mention of schools making the RTI process culturally and linguistically responsive for the student populations they served. Along with using only one measure to select students, some schools reportedly provided the interventions to all students and as core instruction. With the use of a single screening tool, everyone who was identified received the same interventions. This has been the most frequent approach to RTI (Linan-Thompson, 2010; Lipson & Wixson, 2013). In this study, interventions consisted primarily of phonics instruction which targeted one component of reading. Phonics instruction did not necessarily address what individual students needed or contribute to achieving the larger goal of reading comprehension. Although there is potential in using an RTI approach to support students, early implementation of this tiered model of instruction has not been tailored to many of the student populations it was meant to support—including DLLs (García & Ortiz, 2008; Hoover & Baca, 2008; Orosco & Klingner, 2010).

'One-size-fits-all' packaged intervention programs have been emphasized without attention to their effectiveness for diverse student populations, including DLLs (Cummins, 2007; Klingner & Edwards, 2006; Orosco, 2010; Ortiz et al., 2011). In contrast to the use of standard protocols, culturally and linguistically responsive implementation of MTSS/RTI aligns better with the problem-solving option that enables consideration of language proficiency levels and individual learner profiles of strengths and needs (Richards-Tutor, Baker, Gersten, Baker, & Smith, 2016). Given the heterogeneity among DLLs, it is important to discern the specific nature of students' challenges to design and implement instruction or interventions that are derived from the DLL research base. For example, reading interventions employed at text level that go beyond focusing on word-level phonics and fluency skills have been found to significantly improve reading comprehension for DLLs (McIntosh, Graves, & Gersten, 2007).

Early implementation of RTI has typically employed a narrow set of assessment tools that measure discrete component skills in reading English. Many of these tools compare DLLs' performance to that of monolingual speakers without taking bilingual learning, language proficiency levels, or cultural and experiential backgrounds into account (Linan-Thompson, 2010). Use of multiple sources of data is recommended for DLLs, including measures of meaning-based skills—for example, vocabulary and listening comprehension—that compare growth to that of students with similar language and cultural backgrounds (National Academies of Sciences, Engineering, and Medicine, 2017). To better discern how DLLs are learning, it has also been suggested that the screening period be extended to observe how DLLs respond to classroom-based strategies that utilize dynamic assessment techniques (Linan-Thompson, 2010). Of diagnostic note, DLLs that had not been provided with sufficient opportunities to learn have been observed to make rapid and consistent gains when given systematic and explicit DLL instruction. However, with the same type of instruction, DLLs with learning difficulties demonstrated slower rates of progress on repeated assessments, similar to those of monolingual students with learning disabilities. Gathering this type of qualitative data in addition to that provided by typical RTI screening and progress monitoring tools can guide instruction by enriching our understanding of how DLLs learn. By taking a problem-solving approach to MTSS/RTI, culturally and linguistically responsive practices can be infused into all stages of the process: screening, classroom instruction and tiered interventions, and classroom-based assessment (Young & Sánchez-López, 2017).

A descriptive study of early implementation of RTI in a diverse school where 85 percent of students were Latino (Orosco & Klingner, 2010) reported that deficit views of DLLs were prevalent. After two years of implementing RTI, it remained difficult for educators and other practitioners to shift away from their deeply held beliefs. They focused primarily on figuring out 'what was wrong' with individual DLLs rather than on improving the quality and effectiveness of instruction in the learning environment. The evidence-based reading practices for English-speaking students that teachers implemented were not sufficiently responsive to the language and literacy needs of DLLs.

Teachers reported that the prescribed assessment tool was not sensitive enough to the nature of student needs to be helpful in planning instruction. It was noted that the teachers lacked current and relevant literacy materials and resources for their diverse student population. Orosco and Klingner (2010) acknowledged the need for substantial professional development for teachers in DLL pedagogy, taking a sociocultural perspective and an advocacy orientation in implementing RTI.

Educational systems that develop culturally and linguistically responsive versions of MTSS/RTI attend to students' language proficiency, cultural backgrounds, and life experiences as sociocultural resources for learning (Artiles et al., 2004; González & Artiles, 2015; Hamayan et al., 2013; Klingner et al., 2014; WIDA Consortium, 2013). Incorporating sociocultural perspectives into MTSS/RTI models is a critical ingredient in optimizing learning and implementing appropriate interventions for DLLs and DLLsSEN (Orosco, 2010; Orosco & Klingner, 2010).

Taking an Asset Orientation

The growing field of positive psychology can further enhance instruction for DLLs by framing our work with students within an asset or strengths-based orientation that leads us to develop learning environments that promote positive emotion and engagement (Seligman, 2011). Peterson and Seligman (2004) developed a categorization system in *Character Strengths and Virtues: A Handbook and Classification*, modeled on the *Diagnostic and Statistical Manual of Mental Disorders* but with a shift in focus from fixing flaws to one of building strengths. Based on this work, teachers at Geelong Grammar School in Australia worked together to make school-wide changes to the instructional environment. They infused positive educational principles into their curriculum and teaching practices by integrating exercises exploring students' character strengths in literature units and promoting well-being in the general education curriculum. Teachers reported improved learning and engagement in school, including curiosity, love of learning, and creativity among typical learners (Seligman, Ernst, Gillham, Reivich, & Linkins, 2009).

In the field of speech-language pathology, Nelson advocates for practitioners to build on strengths to address areas of need in providing instruction and intervention for children with SLI and counselling for their families (Holland & Nelson, 2013). Holland has been a leader in bringing a wellness perspective to her work as a speech-language pathologist with adults diagnosed with degenerative conditions. These authors, who elevate strengths as resources in intervention, provide a model for shifting practice for those of us whose training has grown out of a deficit orientation.

Valuing Family and Community Resources

Researchers in diversity education have long advocated for a positive, strengths-based view of students, their families, and their communities. Cummins (1994) has promoted an asset orientation in all our interactions with students and families. Delpit (1995) urged recognition of the strengths of diverse learners and teaching to these strengths. Nieto (1996) affirms the diversity of learners through multicultural educational practices based in social justice. The work of Miramontes and Commins (2014) promotes an ability-centered perspective rather than a deficit view to reveal competence among language minority students. Based on sociocultural theory, educators who embrace their students' beliefs, values, and cultural and linguistic practices enhance learning with positive outcomes. In this way, educators show appreciation for the assets students bring to school and their value for diversity (Baca & Cervantes, 2004).

The work of Luis Moll and his colleagues has encouraged educators not only to acknowledge their students' home and community resources but to also build upon these resources to create instruction that is more meaningful and of higher quality than what these students have typically experienced. Using ethnographic approaches, they gathered data through observations, interviews, life histories, and case studies to explore students' assets beyond the classroom, studying everyday practices of Latino families in their homes (González, Moll, & Amanti, 2006). Ethnographic approaches are used in the field of cultural anthropology to gather data through direct observation or participant observation and informant interviews. Using participant observation, the researchers interacted with families and recorded descriptive field notes. These qualitative data were systematically analyzed for patterns and insights into knowledge and dynamics within the families.

Spotlight Study 2.3 illustrates the interactions and collaborative work of teachers and researchers as they uncovered the funds of knowledge of the students they taught and their families (Moll et al., 1992).

Spotlight Study 2.3

A group of teachers and researchers in anthropology collaborated to learn about students and their working-class Mexican immigrant families in Tucson, Arizona. The study included three components: home visits to analyze household resources and dynamics; an in-depth examination of current classroom practices; and after-school study groups where teachers and researchers discussed and analyzed what they had learned from the home visits. Before conducting the home visits, teachers participated in workshops on how to conduct ethnographic observations and interviews. They also learned how to write field notes and manage and analyze the data they would collect. Using these ethnographic approaches, teachers explored their students' relationships and activities in their families and communities to gather information about their funds of knowledge. In the study, researchers used the term 'funds of knowledge' to refer to the bodies of knowledge and skills that families and communities use to survive and thrive. These also included long-standing and functional social networks that connected families to one another within the community.

The ten teachers who participated in this study each selected three households that they would study. They visited 25 homes and conducted 100 observations and interviews during a school semester. Teachers and researchers noticed that the families seemed comfortable and enjoyed sharing stories about their children. They also freely shared information about their work and the ways that family and community members outside their immediate family helped one another. The anthropologists noted that the teachers were held in high esteem by the families, and that they were warmly welcomed and trusted immediately. The researchers noted that it typically takes them far longer to reach this level of trust when studying communities.

The teachers kept track of the funds of knowledge they observed and learned about. They noted that families had a great deal of knowledge and experience related to agriculture, mining, repair, business, medicine, household management, and religion. Some of the families had experience traveling back and forth between Mexico and the US for trade and for family visits.

After the home visits had taken place, the teachers gathered in study groups to discuss what they had observed and learned from the families. They reflected on how their students were actively learning through their social activities and family relationships, often as active contributors to the daily functioning of their households. As they became familiar with the rich repertoires of knowledge and skills among families, the teachers gained a deeper understanding of their students' lives and capabilities that had not previously been acknowledged in school or integrated into the classroom. Their study of household knowledge and skills was then used to design classroom lessons that accessed and built on the students' existing resources. In one example, teachers noticed that many students contributed to the family economically by selling Mexican candy to members of the community. They took that theme and generated a week's worth of activities for inquiry. They brainstormed types of candy they knew about, categorized them, and then generated questions about the different types of candy. Student teams chose a research question to pursue, using all sources of information, including parents and other community members, to answer their question. Parents came to school during this inquiry unit as intellectual resources for the children in the class. One research question was about the kinds of ingredients found in candy. The class gathered their information about all the ingredients in all the candy they had brainstormed and were surprised to find that there were far fewer ingredients in Mexican candy than in US candy samples.

At the end of the unit, one of the mothers came into class to demonstrate how to make *pipitoria*, a Mexican candy treat. While the candy was cooking, the parents talked with the children about nutrition in the US and in Mexico as well as about the kinds of ingredients that were used in the cuisine of both countries. On the last day of the unit, students created advertising and packaged the candy they had made to sell during a school activity. They spent time reflecting on and summarizing their research findings and generating new research questions about the kinds of candy children eat in Africa and in China. And so a unit based on the students' funds of knowledge formed the basis of future inquiry and study. ■

This spotlight study illustrates how exploring the funds of knowledge that our students and their families possess has the potential to enhance practice and pedagogy in ways that naturally engage and promote language learning for the DLLsSEN in our classrooms. Studies such as this promote fuller appreciation of family resources and deeper understanding of community connections. In Classroom Snapshot 2.3, we will look at how valuing family experiences and perspectives is central to developing reciprocal relationships with our students and their families.

In their work with special educators, Kalyanpur and Harry (2012) urge practitioners to reflect on the subtle yet deeply embedded values that shape special education programs and systems and on how these influence their professional beliefs and practices. Kalyanpur and Harry speak of leaning into students' worlds, as in Spotlight Study 2.3, as a means of learning more about and appreciating the families of the children they serve. They emphasize that developing this rapport can support families in considering all their options while navigating their child's special educational experience.

In Classroom Snapshot 2.3, a school team collaborates to support and share resources with a family. Of equal importance is the willingness of the school personnel to learn from and appreciate the family's understanding and perspectives on their child. Families need to know that their contributions are valued. By approaching their relationships with families as reciprocal, educators can gain insights into their world views and into students' life experiences, as illustrated by the work of Moll et al. in Spotlight Study 2.3. Classroom Snapshot 2.3 provides an example of how a reciprocal relationship was developed with one family in a meeting with a school team. While the educators, practitioners, and administrators had information to share, they came to realize that they also had much to learn from the parents in order to enhance the programming for this student with special educational needs.

Classroom Snapshot 2.3

A meeting was set with the family of Javit, a middle school DLL, to identify and make plans to accommodate his moderate cognitive and physical disabilities in the sixth-grade classroom. The family had moved to the area from another school district and had recently denied permission for Javit to attend an upcoming field trip. The teacher wanted to ensure the parents understood that the field trip was an introductory experience integral to the next unit of study. During their trip, the students would gather information by taking pictures for a unit combining science and language arts. The school team had theorized that this immigrant family might need financial assistance for the trip and planned to address this with the parents. They considered how to address this potentially sensitive offer of financial support to encourage permission for Javit to attend the trip.

A teacher who spoke Gujarati, the family's home language, worked with the principal to set up the meeting with the family. They explained the purpose of the meeting and obtained consent for the Gujurati-speaking teacher to attend as the interpreter. It was explained to the parents that the school team members did not speak their home language and were requesting interpretation in order to share information and learn more about their son. The school staff had not previously worked with an interpreter at parent meetings. The speech-language pathologist working with the school, who did have previous experience, previewed key strategies with the team to promote effective communication. These included speaking to and looking at the parents and not the interpreter, as well as allowing time for interpretation by chunking information into reasonable amounts. The interpreter was encouraged to signal should information become too long or complex and to seek clarification or examples for technical terms should she recognize any signs of misunderstanding.

During the meeting, team members took the opportunity to learn more about the student's abilities in his home language and previous school history. The parents' questions and perspectives were invited. In discussing the upcoming field trip, the teacher spoke about its significance for the next unit of study. With open-ended and respectful questioning, she uncovered unanticipated concerns that the parents had about the trip. Javit's mother shared that the family had recently attended a holiday event at a local park amidst a large crowd. When Javit went to the washroom, he became separated from his brother. He was unable to navigate his way back to their location or ask for help in finding them. Although they eventually located him, it was very traumatic and frightening for them all. The parents were worried that the same thing could happen on the field trip. The teacher indicated that school policy was to group students in threes on outings and that she and the educational assistant would both be in Javit's group for safety. She planned to create a pocket identification card for Javit and it was agreed that the parents would preview information about the field trip and safety practices with him in their home language.

After subsequent reflection, the team shared their insights. They felt interpretation services had enabled the family to clarify their understanding about the school logistics and, more importantly, to share their recent experience and understandable concerns. By listening to the family's story, the educators also learned a great deal about the student and his family. The teachers' manner of interaction had facilitated an exchange with parents and resulted in a mutually satisfying plan that they could accomplish together to enable Javit to participate safely in the field trip. Classroom Snapshot 2.3 exemplifies a call to re-envision parental participation as a reciprocal relationship whereby educators value parents' knowledge and input and respect their role as collaborative partners in their child's education (Kalyanpur & Harry, 2012; Young & Westernoff, 1996).

Special Education Approaches for DLLsSEN

We argue that culturally and linguistically responsive instruction benefits all students by making learning personally relevant through recognition of the strengths that individuals bring to the process while affirming their identities. When practicing from this perspective, educators meet the students where they are in multifaceted ways to build toward their next steps in learning (Gee, 2008). This approach remains applicable for DLLs experiencing a variety of learning challenges, whether these are related to a lack of opportunities to learn or to their disabilities. Disabilities can range from mild to moderate or severe in terms of the degree to which they impact learning and the lives of individuals. Although the level of severity is not clearly articulated in most studies, current classroom-based research pertaining to DLLsSEN focuses predominantly on students who experience learning disabilities in the mild to moderate range. This category of LD is among the most frequent identifications for DLLs (Donovan & Cross, 2002).

Considerable research effort has also focused on DLLs who are described as 'at risk' learners for literacy development. The large numbers of DLLs who experience difficulty with reading points to educational systems that have not developed culturally and linguistically responsive instruction for successfully educating increasingly diverse student populations. The challenges and complexities of diagnosing disabilities among DLLs further complicates efforts to distinguish the DLLs who are affected by a disability from those who have not yet experienced sufficient opportunities to learn either English or academic content during their school careers.

Whatever the constellation of characteristics that DLLs bring to the classroom, educational practices need to be grounded in culturally and linguistically responsive principles to facilitate and support students' next steps in learning. For some DLLsSEN with severe disabilities, goals may start with developing ways of effectively communicating their needs in two languages with various partners across different settings. Establishing scaffolds using manipulable objects or pictures and assistive technology may be the priority in educational planning. Examples of assistive technology that can be used to support communication and learning goals include voice output devices and various apps available on mobile devices. For other DLLsSEN, curriculum goals are achievable by starting with culturally and linguistically relevant instruction that is modified and supplemented to meet their learning needs.

Taking a sociocultural approach is particularly important for DLLsSEN, who possess wide-ranging characteristics and capabilities (Orosco & Klingner, 2010). Educators and practitioners mediate learning by providing scaffolding specific to students' level of ability using authentic activities based on curriculum content. For all students, the aim is to facilitate learning while gradually maximizing their independent use of knowledge and strategies. We take the view that DLLsSEN benefit from L2 and bilingual pedagogy as well as content instruction and interventions that are anchored in sociocultural theory. When learning is viewed as a meaning-making process, sociocultural principles are applicable to instruction and interventions across all classroom settings (Bransford et al., 2000; Damico & Damico, 1993). When identified as having SEN, DLLs will continue to benefit from the high-quality instruction they receive from teachers who are knowledgeable about DLL pedagogy. DLLsSEN do not need to be removed from their ESL/bilingual or other general classroom to receive interventions centered on commercially developed packaged 'one-size-fits-all' programs that are disconnected from the curriculum. Through collaboration with special education and ESL/bilingual educators, teachers can design, tailor, and implement general education curricula to meet the needs of DLLsSEN.

Educators may already be familiar with common learning characteristics of students with SEN through their experiences with them. There are general patterns that can be anticipated when planning instruction and intervention. For example, students with disabilities often experience difficulties in acquiring knowledge and skills as readily as their typically developing peers. Additionally, they may have challenges in independently generating ideas and using effective strategies. Educators can respond to such challenges by clearly articulating, demonstrating, and then extensively modeling strategies and by providing extended practice to develop effective use of skills. Teachers can provide specific feedback and encouragement for students as they gradually work towards success (Damico & Damico, 1993; Hamayan et al., 2013). The pace of guided and shared practice needs to be tailored to each student's rate of progress, with practice extended over sufficient time for students to begin to incorporate strategies as their own. Students with SEN may also benefit from personalized tools that they create or that are prepared for them to scaffold use of strategies to their level of ability. These may include visual organizers, references, or technology.

Students with SEN can experience persistent difficulties in applying knowledge and strategies across different contexts. To address this, educators and practitioners can collaborate to design instruction from a sociocultural perspective that enables students to practice using effective meaning-making strategies in authentic contexts. This contrasts strikingly with approaches that use decontextualized skill-building or oversimplified curricula to instruct students with SEN. In general, learners with SEN benefit from greater intensity of support in terms of the resources provided within their ZPD, and they often need these supports for longer than learners without SEN (Damico & Damico, 1993; Hamayan et al., 2013). DLLsSEN benefit from accessing the same topics, content, and curricula as their peers when the pedagogy, materials, and resources are designed to engage them within their ZPD and allow more time for shared and guided practice to make progress.

As we have seen, the quest for evidenced-based interventions for DLLsSEN has led some to assume that what works for monolingual students with SEN applies to DLLsSEN. Worse yet, once a DLL has been identified as having SEN, educators may think that it is appropriate to focus only on special education programming to the exclusion of ESL or bilingual language development. The failure to see language learning as an essential component of instruction for DLLsSEN denies a vital part of the students' education (González & Artiles, 2015). In some school districts, discouraged ESL educators have shared that their colleagues tell them that special education *overrides* ESL instruction. They describe having little or no instructional time or ability to consult with special educators for DLLs who have been identified with SEN. As a result, DLLsSEN receive diminished language instruction and support (Gándara & Rumberger, 2009), although they are entitled to and continue to benefit from language development (Klingner et al., 2014; Orosco & O'Connor, 2014; Zetlin, Beltrán, Salcido, González, & Reyes, 2011). This scenario can also evolve inadvertently in systems which do not recognize that language learning needs overlap and interact with academic content learning needs throughout the school day. The unfortunate social, emotional, and linguistic consequences of attempting to address each area of need separately for blocks of time were illustrated in Spotlight Study 2.1.

Ruiz (2012) urges educators to build on 40 years of L2 learning research in creating programming for DLL students who also have SEN. Spotlight Study 2.4 illustrates how teachers developed enriched programming for a student in a bilingual resource room (Ruiz, Vargas, & Beltrán, 2002). In this example, teachers worked strategically with the student to tailor practices to his learning strengths and needs within an optimal learning environment where both of his languages were used instructionally. This study was coauthored by a bilingual special educator, a resource teacher, and a teaching assistant, who worked collaboratively with Diego, a student who was identified as a DLLSEN after a history of significant difficulty with traditional instruction.

Spotlight Study 2.4

Ruiz et al. (2002) reported that Diego spoke an indigenous Guatemalan language at home, which seemed to align with the 'low' results on assessments of his English and Spanish language skills in kindergarten. He started school in an English kindergarten and then he began attending bilingual classes in first grade. However, teachers mostly used English with him and he spoke very little, resulting in limited oral interaction in school.

By the end of second grade, Diego was observed to be withdrawn and would speak only a few words under his breath. The bilingual special educator, a resource teacher, and a teaching assistant worked collaboratively on a staff development project to create an Optimal Learning Environment (OLE) to accelerate language and literacy based on the earlier work of Ruiz, García, and Figueroa (1996). OLE principles will be further elaborated in Chapter 3.

While awaiting a special education assessment, the educators began to work with Diego in the OLE bilingual resource room. Through interactive instruction and observation of his performance, educators developed a profile of his abilities. They learned that he participated in hands-on projects and applied math calculations to problem-solving when information was read to him in Spanish. They started by specifically tailoring instructional scaffolds to whatever he was able to do independently. For example, teachers accepted and affirmed his drawings as they initiated interactive journaling. While educators focused on what Diego was communicating through his illustrations, they supported him in gradually using more print. The teacher provided intensive mediation for the student to encourage him to speak out loud. Diego initially whispered his ideas to the teacher, who then shared his contributions in the literature study group. As the teachers and peers modeled acceptance of all ideas in their discussions of the text, Diego gradually gained enough confidence to contribute orally.

When Diego was identified as having a learning disability, the educators advocated for him to be placed in the bilingual OLE resource room as opposed to the English special educational setting offered at the school. During his second year in the bilingual OLE resource room, the educators provided compelling examples of his progress as a reader, writer, and speaker in this enriched learning environment. Re-administration of standardized achievement tests revealed that he had achieved more than three years' growth in reading, from a grade equivalent score of K.3 to 3.7, and 3.2 years' growth in writing, from 1.2 to 4.4. ■

Activity 2.3

Approaching the case reported in Spotlight Study 2.4 as a reflective practitioner (Shön, 1987), consider the following questions:

- What resonates with your understanding of the critical components for DLLsSEN in the learning environment?
- What factors appear to contribute to this student's learning and well-being?
- What has not worked for this student in the past?
- Compare your reflections with those from Spotlight Study 2.1 in terms of the features of the learning environments that stand out to you.
- Lastly, what is your take-away—one thing that you can systematically incorporate into your instructional setting with DLLsSEN?

Spotlight Studies 2.1 and 2.4 represent dramatically different educational experiences for two DLLsSEN in their school settings. The students followed similar trajectories in the early grades, but when we met them, Melissa was described as withdrawing from active participation in lessons while Diego was thriving academically and had begun to speak aloud in the bilingual resource room. In both settings, the teachers cared about their students, yet their teaching experiences were markedly different. Melissa's teachers worked in separate classrooms, with different programs and goals, and with no time or resources for coordinating and combining their efforts, knowledge, perspectives, and skill sets. Diego's teachers worked collaboratively in the same setting, with support and resources, to develop optimal instruction while planning and providing highly specific mediation for individual students.

Summary

In Chapter 2, we have summarized theories and foundational research that are relevant to the education of DLLsSEN. Key components have been organized into a framework for culturally and linguistically responsive inclusive learning environments for DLLsSEN (Figure 2.1) that centers on learners as meaning-makers. In this framework, learners participate in educational environments and systems that are designed to effectively support their learning and well-being. In providing instruction for DLLsSEN, collaborative practice is essential, given the complexity and overlapping nature of the types of instruction and interventions they will need.

Educators and practitioners working collaboratively can benefit from each other's perspectives to build upon their knowledge and practices to support DLLsSEN. Coordinated and cohesive programming that is embedded in culturally and linguistically responsive inclusive educational systems proactively addresses the diversity of learners in our classrooms. DLLsSEN benefit from quality L2 and bilingual pedagogy infused with interventions guided by special educational practice, all of which are grounded in sociocultural theory. Chapters 3 and 4 will provide a closer look at classroom and clinically based studies that can guide instruction and intervention for DLLsSEN: Chapter 3 will focus on young DLLs from preschool age to 10 years old; Chapter 4 will focus on adolescent DLLs in middle and high school.

3

Learning Environments for Young Language Learners with Special Educational Needs

Preview

In Chapter 3, we will address research on instructional practices that teachers can use to support their dual language learners with special educational needs in early years and in primary grades up to fifth grade. Most studies in this chapter integrate multiple components of culturally and linguistically responsive practice (see Figure 2.1 on page 39). Elements from the framework that are especially evident in instruction for young DLLsSEN include the use of meaningful contexts, oral communication, and support of multilingualism and multiculturalism.

Much of the research in this chapter focuses specifically on approaches that support literacy and content instruction. It includes both qualitative and quantitative studies set in a variety of educational contexts. The DLLsSEN studied are in general and special education classrooms and, in some cases, are instructed bilingually. The research that we draw upon includes individual case studies, and interventions delivered in small groups and a variety of classroom settings. Studies in preschool are also included as we consider how research findings for very young DLLsSEN can inform intervention for school-age children in the early grades.

Young language learners are enthusiastic, curious, creative, and willing to collaborate with their peers and their teachers. Culturally and linguistically responsive practices that build upon ESL/bilingual learning principles and students' strengths are essential for students to fulfill their learning potential. It is also critical that extrinsic factors in the learning environment be addressed so as to acknowledge their impact on students' academic difficulties. As illustrated in the framework in Figure 2.1, creating culturally and linguistically responsive inclusive learning environments is essential to optimize the academic progress and emotional well-being of DLLsSEN.

While DLLsSEN are the focus of this volume, we will explore a variety of studies with a range of learners to summarize key instructional elements and approaches that support DLLsSEN. Activity 3.1 sets a context within which to examine these instructional practices.

Activity 3.1

Think about a DLLSEN that you have had in class or interview a teacher who has taught DLLsSEN and consider the following:

1 **Linguistic resources:** What languages are used in the student's home? Community? Friend group? Describe the student's stage of English proficiency.
2 **Cultural resources:** What are the student's strengths? Interests? Hobbies? Funds of knowledge? Travel experiences?
3 **Learning characteristics:** What strengths, resources, and strategies does the student bring to learning? What has the student achieved? What are some next steps instructionally?

Create a chart of the student's profile of strengths and learning needs. As you read about the various instructional approaches in this chapter, consider what components may be helpful in teaching this individual DLLSEN.

Oral Communication in Instruction

Oral communication involves speaking and listening in real-time exchanges for authentic purposes between two or more people (Oliver & Philp, 2014). In classroom settings, speaking serves multiple functions including requesting, directing, relating, informing, imagining, and relaying (de Oliveira & Schleppegrell, 2015). From a sociocultural perspective, as students exchange their insights and share connections verbally with their peers and teachers, they co-construct meaning. Expressing their ideas orally also frees students to formulate and revise their thoughts without the stress of immediately producing written text. Creating opportunities for students to talk about what they are learning, reading, and exploring helps them demonstrate how and what they comprehend. Observing and noting the content and nature of the conversation that students engage in can also serve as a type of formative assessment procedure that yields information that teachers can use to adjust their instruction (Jang, 2014).

According to August and Shanahan (2006), oral communication is foundational to students' language and literacy development and integral to their understanding of academic content. For DLLs, use of oral language in both the home language and English is essential in developing print literacy in English (Snow, Burns, & Griffin, 1998). For DLLsSEN, it is especially important to integrate oral language with literacy and content instruction because these students are in the process of learning the language of instruction and may also have difficulties with oral language and reading due to their language or learning disabilities. It is crucial to create frequent opportunities for oral exchanges during reading instruction if students are to engage meaningfully with text and make direct connections between what they know and what they are reading. This process of actively making meaning from text can also increase interest and engagement in literacy instruction.

As we saw in Chapter 2, traditional special education approaches have often focused on the mastery of discrete subskills divorced from a meaningful context, with much time spent on providing correct responses to factual questions. These reductionist approaches have not been found to benefit DLLsSEN (Lopez-Reyna, 1996). Engaging students in Instructional Conversations (ICs) is an approach that has provided an alternative to reductionist instruction (Tharp, 1997; Tharp & Gallimore, 1991).

Developed by Goldenberg (1992/1993), ICs consist of the following ten elements (see Appendix 1 for more details):

1   thematic focus
2   activation and use of background and relevant schemata
3   direct teaching
4   promotion of more complex language and expression
5   elicitation of bases for statements or positions
6   fewer 'known-answer' questions
7   responsivity to student contributions
8   connected discourse
9   a challenging but non-threatening atmosphere
10   general participation, including self-selected turns.

By strategically structuring conversations, teachers create learning environments where students' thoughts are the center of discussions about the stories or texts they are reading. Teachers promote dialogue among students through open-ended discussion of questions and by eliciting students' reflections about what they are learning. By preparing thought-provoking questions about culturally relevant themes, teachers encourage students to participate in these discussions. As mediators, teachers use prompts to draw out students' comments, connections, and thoughts about the text and wait quietly and patiently to create opportunities for students to contribute. With the goal of engaging students in comprehension-fostering activities, ICs encourage students to analyze text and to make relevant inferences and predictions as they develop their critical thinking (Echevarria & McDonough, 1995).

When the IC approach was used in a study with 27 fourth-grade DLL students transitioning from Spanish to English in general education classrooms, it was found to promote high-level comprehension and more complex elaboration of concepts and topics in essays (Saunders & Goldenberg, 1992). In Spotlight Study 3.1, a teacher employed ICs in a bilingual special education classroom to promote oral communication for DLLsSEN.

Spotlight Study 3.1

Echevarria and McDonough (1995) took an ethnographic approach to study the critical ingredients and adaptations of ICs that supported DLLsSEN while exploring the learning opportunities that were created by increasing oral language use. The teacher presented the lessons in the following format:

1 introduce the theme or idea related to the text
2 relate the theme to students' background knowledge and experiences
3 show the text to students and ask prediction questions
4 read the text, stopping strategically to provide opportunities for discussion
5 relate the theme and background knowledge to a text-based discussion
6 conduct some lessons in Spanish and others in English for DLLs.

The 6- to 10-year-old students in the self-contained special education classroom were identified as having language impairments, LDs, or mild intellectual disabilities. Between 10 and 12 students participated in each lesson, of which 9 to 10 were Hispanic DLLs receiving instruction in English and Spanish.

Data were collected over a year and a half and included classroom observations and video recordings of lessons, along with teacher reports and interviews. Analysis of the data indicated that ICs promoted oral participation and student interaction during reading lessons. In reviewing video tapes of the lessons, the teacher observed that all students, including those with language impairments, had frequent opportunities for oral language practice. The theme-based lessons provided a more holistic context for oral participation than the reductionist approaches the teacher had used previously. The use of themes to guide conversation and create cohesion during the lessons appeared to support students' attention. Adaptations made to ICs that the teacher identified as promoting interaction among students were:

• careful selection and presentation of engaging and relevant themes
• getting the level of questioning just right, i.e. not too obvious or too abstract
• recording students' contributions on a chart
• incorporating strategies to support positive behavior. ▦

Let us now examine some of the features of ICs that support DLLsSEN and inform implementation of this approach in other settings. ICs enhance both oral language development and comprehension through conversations about the text that the students are reading in class. With teacher and peer support, students in Spotlight Study 3.1 learned how to provide a rationale for their opinions about the theme and its relationship to their own lives and to the events in the text. The teacher observed that students used more complex oral language as they learned to explain their views by referencing evidence from the text. Descriptive data indicated that the students were exposed to and employed specific vocabulary related to the theme in complex sentences as they discussed their ideas.

Students were encouraged to participate freely and naturally in the discussions by asking questions, giving their opinions, asking for clarification, and sharing their ideas in their home language and in English. The teacher noted that the students initially found it challenging to share their own ideas and opinions as they had little experience doing this with academic content. Prior to using ICs, she had been using scripted literacy programs that focused on students providing specific answers to factual questions. The teacher noted that the DLLsSEN seemed to lack confidence in contributing at the outset. By accepting and building upon their contributions, she encouraged them to share their ideas, opinions, and connections to the text.

The teacher intentionally remained quiet during certain times in the lesson to encourage students' oral participation. Our tendency as educators is to jump in to help and even finish students' utterances, but researchers have shown that longer 'wait times' can lead to increases in the number and length of students' responses (Rowe, 1986).

Teacher interviews and review of the videotaped IC lessons revealed certain patterns. When the teacher actively refrained from talking, the students more frequently took the initiative to start and continue conversations. When they had more time to formulate their answers to questions and prepare their comments, deeper thinking and the use of more complex language became evident in both Spanish and English. When the teacher did contribute to the conversations, she modeled how to provide evidence from the text and asked questions that kept the conversation going. Her response to each student's contributions showed that she valued their ideas, and this appeared to encourage ongoing participation.

Choosing the appropriate theme for the lesson was another critical feature that generated interesting and relevant conversations about the texts. The more the students could relate the theme to their own lives and backgrounds, the more fruitful the conversations were, as the students made more connections to the story or text. When the themes were too obvious or simplistic, the students quickly reached consensus on the answers and so the conversations were shorter. Similarly, formulating relevant questions influenced how much students participated in conversations about the texts. Asking questions that students could relate to was important. It was noted that when the questions set up a scenario with which the students had little experience or if the answer to the question was obvious and simplistic, then the conversations were also brief.

Another adaptation that the teacher found to be effective in supporting DLLsSEN was implementing structures that allowed all students to participate equitably. The teacher began by using 'talking chips' to manage turn-taking. After a speaking turn, students placed a 'talking chip' in the center of the table. In this way, they could see who had already spoken and who still needed to have a chance to talk. Eventually, the class did not have to use the chips as they became aware of letting everyone have a turn in the conversation. The teacher also noted that students were more focused when she recorded their ideas on a chart that was visible to everyone. Students could read along as she wrote. Finally, changing the amount of time allotted to each component of the lesson was an adaptation that appeared to help DLLsSEN to participate for the duration of the lesson. The teacher found that when she shortened her introduction to the lesson, the students sustained their attention during reading and discussions.

Instructional Conversations begin with students' cultural and linguistic resources, and with a focus on language development in students' home language and in English. ICs promote understanding of important concepts through engaging thematic lessons and support reading comprehension by creating many opportunities for students to participate in meaningful conversations. The teacher in this study reported an added benefit—that students were highly motivated to engage in the IC lessons.

Activity 3.2

Thinking about the student profile you created in Activity 3.1, consider the following questions:

- How have you used oral language strategies in your teaching or learning in the past?
- What strategies have you learned in your coursework thus far that promote oral interaction among students?

Note strategies that you can take from Instructional Conversations to implement with your students systematically throughout the next unit of study.

Peer Interaction and Reading Comprehension

Approaches that facilitate peer interaction among students have been found to support the oral language development and reading comprehension of DLLs (Genesee & Riches, 2006; Oliver & Philp, 2014). As students proceed through the elementary grades, they must increasingly rely on their comprehension of text to learn. Yet for DLLs with reading challenges, reading instruction often focuses on skill work at the word level and on literal comprehension rather than on the higher-level understanding required for content learning (Klingner et al., 2006). It is important to support DLLsSEN in comprehending the kinds of texts they will encounter across content areas. DLLsSEN are increasingly instructed in general education classrooms, but they seldom receive specialized support from special educational or ESL/bilingual educators during content area subjects such as social studies and science (Klingner, Vaughn, Arguelles, Tejero Hughes, & Ahwee Leftwich, 2004). Two approaches, Peer-Assisted Learning Strategies (PALS) and Collaborative Strategic Reading (CSR), incorporate peer interaction that can help students make meaning from expository text in content subjects. Both PALS and CSR have been studied in the context of reading instruction for DLLs, including DLLsSEN.

Peer-Assisted Learning Strategies (PALS) is an approach that has been implemented across grade levels with typically developing students and those with special educational needs (Fuchs, Fuchs, & Burish, 2000). It is a systematic class-wide reciprocal peer-tutoring experience whereby partners take turns in reading aloud, listening, summarizing, retelling, and predicting what will come next. This approach has also been studied with DLLs with and without SEN, with favorable results.

Sáenz, Fuchs, and Fuchs (2005) worked with third-grade reading teachers instructing DLLs in 12 classes, each of which included two DLLsSEN. During regularly scheduled reading time, teachers used PALS for 35 minutes three times a week for 15 weeks with half of the 12 classes. The other six classes received the usual teacher-directed reading instruction. The focus in the PALS lessons was on the comprehension strategies of retelling, summarizing, and prediction. The teachers selected the materials and topics to instruct students in the use of these comprehension strategies. Student pairs with dissimilar levels of achievement worked together using the strategies, changing partners every three to four weeks. The data analysis focused on 11 students from each class, including the two with LD and nine described as low-achieving, average, or high-achieving.

All DLLs participating in PALS instruction demonstrated improved reading comprehension based on adapted measures of passage reading and response to questions. The DLLsSEN in the PALS classes demonstrated significant growth between their pre- and post-test reading comprehension scores. They also made significantly greater gains in understanding what they read in comparison to their DLLsSEN counterparts who received the regular whole-class teacher-led reading instruction. Both teachers and students reported a high level of satisfaction with the PALS approach in their responses to questionnaires.

This highly systematic interactive approach aligns with DLL pedagogy as it provides frequent and extended opportunities for students to use oral language with peers. Working in pairs, DLLs have ample opportunities to read aloud and discuss the text. They practice higher-order thinking as they summarize and retell what their partner has read, as well as formulating their summaries and predictions from what they have read. Texts can be differentiated for a variety of reading levels and stages of English development. DLLs benefit from their partner's feedback to revise and refine their oral language as they talk through their thinking. Partner discussion gives DLLsSEN many more occasions to respond to and receive feedback in less threatening contexts than whole-class teacher-led activities. The researchers noted that the collaborative and interactive nature of the activities provided a positive affective learning environment. Since reading comprehension is crucial for students to gain access to content area curricula from early on, the use of interactive approaches to enhance reading comprehension has important implications for student achievement across content areas as they proceed through the grades.

Klingner and Vaughn (1996, 1999) have investigated the use of Collaborative Strategic Reading (CSR), another multifaceted approach to instruction that supports DLLsSEN. This approach grew out of 'reciprocal teaching', which involves students working together to jointly construct the meaning of a piece of text, using four comprehension strategies: predicting, clarifying, summarizing, and questioning. Students described as 'poor comprehenders' significantly improved their understanding of text by taking turns in leading their partners to use the strategies (Palincsar & Brown, 1984). Based on the success of reciprocal teaching as an intervention with partners, CSR was further developed as an instructional approach for class-wide application by Klingner and Vaughn. Teachers modeled use of the comprehension strategies and then guided students in small groups as they took turns in leading the discussions while applying the strategies to a variety of texts.

CSR centers on teaching four sets of effective comprehension strategies:

- 'preview': brainstorming and predicting
- 'click and clunk': monitoring understanding
- 'get the gist': finding the main ideas
- 'wrap up': generating questions and reviewing key ideas.

As the students become more independent in their use of these comprehension strategies, teachers can shift from teaching the strategies to using them to deliver subject content.

CSR has evolved over time to become an approach used in inclusive settings with heterogeneous groups of students. Cooperative learning principles (Johnson & Johnson, 1989) were added to provide structure (Klingner & Vaughn, 1996). Strategy instruction and practice were provided for the whole class, followed by application of the strategies in small groups using expository texts. In keeping with the cooperative learning principles, students took responsibility for aspects of the discussion. Individual students took turns to lead their small group in the use of specific strategies; for example, acting as the 'clunk expert' or the 'gist expert' (Klingner & Vaughn, 1999). See Appendix 3 for more details on CSR.

There have been numerous studies of the implementation of CSR with students with LD in inclusive settings among diverse populations across elementary and middle grades (for example, Klingner & Vaughn, 1996, 1999, 2000; Klingner, Vaughn, & Schumm, 1998). Overall, results have been positive for improving English reading comprehension while increasing opportunities for oral language practice through peer interaction for DLLs with and without LD.

To explore the application of these reading comprehension strategies to content subjects, Klingner et al. (1998) used CSR during a social studies unit in heterogeneous fourth-grade classrooms. All the students showed growth in content knowledge; however, the DLLs and students with LD also demonstrated gains on measures of reading comprehension. The researchers recommended implementation of CSR for periods longer than the 11 days they had provided, as the changes were not yet statistically significant. To further support DLLs, they suggested that teachers preview the content with the whole class to build and/or connect to their students' background knowledge, prior to reading and discussing the texts in small groups. When transcripts of the students' discussions were analyzed, it was noted that they centered on vocabulary strategies—'click and clunk'—and meaning-making strategies—'get the gist'. In another study, classroom teachers employed CSR during fifth-grade English ESL science classes (Klingner & Vaughn, 2000). Students improved their vocabulary knowledge significantly from pre- to post-testing. Analysis of transcripts revealed that while using CSR, students spent most of their time engaged in strategy discussions related to academic learning and assisting one another.

In Spotlight Study 3.2, Klingner et al. (2004) implemented CSR in a fourth-grade classroom to examine the impact on reading comprehension and strategy knowledge for students with LD in a highly diverse urban school district. Researchers also explored teacher characteristics and implementation factors in these inclusive classrooms.

Spotlight Study 3.2

This year-long study by Klingner et al. (2004) involved ten classrooms across five highly diverse schools in a large school district in the US. Most of the student population was Hispanic—92–97 percent in all schools—and 25.6–51 percent were DLLs. The students who participated were described as either low-achieving, having LD, or average/high readers based on an English reading assessment. Although detailed information was not provided, given the diversity of the student population, many of the students with LD may well also have been DLLs. The study involved five teachers in two schools who implemented CSR with 113 students. The comparison group comprised five teachers and their 98 students attending three different schools. Instruction was provided in English by these general educators, all of whom had a comparable number of years of experience. None of the teachers had special education qualifications and only one teacher in each condition had an ESL endorsement.

The teachers implementing CSR participated in professional development pertaining to this approach. They viewed model lessons and video tapes of students using CSR, and practiced the strategies together. Teachers were then asked to use CSR in their classrooms twice a week over the next school year. Comparison teachers did not receive professional development and continued to instruct in their typical manner.

All teachers were observed instructing social studies lessons. Teachers using CSR were videotaped and provided with constructive feedback on their implementation of the critical components of the approach. An implementation validity checklist was employed by researchers. The CSR teachers and the students who were identified with LD participated in interviews. Each student's reading was assessed with comprehension subtests of the Gates-MacGinitie Reading Tests (MacGinitie & MacGinitie, 1989).

Overall, the students who were instructed using CSR showed greater improvement in reading comprehension than students who were not. Importantly, students made greater gains when their teachers implemented CSR at high levels of quality. Students who participated more often in the high-quality CSR lessons showed the greatest gains in content knowledge as well. The students with LD showed more improvement in understanding and using reading comprehension strategies than their LD peers in the comparison classes (Klingner et al., 2004). ▪

Students with special educational needs are increasingly instructed in inclusive environments and can therefore benefit from strategic approaches to understanding expository texts in their content area classes. This study suggests positive impacts on reading comprehension for students who learn how to use these specific strategies in interaction with peers. Generally, students in classes with teachers who had provided high levels of implementation made the greatest gains, although some variations emerged. For example, the comparison students showed improvement in one classroom where the teacher was already providing regular strategy instruction in her content area.

Instructional Conversations, Peer-Assisted Learning Strategies, and Collaborative Strategic Reading were designed and implemented in inclusive classroom settings with DLLsSEN. When students require more intensive instruction and intervention, it is essential that they continue to receive ESL/bilingual instruction in addition to meaningful support that addresses their learning needs as DLLsSEN. We have looked at approaches that help teachers support students' oral communication. We have also reviewed research and examples of peer interaction that are all used to promote reading comprehension. In the next section, we will describe research showing how educators and practitioners can engage students' home languages in a range of instructional settings. Strategic use of home language supports the language, literacy, and academic development of DLLsSEN while affirming their identities.

Activity 3.3

Thinking again about the student from Activity 3.1, take a moment to reflect on how systematically using oral communication strategies and peer interaction structures could support reading comprehension for all students, including DLLsSEN, in your setting. What is one aspect of the approach described in Spotlight Study 3.2 that you could add to your repertoire of strategies to implement with your student(s)?

Use of Home Languages

As we saw in Chapters 1 and 2, employing students' home languages in academic instruction has been shown to benefit DLLs' language, literacy, and academic performance. Unfortunately, when it comes to DLLsSEN, developing and using their home languages has often been viewed as a disadvantage. A common myth is that the development of two or more languages for children who are diagnosed with disabilities is burdensome, problematic, and unnecessary for academic purposes (Hamayan et al., 2013; Paradis et al., 2011). It is often thought that the demands and complexity of speaking multiple languages would tax the language and learning capacity of children with disabilities. This line of reasoning is not supported in the lives of DLLsSEN or in the research. For bilingual and multilingual families, use of all their languages is often essential in their lives. It is to the advantage of DLLsSEN that they learn to understand and speak the languages of their home and community to the level of which they are capable as they interact in their daily activities. The convergence of research findings affirms what children with disabilities who experience continued exposure to multiple languages have shown us: DLLsSEN can and do develop facility with more than one language. They become bilingual and even multilingual. Studies of home language use have been conducted in clinical and classroom settings, and the findings support the use of home languages for students who experience a range of special educational needs.

Instructional challenges arise when educators and practitioners do not speak the languages spoken by students and their families. Although it is clearly an asset for professionals to be bilingual, their specific languages may not match the wide variety of languages spoken in increasingly diverse schools and communities. Along with efforts to recruit bilingual speakers of the most frequently spoken languages, there are other approaches that can support the use of home languages for DLLsSEN.

After reviewing research studies showing the benefits of bilingual intervention approaches, we will look at examples of how to incorporate students' home languages into instruction and intervention. When teaching multilingual learners, teachers can systematically welcome all the students' languages into the classroom. Teachers can also engage parents (and other caregivers) in using home languages to support academic activities and partner with bilingual colleagues and home language classroom assistants to implement bilingual units of study. Classroom Snapshot 3.1 illustrates how two educators changed their classroom environment by inviting their students' languages into their classroom. They decided to add multilingual greetings to a song they had routinely sung in English when they met on the carpet at the beginning of each class.

Classroom Snapshot 3.1

In a multilingual kindergarten classroom, the greeting song was introduced in English and then adapted to incorporate greetings in multiple languages. The educators modeled by teaching the children greetings in their home languages to add new verses. The children readily used Spanish and Mandarin greetings that many of them were familiar with from popular children's television programs. A number of children willingly volunteered their home language greetings to sing a verse with the group. Some children also changed the accompanying gesture from the hand-waving that was part of the English version of the song to their culturally specific variation—for example, a head nod or prayer hands. Instructors continued to invite children who were initially reluctant to teach the class how to greet someone in their home language. As the school year proceeded, so many students wanted to participate that the song was sung in three different languages daily to include all the languages in the classroom (Young, 2005). ■

The learning environment changed when the educators actively welcomed students' languages into the classroom and systematically incorporated them into daily routines. As the students' multilingual identities were affirmed, they gradually began to talk about and use their home languages when opportunities were created during instructional time. Prior to this, one student had been overheard discouraging another student from speaking her home language in the classroom (see Classroom Snapshot 3.1). The educators recognized that it was important to incorporate home languages in inviting ways, with ample modeling, in multiple contexts throughout the day. While there was no requirement for students to participate in singing the greeting song in their home languages, once they became familiar with this daily practice they all chose to participate. The activity was well within their language and developmental levels (Westernoff, Young, & Shimotakahara, in press).

Theoretical perspectives that focus on meaning-making in education also support the use of home languages in instruction and intervention. The accumulating evidence suggests that employing students' home language(s) in academic instruction is beneficial for DLLs in developing both English language and literacy (García & Kleifgen, 2010). Bilingualism has also been acknowledged as providing cognitive benefits for children (Bialystok, 2001). In addition, social-emotional benefits have been found for bilinguals who more often maintained close family and cultural community connections as adolescents (Kohnert, 2010). In the following section, we will examine research that supports the use of home languages with young DLLsSEN in a variety of settings.

The Early Years

Bilingual or multilingual language learning begins years before children enter formal schooling. There is evidence of infants recognizing features of language that they heard before they were born. For example, young infants recognize their mothers' voices and passages that were read to them in utero (DeCasper & Spence, 1986). More recently, it has been reported that infants even recognize specific speech sounds that they were exposed to six weeks prior to their birth (Partanen et al., 2013).

Activity 3.4

Watch the online TED Talk by Patricia Kuhl (2011) entitled *The Linguistic Genius of Babies*. Consider these questions in relation to the information in the video:

- What can we do to advocate for early bilingual or multilingual development?
- What messages from this video can we share with colleagues, families, students, and health providers?
- How might we respond to a colleague who believes a student has 'no language' when referring to a simultaneous or sequential bilingual learner in the early stages of English development?

Early life experiences include exposure to more than one language for many infants worldwide, and these experiences influence language learning and later performance in the classroom. Young children's understanding and use of words in preschool have been found to be predictive of reading comprehension in later grades. Let us consider how key findings regarding bilingual interventions during the preschool years may inform our practices with DLLsSEN during their school years.

Studies that involve young DLLs with SLI consistently conclude that interventions using both languages are more effective than those only using one language (Kohnert et al., 2005; Restrepo, Morgan, & Thompson, 2013). Several studies have compared bilingual to English-only interventions in classroom-based preschool settings (Gutiérrez-Clellen, Simon-Cereijido, & Sweet, 2012; Restrepo et al., 2013; Simon-Cereijido, Gutiérrez-Clellen, & Sweet, 2013; Simon-Cereijido & Gutiérrez-Clellen, 2014). These studies of Spanish–English preschoolers with SLI provide examples of bilingual approaches to language learning and intervention that promote vocabulary and oral language development in both languages.

Restrepo et al. (2013) conducted a large-scale study to investigate different approaches to intervention for DLLsSEN in preschool. It included 202 bilingual children aged 4 to 5 years who were diagnosed with SLI. The children were divided into four intervention groups, each receiving 45-minute sessions four times a week for 12 weeks. Each group received one of the following interventions: English vocabulary, Spanish–English vocabulary, English mathematics, or Spanish–English mathematics. The two vocabulary interventions consisted of dialogic reading with hands-on/interactive vocabulary activities using objects that targeted 45 words from the story. The comparison group of 54 typically developing DLLs received the regular preschool classroom instruction without interventions. Dialogic reading is an approach that uses interactive strategies during story reading with children designed to encourage their engagement and active participation—i.e. promote dialogue—while modeling vocabulary and language (Whitehurst et al., 1988).

Restrepo et al. (2013) found that the bilingual vocabulary intervention facilitated receptive and expressive acquisition of the instructed words in both languages for these DLLs with SLI. The children who received English-only vocabulary intervention demonstrated significant gains in English vocabulary but did not show improvement with the corresponding words in Spanish. The Spanish–English vocabulary group made significant gains on receptive, expressive, and conceptual vocabulary measures in comparison to the children who received the mathematics interventions. They also learned more words in each language when compared to typically developing bilingual peers who received the regular preschool classroom instruction without interventions. These young DLLsSEN benefited the most from focused instruction in both of their languages.

In another preschool classroom-based intervention study, researchers worked with 185 DLLs with SLI and then followed their progress into kindergarten (Gutiérrez-Clellen et al., 2012; Simon-Cereijido et al., 2013). In addition to their regular speech-language services, these young Spanish–English speakers participated in the same curriculum-based hands-on activities and academic enrichment as their peers. Activities included repeated reading of stories, retelling, manipulatives, and picture-sorting activities to promote vocabulary and numeracy skills. Educators received professional development to employ the following intervention strategies:

- explaining the activities with simple phrases
- using a slow speech rate
- adding stress and intonation to introduce vocabulary
- recasting or restating the children's utterances
- requesting repetitions
- supplementing with paralinguistic cues, such as gestures and pantomime
- encouraging and interacting enthusiastically with the children.

The experimental group received interventions in both Spanish and English and the control group received the interventions only in English. The interventionists were bilingual teachers and paraprofessionals who provided 45 minutes of this enriched programming four times per week for 12 weeks in their preschool classrooms.

The researchers reported that the children receiving the Spanish–English interventions made equal or better gains in English than those receiving English-only interventions. The Spanish–English group improved significantly in both languages, showing increases in the length and grammatical complexity of their spoken language. Both of these studies demonstrate the benefits of using the home language along with English in group interventions for young DLLs with language impairment.

The advantages of employing home languages in intervention have also been found in individual case studies with young children. Thordardottir, Ellis Wesimer, and Smith (1997) compared monolingual to bilingual treatment in the development of oral vocabulary for a young Icelandic–English bilingual child aged 4 years 11 months diagnosed with SLI. He received a total of 12 hours of intervention over 12 weeks. They alternated the languages used in intervention from week to week. English was used to learn one set of words, and Icelandic and English were employed to target an equivalent set of vocabulary. They found that significant learning of the targeted words occurred in both conditions, with somewhat better outcomes evident with the bilingual instruction.

In a longitudinal case study, a bilingual speech-language pathologist (SLP) provided treatment in Korean and English for a 3-year-old Korean–English bilingual child with language delays, and guided his mother in using the same techniques in Korean at home (Seung, Diddiqi, & Elder, 2006). For this child, who was initially recognized as having language impairment and later diagnosed with ASD, treatment addressed wide-ranging communication skills. Goals included the development of precursors of verbalization, including joint attention, gestures, and pretend play, as well as expressive and receptive language, and pragmatic skills. Pragmatics interventions targeted social interactions, such as negotiating a choice of toys, transitions between tasks, social greetings, and turn-taking.

In the twice-weekly sessions, the SLP spoke Korean for the first 12 months, with a gradual shift to English over the next six months and then predominant use of English over the last six months of treatment. The child's mother observed the therapy sessions from outside the room and joined sessions at times. The child demonstrated improved language performance on standardized measures taken before and after treatment. Overall progress in both languages was evident on the follow-up assessment six months later. The authors reflect on the critical need for culturally responsive interventions using the child's home language as early as possible to promote foundational skills for language development. This study illustrates the benefits of providing comprehensive bilingual interventions with sufficient intensity over an extended period and partnering with parents for ongoing use and development of home languages.

These studies of children of preschool age reveal that bilingual interventions, provided in groups or individually, promote the development of both languages for young DLLs with SLI. Despite the challenges that they face with language learning, early bilingual intervention can equip these young learners with more developed linguistic skills as they enter school.

Partnering with Parents

When educators do not speak the home languages of the students they serve, collaboration with parents offers an indirect avenue to promote students' home language development. Kohnert et al. (2005) advocate for intentionally developing and maintaining home language and specifically planning for the transfer of skills across languages during intervention with young children with disabilities. Systematically teaching and modeling language facilitation techniques that parents can use to promote their children's oral communication abilities has been shown to be effective for young monolingual children. Facilitation strategies include following the child's lead in interactions, modeling, expanding, and extending talking turns using toys and books. Girolametto, Verbey, and Tannock (1994) review a number of studies of intervention techniques that parents can employ in their daily interactions with their children.

Studies involving parents of young at-risk DLLs who learned to use techniques to stimulate language and read books and showed growth in the children's bilingual abilities. (See Cheatham, Santos, & Kerkutluoglu, 2012, for a detailed review.) Teaching parents how to use home languages in this way with young DLLs with SLI has had positive results, as is revealed in a number of studies that give us insight into indirectly providing interventions in home language by partnering with parents.

In one study, an SLP taught 24 mothers how to employ language and literacy activities in Spanish with their 3-year-old children who had language delays (Ijalba, 2015). The parents participated in six meetings to learn about language stimulation techniques to use in everyday conversation with their children. Techniques such as modeling and restating children's utterances in authentic interactions encourage meaningful practice of language. The natural setting promotes understanding of the meaning relayed by the therapy targets—for example, verb tenses, pronouns, and questions. The similarity between therapy and daily activities can facilitate acquisition and use of the language skills beyond the intervention setting.

The SLP created six interactive books with accompanying manipulatives that centered on familiar topics and daily activities suggested by parents. The parents practiced the language stimulation strategies in Spanish with a new book each week and in everyday conversations at home. The DLLs with SLI in the first treatment group demonstrated growth in vocabulary in both languages. On a conceptual vocabulary measure, gains were also evident when compared to a second group of peers who had not yet received this intervention. These results suggested that Spanish language intervention supported transfer to English even when the intervention was conducted only in the home language. After participating in this study, the mothers used Spanish more frequently and read more often with their children compared to those in the second treatment group. Ijalba points to the importance of educating and coaching parents, along with providing multilingual resources, to continue to develop the home language for children with language delays.

In another study that included younger children, SLPs provided direct interventions in English and partnered with mothers to do the same in Spanish (Tsybina & Eriks-Brophy, 2010). Parents read books interactively— i.e. dialogically—with the goal of promoting their children's vocabulary development in both languages. By using dialogic strategies when reading books, the parents invited conversation about the book and encouraged their child's oral participation in telling the story with them.

Tsybina and Eriks-Brophy (2010) modeled dialogic reading for mothers of young Spanish–English bilingual children aged 1 year 10 months to 3 years 5 months who had marked expressive vocabulary delays. An individualized parent education program was also provided which included modeling, discussion, practice, and feedback, along with Spanish-language handouts on dialogic book reading. Weekly training sessions continued with demonstration and discussion of strategies used by the SLP, together with feedback for the parents after their Spanish reading sessions.

Thirty 15-minute sessions using dialogic reading techniques targeting specific vocabulary were provided in each language in the children's homes. In consultation with the children's mothers, specific words were selected for each child based on typical early functional words. English book reading was provided by the SLP and Spanish book reading by the mothers. Dialogic reading was practiced in English and Spanish with six of the children for six weeks; six others in a comparison group received the intervention later.

With explicit ongoing support for the mothers in implementing dialogic reading, these children who had marked challenges with learning vocabulary increased their spoken use of the target words in both languages. The children continued to use these words when reassessed six weeks later; however, general growth in vocabulary was not evidenced. Researchers considered that the intensity or nature of the intervention may not have been sufficient for generalization after only six weeks of implementation, given that the children were in very early stages of vocabulary development. However, the mothers were pleased with the training and saw the benefits of reading books with their children in this interactive way. They felt that they would continue to use the techniques when reading stories with their children (Tsybina & Eriks-Brophy, 2010).

In Classroom Snapshot 3.2, we see how an interactive reading strategy such as dialogic reading can be used in an inclusive kindergarten classroom setting.

Classroom Snapshot 3.2

An SLP who collaborated with a kindergarten teacher led an interactive reading lesson. She introduced the story *Mr Gumpy's Outing* (Burningham, 1990) while showing the back and front cover of the book so that children could talk about what they saw and predict what they thought the story would be about.

The children named the animals in English and Ojibwe with the support of the home language instructor. When the children noticed a boat on the cover, the SLP made connections and built upon their knowledge. She asked the children questions about their experiences with boats. 'What kind of boats have you been in? Who went with you? What did you do?' Then she said, 'Let's see where Mr Gumpy goes in his boat', while showing the pictures. The SLP began to read the story aloud, using an animated voice and accompanying gestures to demonstrate actions. After listening to the first few pages, the children recognized the pattern of the narrative: a series of animals ask Mr Gumpy to go on his boat. The SLP paused to encourage the children to participate orally in telling the story as each animal was introduced.

SLP reads or tells the story	Children respond
'Then along came a … [pausing for the children's predictions, before showing the pictured animal]	'Cat', 'Nimoosh', 'Chicken'
'The waabooz / rabbit asked …'	'Can I come?'
'Mr Gumpy said …'	'Yes'
'But don't …'	'Hop', 'Jump'

As she continued to read the story aloud, the SLP discussed words and concepts from the story by using the pictures, acting out actions—'squabble', 'bleating', 'tip over', 'float'—and making personal connections to the students' lives; for example, types of boats or using life jackets. The names of the animals were referenced in both Ojibwe and English throughout. As the story proceeded, the children increasingly joined in, telling more of the narrative while using the actions and gestures. With repeated readings of the same story across a number of classes using dialogic strategies, the children took on more of the retelling and dramatization of the story. Related activities were also used to extend and deepen vocabulary and concepts, including a sink/float experiment in science and a review of animal vocabulary in the home language (Young, 2010). ■

Home Languages in Classroom Instruction

Longitudinal studies of program models for typically developing DLLs have continued to show that the longer the home language is used in instruction, the better the students' academic achievement, English proficiency, and literacy attainment. The greatest advantages were for DLLs in dual language programs where they received half or more of their instruction in their home language for at least five years (Francis, Lesaux, & August, 2006; Genesee et al., 2005; Lindholm-Leary & Borsato, 2006; Rolstad, Mahoney, & Glass, 2005; Thomas & Collier, 2002).

In a post-hoc study of outcomes on standardized assessments for DLLsSEN, Myers (2009) found equivalent or slightly better results for students in dual language Spanish–English programs compared to those receiving English-only instruction. These outcomes were similar for DLLsSEN with different special educational needs including learning disabilities, emotional disturbance, developmental delays, and other health impairments.

In summary, DLLs with and without special educational needs reached higher levels of English proficiency, including literacy and overall academic achievement, the longer they received instruction in their home language. In addition to advocating for optimal program models for our students, our challenge, as educators and clinicians, is how to make the classroom learning environment one which encourages additive and dynamic bilingualism by continuing to promote the development of children's home languages, especially for DLLsSEN.

An experimental study of school-age DLLs with language impairment explored the direction of transfer across languages by measuring effects of bilingual interventions on both languages (Ebert, Kohnert, Pham, Disher, & Payesteh, 2014). In addition to the issue of transfer across languages, this study was designed to look at cognitive domains to shed light on deeper aspects of language impairment since the underlying causes of language disorders are not yet clear. There are differing views on the role of cognition in the development of language. General cognitive theories suggest that subtle weaknesses in skills such as attention, memory, and processing speed directly contribute to the more apparent language difficulties experienced by those with SLI (Leonard et al., 2007; Kohnert & Ebert, 2010). Spotlight Study 3.3 investigates this relationship between cognitive skills and language development in DLLsSEN.

Spotlight Study 3.3

Ebert et al. (2014) designed and implemented three interventions for 59 Spanish–English school-age students—5 years 6 months to 11 years 2 months—who were diagnosed as having moderate to severe primary language impairments (PLI). The students were described as speaking Spanish at least 'most of the time' at home; however, English was the language of instruction at school. Only four of the students received some Spanish support in their classrooms.

Students received either one of two language interventions or a cognitive intervention. Both language interventions focused on vocabulary, grammatical structures, and auditory comprehension of directions. One was provided in English; the other was bilingual—in Spanish typically 80 percent of the time, with the remainder in English. The cognitive treatment focused on processing speed and attention skills using non-linguistic materials in games. All three interventions were provided by SLPs who employed language facilitation strategies with a combination of interactive and computer-based games. In addition to 30 to 60 minutes of their weekly speech-language therapy, the students received an intensive schedule of 75 minutes of intervention four times weekly for six weeks—a total of 45 hours of treatment. The students' progress was compared to that of a group whose treatment was delayed.

All students improved their performance on the specific intervention tasks. As with previous vocabulary treatment studies with young bilingual children, these school-age children learned the specific vocabulary targeted during intervention (Perozzi & Sánchez, 1992; Restrepo et al., 2013). The students also showed overall growth in the general skill areas based on pre- and post-treatment measures. This suggested that DLLs with moderate to severe PLI can generalize improvement with practiced items to novel items in the skill areas targeted. The students who received the intervention only in English showed significant progress with that language but little transfer to Spanish language skills. Those students receiving bilingual treatment made gains in both of their languages, Spanish and English, though there were greater gains in English than in Spanish. The treatment of non-linguistic cognitive skills, including attention and processing speed, resulted in improvements on some measures of language performance in both languages, again with somewhat greater effects in English (Ebert et al., 2014). Ebert's team concluded that DLLs with PLI require direct interventions with significantly greater intensity in their home languages, often minority languages, in order to continue to develop and maintain them. Given that both language interventions improved English but the bilingual interventions resulted in gains in both languages, bilingual intervention showed clear advantages. ■

For typically developing DLLs who receive their schooling in English-majority settings, the tendency is for their home language development to slow, plateau, or regress when the instructional focus is on developing English (Wong-Fillmore, 1991; Kohnert, 2002; Pham & Kohnert, 2014; Sheng, Lu, & Kan, 2011). This study by Ebert et al. (2014) suggests that DLLs with PLI may be even more vulnerable to language loss than their typically developing peers. They therefore require targeted support, frequent opportunities to practice, and ongoing encouragement to maintain and continue to develop their home languages.

The changes that Ebert et al. (2014) found in the language abilities of students who received the non-linguistic cognitive treatment signal potential connections between cognition and language which support the general cognitive theories of PLI discussed above. This perspective points to subtle cognitive weaknesses related to attention and processing speed that may contribute to language impairment. Ebert et al.'s research suggests that these areas of weakness can be improved and do support language development for DLLs with PLI. Improvements in language, as the result of the cognitive interventions, provide insight into the close link between domains of language and cognition. These results encourage the collaboration of practitioners across areas of specialization—for example, SLPs, interventionists, and school psychologists—to facilitate and inform intervention approaches and assessment practices for DLLsSEN.

Home Languages in Multilingual Educational Settings

In educational settings where many different home languages are represented or where teachers do not speak the students' home language, educators have found creative ways to help students use and further develop the language they began learning at home. Engaging classroom instructional assistants and volunteers who speak different languages is one way to support students' multiple home languages at school.

In three self-contained special education classrooms, English-speaking teachers collaborated with their bilingual teaching assistants to provide instruction in the home language of the DLLsSEN with severe disabilities (Clark & St. John, 1995). Together, they planned and created narrative-based bilingual units for all their classrooms. The teaching assistants previewed stories in the home language using interactive activities prior to English instruction by the teachers. The narrative-based units were used for up to a month, providing extended and repeated opportunities for students to hear and use the vocabulary to talk about the stories in a variety of related activities. The students readily engaged in manipulating laminated visuals and employing story frames to retell stories with one another. Clark and St John described notable increases in the students' engagement in instruction and oral expression during the lessons.

Another way to create learning environments that support multilingualism for DLLsSEN is to systematically welcome and use multiple languages in the classroom. As educators, we can demonstrate our curiosity by learning frequently used words and phrases in the students' home languages and employing these in daily classroom activities. During whole-class activities, teachers can ask students to talk to peers from the same language background before contributing to the whole-class discussion. Learning key vocabulary related to units of study in multiple languages can be part of previewing lessons as a class. Chumak-Horbatsch (2012) provides numerous activities for exploring and integrating all the students' languages into preschool and early elementary classrooms. Classroom Snapshot 3.3 provides an example of how a teacher and an SLP who co-instructed in a kindergarten language intervention program actively engaged students in using their multiple home languages (Westernoff et al., in press).

Classroom Snapshot 3.3

Students who participated in a Kindergarten Early Language Intervention (KELI) program were nominated in their first year of kindergarten by their teachers as needing additional oral language and literacy support. Students who qualified attended their half-day kindergarten classes every day and then spent two additional half-days in their KELI class, in a group of eight children. The curriculum was collaboratively designed by SLPs and kindergarten teachers to maximize opportunities for oral language practice and early literacy experiences in the context of narratives. In this classroom, 12 to 15 languages were typically spoken among the 32 students attending each year. While the major focus of instruction was on the development of children's oral language, one of the highlights of the work in this KELI classroom was how practitioners actively engaged and affirmed the children's multilingual and multicultural identities. Although the instructors in this class were bilingual, they did not speak any of the children's home languages. They built a sociocultural learning environment to welcome multilingual children and their families. Their journey began with learning words from parents at intake interviews and progressed to engaging the children's use of home languages in greetings and songs, and eventually to previewing content vocabulary in multiple languages. The following scenario took place when students were engaging in free-choice activities in different centers in the classroom. The house center, with its toy kitchen and plastic foods, dishes, and cooking utensils, provided the context for the interaction between the students and a teacher.

Two students arrived at the house center with the teacher and began to take out food and utensils to put on the kitchen table.

A Tamil-speaking girl was naming items as she placed them on the table: 'Cup, bowl, arici [அரிசி, 'rice' in Tamil].'

A boy who also spoke Tamil, looking directly at the girl and shaking his head, said: 'No Tamil [words] here.'

The teacher smiled and, holding up plastic rice, said: 'I don't know how to speak Tamil! How do you say "rice"?'

The boy quietly replied 'Arici', as the girl looked on.

> The teacher repeated 'Arici' and then asked: 'How do you say "bowl" in Tamil?'
>
> Both children replied 'Kinnattil [கிண்ணத்தில், 'bowl' in Tamil].'
>
> The teacher attempted to pronounce the Tamil word twice while the children repeated the multisyllabic word back for her.
>
> Then the teacher held out the bowl, saying, 'Can I have arici?' The children looked at each other and smiled as the girl put rice in the teacher's bowl. ■

Such interactions can be powerful experiences for DLLs. When educators take an interest in learning and using words in their students' home languages, they show that these languages are valued in the classroom. By practicing saying new words in their students' languages, educators show their vulnerability as learners and model risk-taking for students. By making mistakes in a casual way and continuing their efforts, they also demonstrate how errors are a normal part of learning language. In this kind of classroom environment, with encouragement and modeling by teachers and peers, reluctant participants may gradually begin to offer words from their home languages. End-of-day messages to the students can be used to prompt them to ask their families how to say and write words that could be added to the multilingual word bank.

In kindergarten classrooms where we have taught and observed, previewing vocabulary in children's home languages for an upcoming lesson has been a valuable strategy for supporting multilingualism. Educators and practitioners can partner with DLLs' families to support and sustain home language development, even in multilingual settings. In an example from a multilingual preschool classroom, homework activities were provided to collect and use key vocabulary in the students' multiple languages. Parents were encouraged to talk about the vocabulary related to an upcoming unit of study. Adults and older siblings recorded the words in their home languages, providing the written form and the transliteration that allowed teachers to try to say these words in class.

In this example, all the homework came back the next day. Family members had completed the chart with their children, showing how they write and pronounce the key vocabulary in their home languages. The teacher did not know to what extent the children and their parents had interacted orally at home, but she immediately noticed that the children appeared more engaged during the English read-aloud. They stayed seated on the carpet longer, were less fidgety, and participated more orally (Sánchez-López, 2011). Inviting parents to preview concepts by talking with their children in their home languages appeared to positively affect understanding and engagement for these young children.

Another way to support and affirm DLL's multilingual and multicultural identities is through creating dual-language projects. The Early Authors Project (Bernhard et al., 2006) provides an example of dual-language books created in 32 childcare centers in Florida. Over a 12-month period, 112 educators and interventionists provided monthly parent workshops and partnered with 800 families and 1,100 children to create dual-language books. The stories centered on the children and their families' lives and were written in English, along with Haitian Creole or Spanish. Writers imported their own pictures and the laminated books were displayed at a children's museum for a month. Bernhard et al. (2006) followed 325 of these DLLs, including both participants in the Early Authors Project and a control group, during the year. Results of pre- and post-assessments revealed greater growth in both language and literacy skills for the early authors. The researchers attributed gains to strengthened self-identity and improved self-esteem for these young DLLs. They recommended that this approach to incorporating home languages be used preventatively in the early years to realize benefits in advancing school readiness skills in language and literacy abilities among at-risk DLL populations. This is based on the hypothesis that children engage in learning to the extent that their identities are affirmed and valued, and that their languages, cultures, and life experiences are viewed as assets in the process (Fu & Matoush, 2015).

Culturally and Linguistically Responsive Inclusive Learning Environments

In this chapter, we have described research and real-world examples of instruction and intervention that support oral communication skills among young DLLsSEN, foster peer interaction, promote comprehension, and utilize students' home languages. The approach described below exemplifies implementation of multiple elements of the framework for creating culturally and linguistically inclusive learning environments for DLLsSEN presented in Chapter 2 (see Figure 2.1 on page 39).

This framework takes an asset orientation and addresses learners as meaning-makers. DLLsSEN benefit from effective instructional practices that include a focus on oral communication and conceptual understanding, and are embedded in meaningful contexts that affirm students' multilingualism and multiculturalism. The Optimal Learning Environment (OLE) developed by Ruiz et al. (1996) is a comprehensive instructional approach that exemplifies many of the features present in Figure 2.1. OLE is designed to work with DLLs experiencing academic challenges from the perspective of educating 'gifted' students—one that acknowledges, values, and incorporates their strengths into the curriculum. Figure 3.1 outlines the teaching principles embedded in OLE.

1	student choice
2	student-centered teaching
3	whole-part-whole approach
4	active participation
5	meaning first, followed by form
6	authentic purpose
7	encouraging approximations
8	immersion in language and print
9	demonstrations by teachers and peers
10	responsiveness to ideas, experiences, and efforts
11	a community of learners with students, parents, and teachers
12	high expectations among teachers, parents, and students

Figure 3.1 The Optimal Learning Environment (OLE) Project (Ruiz et. al, 2002, summarized and adapted from Ruiz et al., 1996)

This approach was featured in Spotlight Study 2.4, which illustrated Diego's academic turnaround as a bilingual student who had experienced significant challenges in his first three years of school. When educators in a bilingual resource classroom tailored their instructional practices based on OLE principles, he grew academically and made remarkable social and positive behavioral changes in just a few years.

In another study, Goldstein (1995) brings these principles to life for 11 first- and second-grade DLLsSEN in a bilingual special education classroom. Educators incorporated the OLE principles with DLLsSEN while embracing their students' lived experiences through **critical literacy**. The teachers guided young DLLsSEN to deeply explore relevant literature by discussing how the characters and events in stories related to their own lives. When the teachers read books aloud, the students were encouraged to generate a personal point of interest from the story. Although students were initially hesitant to share, the teachers asked specific questions: 'What did you like best/least about the story?' and 'How are you like the character in the book?' They wrote the students' exact oral responses on a chart. Students then recorded their statements from the charts in personal folders to practice writing and reading their own sentences. The charts were used daily to build vocabulary and reference ideas for discussions. Key vocabulary was selected to add to the classroom word bank.

By the end of each unit, students had discussed their feelings, identified key events, and shared personal experiences that they felt were like those of the characters in the books. Referencing the word banks, they composed original sentences and illustrated their experiences in personal journals with the support of the teachers. The students periodically read from these journals to their peers. The charts also served as a reading log for the class. After their study of each book was completed, the charts were bound into a big book to add to the classroom library for independent reading.

Units were built around stories that depicted familiar cultural and social themes that the students could readily relate and respond to personally. The voices and life experiences of these young DLLsSEN were acknowledged through their illustrations and oral and written responses. They shared personal experiences orally and in writing as they made connections to the narratives and generated activities to document their observations and insights. By incorporating the elements of OLE, the educators addressed multiple aspects of instruction for young DLLsSEN. They enhanced the quality of instruction as well as the social-emotional climate and culture of the classroom. An enriched, asset-oriented, comprehensive, and cohesive learning environment was created for their students.

Summary

In this chapter, the research summaries and classroom case studies have illustrated important characteristics of teaching and learning that influence young DLLs and DLLsSEN. Key elements of instruction and intervention for young DLLsSEN include the development of oral communication and interactive learning with peers. Investing in young children's bilingualism is another integral element of instruction that supports their academic, social, and lifelong development. We have provided examples of educators and practitioners incorporating the home languages and cultures of DLLsSEN in very diverse settings. The research reviewed in this chapter clearly indicates that implementing these evidence-based practices improves learning outcomes for DLLs and DLLsSEN. These are in stark contrast to reductionist bottom-up educational practices that have too often been the primary mode of instruction for DLLs, students with SEN, and DLLsSEN. To optimize learning environments for young DLLsSEN, instruction needs to be engaging, relevant, and meaningful to the students. Interactions in classrooms and schools must affirm students' identities as multilingual and multicultural individuals. Culturally and linguistically responsive inclusive learning environments are designed to engage DLLsSEN in learning experiences that build on their strengths, enhance their confidence, and uphold them as capable learners.

4

Learning Environments for Adolescent Language Learners with Special Educational Needs

Preview

This chapter begins with a discussion of some of the characteristics of adolescent DLLs and the learning environments that pose challenges as well as opportunities for them and their teachers. We will then turn to the characteristics of instruction that benefit DLLsSEN. Building on what has been learned about optimizing instruction for younger learners in Chapter 3, we will review available classroom-based research pertaining to adolescent DLLsSEN. Some studies of typically developing DLLs in middle and high school classrooms are included, as they provide important insights into aspects of instruction that are critical to DLLs identified as having SEN. We will review research designed to identify and evaluate instructional practices that can assist teachers in supporting DLLsSEN in the classroom. Collaboration among educators and clinicians remains essential so that ESL/bilingual instruction and special educational programming for DLLsSEN are integrated rather than isolated. The chapter closes by addressing professional development that can support teachers as they incorporate these practices into instruction for DLLsSEN throughout the school day.

Although there is a paucity of classroom-based research specific to adolescent DLLsSEN, there are many studies that address adolescent DLLs who struggle with reading, and others that focus on monolingual adolescents with disabilities. Unfortunately, even when DLLs and students with SEN have been included in study samples, specific outcomes for DLLsSEN are not always reported (González & Artiles, 2015). In other studies, although DLLs have formed a large percentage of the student population, neither the number of students with disabilities nor their outcomes have been reported in ways that allow us to determine how they fare in different learning environments. Therefore, we have drawn on available research that is specific to DLLsSEN, along with studies that focus on elements of instruction that optimize learning for adolescent DLLs, and discuss how these findings can inform instruction and intervention for DLLsSEN.

> **Activity 4.1**
>
> Take a moment to review the framework for culturally and linguistically responsive inclusive learning environments for DLLsSEN (Figure 2.1) on page 39.
>
> Think about the different components of the framework and the instructional practices, strategies, and approaches that you already implement with your adolescent DLLsSEN. Alternatively, with a colleague, brainstorm practices that you have observed or could implement going forward.
>
> In a notebook, write down your ideas and some examples for each element of the framework. For instance, you could note ideas about how you have affirmed or would affirm learners as meaning-makers. What strategies might you use to integrate your adolescent students' home languages and cultures into instruction?
>
> As you read this chapter, add any approaches and strategies to your inventory that may be useful in your work with adolescent DLLsSEN.

Characteristics of Adolescent Learners

In order to provide a meaningful context for our examination of classroom-based research for educators working in Grades 6 to 12, we first need to consider the unique strengths and challenges of the learners. Adolescent learners are in the process of developing their identities and learning more about life as they mature. They have a great deal to talk about, hold opinions on a wide range of issues, and are often willing to support causes bigger than themselves. Many adolescents are interested in and care deeply about the world—its beauty, its people, and its injustices. Given the opportunity and guidance, they will speak out, contribute, and help to make things better for others.

Educators who have taught adolescent DLLs know how creative, tech-savvy, independent, full of humor, outspoken, and self-directed these students can be. They have fascinating life stories to talk and write about, record digitally, or dramatize to share with a wider audience. Adolescent DLLs may have responsibilities in helping to take care of their younger siblings or translating for their families in a wide range of community settings. Many are balancing responsibilities at home, school, and work (National Academies of Sciences, Engineering, and Medicine, 2017). Some students have traveled extensively and can bring personal experience and a global perspective to topics that are studied at school.

An important practice shared by culturally and linguistically responsive educators involves getting to know their students. By learning about their worlds, languages, cultures, families, and communities and by incorporating elements of these into lessons, educators show their students that they value them and are interested in their lives (Gay, 2000; Moll et al., 1992; Nieto, 2003; Klingner et al., 2014). Building instruction on the many strengths and resources of typically developing adolescent DLLs is also indispensable in optimizing their learning. This becomes even more crucial when teaching DLLsSEN. Adolescent DLLsSEN have developed their own set of strengths, resources, and interests, and yet they may face significant ongoing challenges in school. They bring a wealth of school experience that has shaped them as learners and can provide insights into the kinds of supports, strategies, and approaches that have worked for them and those that have not. Like other adolescent DLLs, DLLsSEN face challenges within time constraints as they continue to develop academic language and literacy while learning increasingly complex content material. They have 'double the work' (Short & Fitzsimmons, 2007) to accomplish in the same timeframe as their native English-speaking classmates.

The heterogeneity among DLLs, which was discussed in Chapter 2, only increases in adolescence. Like their younger counterparts, adolescent DLLs come to school with different linguistic, cultural, and educational experiences, as well as varied socioeconomic backgrounds. Some students have had limited opportunities for formal education in their previous country or countries of residence. Others may have had a great deal of formal education, as well as opportunities to study English (Schonewise & Klingner, 2012). Some adolescent DLLs have lived in English-speaking countries from a young age and experienced bilingual or multilingual education throughout their elementary schooling, while others have received all their education in English. Some have had the opportunity to develop literacy in both their home language and English or another language of instruction, while others have experienced subtractive language learning environments in their early grades, losing facility with their home language over time (Wong-Fillmore, 1991; National Academies of Sciences, Engineering, and Medicine, 2017). Even when students have retained use of their home language for oral communication, they may not have had the opportunity to learn to read in that language. They may still be in the process of developing literacy in both their home language and the language of instruction.

In addition to coming to school with a range of educational experiences, adolescent DLLs who are newly arrived immigrants and refugees must negotiate unfamiliar cultural contexts (Ruiz-de-Velasco, Fix, & Clewell, 2000). They may also encounter bullying, prejudice, and harassment and/

or be dealing with physical and mental health issues. While adjusting emotionally, they are acquiring the language in which they must help their families to navigate multiple experiences at school and in the community.

Understanding the unique backgrounds, strengths, and challenges of adolescent DLLsSEN will assist educators in creating meaningful and caring learning experiences for them. In the following sections, we will look at characteristics of supportive learning environments for adolescent DLLsSEN.

Learning Environments

Adolescent DLLsSEN require learning environments where their special educational needs as well as their language, literacy, and content area needs are met. As noted in our framework in Figure 2.1, optimal instruction is comprehensive, cohesive, and integrated across learning environments. This necessitates a great deal of coordination and collaboration among educators who support DLLsSEN. A challenge to coordinating instruction is the departmentalized organizational structures of many middle and secondary schools. Teachers often work in 'silos' related to their content areas. This makes it challenging for ESL/bilingual teachers, special education specialists, and content classroom teachers to align schedules for regular opportunities to plan and coordinate their instruction. However, collaborative efforts among teachers, related school personnel—such as counselors and social workers—and families go a long way in supporting learners to meet increasing academic demands and navigate the social milieu through the middle and secondary school years (Cloud, Lakin, Leininger, & Maxwell, 2010).

All students benefit from experiencing success and a sense of belonging, which promote continued engagement and learning (Sánchez, Colón, & Esparza, 2005). Creating a supportive and nurturing learning environment contributes to adolescent DLLs and DLLsSEN thriving and remaining in school (National Academies of Sciences, Engineering, and Medicine, 2017). Building flexibility that allows students to speak freely during content area discussions is one example of creating such an environment. Educators can also welcome and value students' languages and cultures as they encourage students to exchange ideas in all their languages (Doherty & Hilberg, 2007). When teachers invite students' languages into class and guide them as they build connections through translanguaging (García & Wei, 2014), they are encouraging their students to use all their linguistic resources while affirming them as multilingual learners. As with younger students, Brice and Roseberry-McKibbin (2001) suggest that teachers and practitioners learn phrases or words in their students' home languages to promote understanding and encourage oral expression, especially when the students' area of need involves language impairment. Incorporating these elements into learning environments helps adolescent DLLsSEN feel that they belong and are safe to express themselves. Partnering students with peers who speak the same language, hiring more multilingual teachers, and engaging home-language instructional assistants facilitates students' access to the curriculum content. Making instruction culturally and personally relevant is another way to enhance the learning environment for adolescent DLLs and DLLsSEN (Schonewise & Klingner, 2012).

Within these nurturing learning environments, teachers need to support adolescent DLLs and DLLsSEN to successfully navigate the increasingly complex academic content, language, and literacy demands of the middle and secondary curriculum (Bailey, 2007; Schleppegrell, 2004; Cook, Boals, & Lundgren, 2011). Students must learn a great deal of highly specific academic language related to a variety of content subjects (Cook, Wilmes, Boals, & Santos, 2008; Hakuta, Butler, & Witt, 2000; Short & Fitzsimmons, 2007). The range and complexity of academic language required to understand lectures, texts, and discussions in sixth to twelfth grade classrooms makes the integration of language and literacy goals essential in all content area classes, not just in ESL/bilingual language classes (Cummins, 1991; Wong-Fillmore & Snow, 2000; Schleppegrell, 2004). In elementary grades, teachers address literacy during time allotted for reading instruction and during content area instruction. Educators who teach in middle and secondary grades are often content specialists but may not have had additional training to teach DLLs the academic language and literacy specific to their subject areas (Massey & Heafner, 2004; Vacca, Vacca, & Mraz, 2005). Given the expected time it requires to develop academic language, DLLs—and especially those with SEN—will often continue to need explicit instruction in content-specific language and literacy through these upper grades. The following section will describe characteristics of instruction that support typically developing DLLs and that are also relevant to instruction for adolescent DLLsSEN.

Characteristics of Instruction

Caring teachers who develop strong connections with their students and affirm their cultural and linguistic backgrounds help them to participate fully and succeed in the academic activities of the classroom (Noddings, 1999). Teaching adolescent DLLs requires that educators and practitioners understand the cognitive, linguistic, and social-emotional changes adolescents are going through (Lerner & Steinberg, 2009). Adolescent DLLsSEN may have experienced significant learning challenges in school and consequently lack confidence in their abilities. Addressing the social-emotional needs of adolescent DLLsSEN is therefore essential to their continued development and academic progress. Affirming them as successful, capable learners can support them as they navigate the often tumultuous adolescent years.

Effective teachers deliver culturally relevant instruction and provide their adolescent DLLs with opportunities to develop oral language and literacy through interactive and collaborative approaches (Fletcher, Bos, & Johnson, 1999) while making content comprehensible (Cloud et al., 2010). As we learned in Chapter 3, young DLLsSEN benefit from instructional approaches that focus on oral communication, language and literacy development, and highly engaging and comprehensible content area instruction. In the same way, adolescent DLLsSEN continue to benefit from scaffolded instruction that is appropriate to their current ZPD.

When working with adolescent DLLs, educators must also consider that students' learning needs may not have been fully met by the amount and quality of previous instruction that they have received. Additionally, it is important to understand and build upon the specific scaffolds and strategies that have been effective in addressing individual learning needs. Instruction must be multifaceted to address the unique and wide-ranging learning profiles of adolescent learners with special needs. These students benefit when teachers and practitioners collaborate to draw upon the pedagogy, research, and experience they each bring from their various fields: language learning, teaching adolescent learners (Biancarosa & Snow, 2006), and special education (Klingner et al., 2014).

Culturally and linguistically responsive instruction that is meaningful and understandable for DLLsSEN supports academic language and literacy development while addressing students' specific area(s) of disability (García & Ortiz, 2008). Teachers can integrate various strategies and scaffolds into their instruction to support DLLsSEN, promote their success as learners, and reduce frustration. Effective educators can learn about and address cultural factors that impact learning (Klingner & Soltero-González, 2009) as well as linguistic considerations that influence the academic performance of DLLs. Additionally, when educators understand the process of L2 acquisition, they can better differentiate instruction for students across a range of language proficiency levels. For example, if students are at the beginning stages of learning English, the science teacher could find images and diagrams that illustrate the big idea being taught and help students develop oral language related to the key concepts in preparation for delving into the texts. Teachers can also differentiate instruction by taking students' diverse learning characteristics into account when planning and implementing lessons in order to give every student access to the thinking, academic language, and curricular material in a unit of study. They can differentiate instructional activities by basing them on students' interests, abilities, language proficiency levels, and preferred learning styles. Teachers may vary delivery modalities, incorporating simulations, music, videos, and technology. They can also provide extension activities using popular culture and projects to maximize access and engagement for DLLsSEN. All the while, learning scaffolds can be built into instruction to address the characteristics of language learners and those with disabilities. Examples include print and diagrammatic references, such as graphic organizers, mind maps, and content glossaries.

Learning about the grammar and orthography of students' home languages helps educators to better recognize how these influence DLLs' oral language, reading, and writing in the language of instruction. For example, Spanish speakers mark adjectives to agree with plural nouns and place them after the noun—as in *carros azules*. Thus, in English they might say or write '*cars blues' rather than 'blue cars'. Knowing about such language features can help teachers understand why students may use these structures when speaking or writing in English. As students make connections between their languages, teachers can model and guide them in cross-linguistic analysis. Comparing and contrasting elements of the home language with English is a valuable instructional approach to use with DLLs (Hill & Miller, 2013). Students can be encouraged to access all of their linguistic resources as they strive to make sense of the world and the new language they are learning.

Academic Language

It is expected that adolescent learners can decode and comprehend text effectively to learn grade-level content. Thus students with SEN who have difficulties with reading continue to need specialized literacy support and adaptations across content classes (Hock et al., 2009; Kim, Linan-Thompson, & Misquitta, 2012). Additionally, DLLsSEN may experience challenges with learning and retaining new information and organizing ideas. They may not use strategies as consistently, effectively, or efficiently as their classmates. These characteristics all impact the students' facility in developing the language and literacy needed to understand content area texts.

DLLsSEN often qualify for continued support as language learners through middle and secondary school. Unfortunately, however, many DLLs are exited from those services in elementary grades. One reason for this is that DLLs may have developed the ability to use language in certain social contexts, leading educators to believe—incorrectly—that any problems a student has are not related to language development but rather to cognitive limitations or a lack of effort or attention. Researchers have shown that it takes several years for DLLs to develop understanding and use of academic language at these grade levels (Cummins, 1984, 2008; Thomas & Collier, 2002). It follows, therefore, that DLLs and DLLsSEN will benefit from continued, focused, and explicit instruction to address academic language development and literacy learning within their content area classes.

We are reminded by Baker et al. (2014) of the challenges that adolescent DLLs face when they must simultaneously learn academic language, literacy, and content:

> For the learner to undertake this complex process of comprehending and producing academic text, deep and flexible knowledge of the often abstract and complex words and phrases used in this particular register is needed.
>
> (Baker et al., 2014, p. 3)

Vocabulary Development

Adolescent DLLs and DLLsSEN require rich, intensive, and explicit vocabulary instruction (Lesaux, Kieffer, Faller, & Kelley, 2010) across their content area classes. Building students' academic vocabulary will help them understand the complex concepts presented in the texts they encounter in middle and high school. While the following examples focus specifically on effective vocabulary instruction for DLLs, DLLsSEN also benefit. As in the studies with younger learners explored in Chapter 3, approaches used with adolescent DLLsSEN are often multifaceted. Effective vocabulary instruction centers on meaning-making that incorporates a number of elements including oral communication, peer interaction, language and literacy activities, and the use of students' home languages.

In a review of 11 studies, Cisco and Padrón (2012) found that DLLs benefit from learning vocabulary incidentally in speaking with others or through reading extensively as well as through explicit instruction. DLLs are in the process of learning English words and may not recognize and understand all the words they encounter when they read grade-level text in that language. DLLs are also learning the grammar of the language, and are therefore developing their use of contextual and linguistic clues to decipher unfamiliar vocabulary in the target language (Nagy, 2007). Considering the connection between DLL vocabulary development and reading comprehension, Cisco and Padrón (2012) affirmed the need for both oral and written vocabulary development as an integral element of reading comprehension for DLLs.

For DLLsSEN with language-based disabilities, they may struggle to understand vocabulary in what they hear or read. Although they may grasp general concepts, DLLsSEN may misunderstand words with multiple meanings or the application of related terminology in different contexts. They may use vague or non-specific vocabulary that does not fully express their intended meaning when speaking and/or writing in both languages. DLLsSEN can benefit from explicit instruction to systematically develop the vocabulary that is used in their content subjects (Nagy, García, Durgunoğlu, & Hancin-Bhatt, 1993).

Schonewise and Klingner's (2012) review of factors impacting adolescent DLLs' content area literacy development summarized a variety of ways that teachers can develop their students' academic vocabulary:

- use the visual support of pictures, photographs, charts, diagrams, maps, multimedia, and real objects to preview and illustrate new ideas and concepts that students will encounter in the lesson
- highlight and list targeted words on the board to provide a print reference to support oral lessons
- connect new information to students' background knowledge, prior experiences, and interests
- explicitly instruct strategies to help adolescent DLLs figure out the meanings of unfamiliar words by using contextual clues and word analysis
- develop semantic webs and semantic feature analysis charts, as well as concept and word maps.

Like younger DLLs, adolescents need opportunities to practice using new vocabulary in a variety of contexts while engaging in activities that promote higher-order thinking, such as problem-solving, predicting, organizing, synthesizing, and evaluating.

Vaughn et al. (2009) found that DLLs' knowledge of words, concepts, and content improved when they implemented vocabulary instruction in seventh-grade social studies classes. This approach combined explicit content area instruction with the use of graphic organizers and videos to build conceptual understanding and promote discussion as students worked collaboratively with peers. In a study with sixth-grade DLLs (Lesaux et al., 2010), teachers introduced vocabulary by reading short and engaging texts that included specific academic terminology and provided multiple exposures to the target words. Students had many opportunities to use the vocabulary in discussions of the passages during pair-work and whole-class instruction. DLLs' vocabulary comprehension was found to improve significantly with this combination of techniques.

DLLs need to expand and deepen their understanding of content-specific vocabulary to access and comprehend grade-level texts they read in English (Lesaux et al., 2010). Helping DLLsSEN develop strategies for accessing content area information from texts is essential. For DLLs with SLI or reading disabilities, understanding vocabulary may be a particular area of focus to support listening and/or reading comprehension. They may be especially challenged by words with multiple meanings and idiomatic expressions. They are still developing their knowledge of syntax and morphology in English and this contributes to the difficulty they may experience in learning the meaning of words in the language of instruction.

Content area curriculum at the middle and secondary school levels requires students to understand very technical and subject-specific vocabulary. In Spotlight Study 4.1, researchers looked at the effectiveness of teaching strategies that adolescent DLLsSEN could use for predicting and analyzing the meanings of morphemes in science-related vocabulary.

Spotlight Study 4.1

Helman, Calhoon, and Kern (2015) explored the use of contextual clues and a morphemic analysis strategy to increase students' ability to predict and analyze science vocabulary. The study involved three DLLs attending ninth and tenth grades in high school who were identified as having specific learning disabilities. Their English reading skills ranged from fourth- to sixth-grade level. According to the WIDA English language proficiency standards (WIDA Consortium, 2007), the students were at Stage 3 or 4 on a six-stage scale of language development. Thus they were in the middle stages of developing English and still qualified to receive ESL services. The students participated in general education and received reading and writing instruction during a daily 60-minute block in their ESL classroom. It was during this block that students received the intervention. These DLLsSEN were not enrolled in a science class during the time of the study.

Before the intervention was implemented, each student received six training lessons, three days per week for two weeks. During these sessions, students learned the Clue Word Strategy (CWS) from the ESL teacher and continued to receive the typical vocabulary instruction in their general education classrooms, which they attended with native English speakers. The ESL teacher prepared them by providing the meanings of various morphemes, as well as information on how to identify morphemes, and then gave students the opportunity to study the steps of the CWS process. The CWS steps require students to:

1 read a sentence containing a target science word
2 look for contextual clues surrounding the unknown word
3 re-read the sentence
4 write the target science word
5 break the science word into its morphemes
6 write the meaning of each morpheme
7 predict and write the meaning of the target science word
8 check the dictionary for the correct meaning.

After the training in strategy use, the intervention phase began. This lasted three weeks and each CWS lesson took 45 minutes. The CWS intervention consisted of the set of steps listed above, which students followed to help them derive the meanings of unknown science words based on the instructional context and the form of the word itself, i.e. morphology.

The teacher began with a demonstration using the CWS steps followed by teacher-led practice, guided practice, and then independent practice. In each 45-minute lesson, the teacher taught one science morpheme and three new science words using the CWS steps. Each student worked in their vocabulary binder, which included:

- three CWS graphic organizer sheets for each lesson
- a list of CWS steps
- answer key sheets
- guided note sheets for the training lessons
- blank note sheets.

The CWS graphic organizer used during teacher-led instruction included directions, a sentence with the target science word, the CWS steps, and a graphic organizer web. The graphic organizer included boxes into which students could write each morpheme, its meaning, and a definition for the target word.

A poster showing the CWS steps was displayed on the wall to help students remember what to do and promote their independence. The teacher explained the CWS strategy, reviewed key terms, used interactive questioning procedures, and provided corrective feedback during the 45-minute intervention lessons. CWS probes showed that all three students could list the steps in the process and used the CWS strategies during the intervention. There was also improvement in students' ability to identify the meanings of unknown science morphemes, define science words, and list CWS steps for identifying context and morphemes.

The DLLsSEN improved in defining the target science words, writing the words appropriately in sentences, and identifying and writing the meanings of morphemes. They also improved in their ability to write the meanings of isolated morphemes. Students were given the opportunity to rate their satisfaction with the intervention and their participation. Overall, they were satisfied with the effectiveness of the intervention and all students reported that they would recommend this strategy to their peers. Two of the three students maintained their gains and generalized the use of morpheme definitions to analyze unknown science words when reassessed two months later. Results suggested that these DLLsSEN could use morphemic and contextual analysis strategies given a short intensive schedule of explicit and systematic instruction that focused on strategy use for understanding science vocabulary. ■

Spotlight Study 4.1 provides an illustration of small-group vocabulary instruction in an ESL classroom that could be applied to reading in other content subjects as well. It highlights the importance of cognitive strategy instruction with systematic steps, multiple opportunities for practice, graphic organizers, and print references.

Reading Comprehension

For adolescent DLLsSEN, reading comprehension is often an area of particular challenge that warrants additional attention as students are increasingly expected to learn from content area texts in middle and high school. Reading comprehension must therefore become a focus for students to better access grade-level content. Their level of reading in their home language is an important predictor of their reading in English. When DLLs are proficient readers in their home languages, the process of reading is familiar and supports learning to read in English (Jiménez, García, & Pearson, 1996; Krashen, 1985). Adolescent DLLs can benefit from explicit comprehension strategies in the language of instruction (August & Shanahan, 2006; Genesee & Riches, 2006). The use of these strategies supports older students to actively engage in learning (Schonewise & Klingner, 2012). The following sections will highlight research pertaining to reading comprehension strategies that teachers can employ with DLLsSEN.

Jiménez (1997) studied the effectiveness of cognitive strategies designed to improve reading comprehension for five middle school DLLs described as having reading difficulties. Instruction focused on how to:

- derive meaning from unfamiliar words
- incorporate prior knowledge
- create questions
- use both of their languages during instruction.

Teachers employed think-aloud activities to model strategies while reading a variety of culturally relevant texts. Given this focused explicit instruction, these DLLs were, in spite of their reading difficulties, successful in applying the strategies and extended their use to other contexts. The students expressed positive attitudes towards their improved comprehension and showed increased motivation to read.

A familiar approach to developing reading comprehension for monolingual English speakers is the use of Guided Reading during small-group literacy instruction (Fountas & Pinnell, 1996). Guided Reading lessons typically include the following components (Pinnell & Fountas, 2011):

- selecting texts at the students' instructional level
- introducing the text through pre-reading activities
- students reading the text softly to themselves or aloud with some interaction or prompting by the teacher
- a guided discussion of the text
- a focus on students' comprehension
- teachers explicitly instructing on elements of the text
- working with words to strategically determine their meanings
- extending understanding through writing or other activities.

Teachers provide differentiated literacy instruction to groups of four to six students based on their strengths and needs. The teacher acts as a guide to help students make meaning and build skills and strategies for comprehending a wide range of fictional and informational texts. A number of aspects of this approach align with pedagogy for DLLs and DLLsSEN. Small-group instruction with the use of books at differentiated reading levels is beneficial for all students. Guided Reading creates many opportunities for students to interact with teachers and peers to co-construct meaning from text and to practice oral language in meaningful contexts. Listening, speaking, and writing are integrated with reading through conversations and related activities before and after reading. The lesson format is structured and predictable, which supports learning for DLLs and DLLsSEN, and it includes a systematic evaluation of progress in context. In the next section, we will describe how this approach has been adapted for use with DLLs and then discuss benefits for DLLsSEN.

Modified Guided Reading

Modified Guided Reading (MGR) has been adapted for use with DLLs across grade levels (Jiménez, 1997; Krashen, 1985). Modifications for DLLs include: detailed vocabulary instruction; focus on semantics, syntax, and morphology of English; and use of culturally relevant texts. (See Appendix 2 for a detailed outline of a Modified Guided Reading lesson.)

In a study by Avalos, Plasencia, Chavez, and Rascón (2008), DLLs made gains in English reading comprehension using MGR. These authors completed a pilot study in two middle school classrooms that included 23 DLLs who had been in the US for between 24 and 48 months. Although they were in the early stages of English development, assessment indicated that most were reading below grade level—from pre-primary to fourth grade—in both Spanish and English. For DLLs, the authors also modified time and intensity by increasing the length of sessions from 20 to 30 minutes and the number of sessions devoted to a single text from one to three. Vocabulary work focused on morphological and phonemic awareness, phonics, semantics, and syntax in meaningful contexts. Reading, writing, speaking, and listening were integrated into each lesson through a variety of passages. The DLLs received 24 to 36 30-minute small-group sessions.

After nine months, DLLs participating in MGR demonstrated average gains of 1.3 to 1.8 grade levels in English reading based on the results of informal reading inventories. The students overwhelmingly reported positive attitudes towards MGR, expressing satisfaction and reflecting that they had learned more about reading, writing, and speaking English during MGR sessions than in previous reading instruction. They felt this approach had helped them to learn about English sounds and letters while reading meaningful text. The DLLs indicated that working in small groups facilitated their understanding of what they were reading, as they could readily ask questions to clarify. The students enjoyed listening to the teacher read aloud and expressed interest in continuing to use MGR.

This study provides an example of an instructional approach used with monolingual students that was modified to benefit DLLs who struggle with reading. This approach also encompasses multiple features of the learning environment outlined in the framework for culturally and linguistically responsive inclusive learning environments that are essential for DLLsSEN (Figure 2.1). For instance, instruction during MGR focuses on comprehension while developing literacy and oral language in the meaningful context of literature. Home language use was encouraged in oral discussions and could be extended to include dual-language texts, dictionaries, glossaries, or wall charts for key vocabulary. Time allocation was increased in the study, with lengthier sessions and a greater number sessions for each text. This increase in frequency and intensity offered students more time to build comprehension through recurrent exposure to and use of the concepts and vocabulary. Small student groupings enabled more individualized scaffolding to facilitate understanding, and the vocabulary work could be used to target specific skill areas in context. That these adolescents engaged, experienced progress, and recognized improvement in their learning speaks to the overall benefit of implementing MGR.

Another approach that supports reading comprehension for adolescent DLLs and DLLsSEN is Collaborative Strategic Reading (CSR), which we will examine next. One of the strategies that students learn to use in CSR—'get the gist'—is introduced in Activity 4.2.

Activity 4.2

'Get the gist' involves identifying the most important idea in a paragraph. The goal is for students to restate in their own words the most important point as a way of making meaning from what they have read (Klingner & Vaughn, 1998). They are taught to identify the most important 'who' or 'what' in a text and then to briefly state the critical information about the 'who' or 'what' (Boardman, Klingner, Buckley, Annamma, & Lasser, 2015). The students discuss their 'gists' after each paragraph and record them in their learning log.

While reading the next section about CSR and Spotlight Study 4.2, use the 'get the gist' strategy orally or make written notes. At the end of the section, consider how this strategy worked to make meaning. How would you adapt it? How might your current or future students benefit from this strategy?

Collaborative Strategic Reading

Collaborative Strategic Reading (CSR) was introduced in Chapter 3 as an example of reading instruction with the goal of improving understanding of expository text. The design of CSR, with its multiple scaffolds, meaningful text-based strategies, and teacher modeling, addresses language and literacy learning during content area instruction for DLLs and those with SEN. Students receive explicit instruction on reading for meaning and on using strategies to access information. Pre-reading strategies are used to access background knowledge and to make connections to prior learning related to the topics. Use of visual organizers also supports comprehension by explicitly building schemata. Strategies for recognizing and exploring the meanings of unfamiliar words provide methods for developing content-specific vocabulary in context. The format of CSR integrates listening, speaking, reading, and writing for making meaning. For example, oral language use is integrated with scaffolds, such as question starters and discussion frames, to create frequent opportunities for purposeful conversations with peers. The nature of the strategies requires higher-order thinking skills, as students are asked to return to the text to justify their thinking and generate questions. Ample opportunities are provided for learners to develop understanding of oral language and text while using academic language in discussions and in writing using CSR learning logs—for example, to inform or argue using evidence. This approach can change the way teachers think about and interact with their students by offering instructional tools that optimize students' use of language and that allow them to show what they know and have learned while working collaboratively (Boardman & Blake, 2014).

Spotlight Study 4.2 provides an example of an early version of CSR instruction for seventh- and eighth-grade DLLs with LD in an inclusive classroom (Klingner & Vaughn, 1996).

Spotlight Study 4.2

In contrast to the prevalent emphasis in instruction on word identification and memory for facts, Klingner and Vaughn (1996) chose to explore comprehension using CSR strategies to develop students' understanding of text through oral discussions with peers in inclusive settings. Students received focused instruction on strategies that targeted higher-order thinking—for example, predicting, summarizing, and posing questions—as opposed to factual recall.

They studied the use of these reading comprehension strategies with 26 DLLs with LD in seventh and eighth grade. All the students received a modified version of reciprocal reading using social studies passages for 40 minutes per day over a period of 15 days. Reciprocal reading is a collaborative approach to reading instruction where teachers first model and guide students to take turns in leading discussions about the text using comprehension strategies (Palincsar & Brown, 1984). As outlined in Chapter 3 (see also Appendix 3), strategies included the following:

- pre-reading strategies ('preview'): predicting and brainstorming
- during-reading strategies ('click and clunk' and 'get the gist'): monitoring understanding, clarifying vocabulary, and finding the main ideas
- post-reading strategies ('wrap up'): generating questions and reviewing key ideas

Initially, the instructors modeled and demonstrated the strategies using think-aloud techniques while reading social studies passages with the students. Cue sheets were then employed by the students to practice using the strategies in discussions with their peers. Guidance and feedback were provided as the students took turns in leading their group of seven or eight students to apply specific strategies. The instructor's role gradually shifted to one of facilitating as the students gained experience in the collaborative use of the strategies. Students were encouraged to use their home language throughout to support their understanding of vocabulary and the ideas they were discussing.

In the second part of this study, the DLLs with LD interacted with other students in one of two ways: in cooperative learning groups of same-age peers or in pairs for cross-age tutoring. Although both approaches had been explored with students with LD and were recommended for DLLs, this study focused on students who were DLLs and had been diagnosed with LD. The students in the cooperative learning groups continued using the strategies independently in smaller groups of four to five same-age peers who had all received the initial strategy instruction. The cross-age tutoring students received group instruction on best practices in tutoring. Next, they were each partnered with a younger sixth-grade student with LD, for whom they modeled the strategies for two sessions. The younger partners were then invited to utilize the strategies, working toward taking turns 'being the teacher' as they read text passages.

Overall, all the DLLs with LD in this study improved their reading comprehension, as reflected in their enhanced performance on standardized measures of reading in English—the Gates-MacGinitie Reading Test (MacGinitie & MacGinitie, 1989). Qualitative data included student interviews and researchers' logs. Reading comprehension was also assessed in terms of students' responses to questions based on a set of passages developed by Palincsar and Brown (1984). The students continued to show progress as they worked through social studies texts in both the cooperative learning and peer tutoring formats. Gains were evident on weekly assessments during strategy instruction, as well as during the peer interaction phase with less direct instruction. Students also maintained improved levels of comprehension when assessed one month post intervention.

The researchers reported that the range of students that benefited from the CSR interventions was greater than expected. DLLs with LD who had basic decoding and oral language skills in English before instruction appeared to make the most gains. Within this group there were students who had English decoding skills at or above fourth-grade level but experienced greater challenges comprehending English text. Other students had more limited English decoding skills—between second- and fourth-grade level—but stronger reading comprehension skills in English. Even students who were in the early stages of developing oral language proficiency in English and who did not yet have well-established decoding skills made progress with the CSR intervention.

Using strategy cue sheets can be particularly helpful for students with LD, as they provide a ready reference for strategies and organize students' discussions with their peers. The visuals and graphics that accompanied the text references can support both DLLs and students with SEN to understand and continue to implement the strategies beyond the initial instruction. The researchers attributed students' gains to the structure provided for them to learn and practice the strategies with each other while developing their understanding of meaningful texts. They also suggested that the high degree of student engagement evident in the tasks and in their use of the home language was likely to have contributed to their progress (Klingner & Vaughn, 1996). (See Appendix 3 for a CSR lesson outline.) ■

Teaching reading comprehension strategies using CSR has been effective, with the best outcomes for students who have regular opportunities to use them a minimum of two times weekly (Klingner et al., 2004). By adopting this approach and collaborating across disciplines, teachers can introduce and systematically employ CSR with sufficient frequency across various content subjects for students to experience the benefit. In this way, special educational strategies and language learning pedagogy are integrated into content area instruction. DLLs and DLLsSEN can continue to develop both language proficiency and reading comprehension while improving their access to curriculum content. Integration of CSR into subject content addresses multiple goals for content area teachers who typically instruct large numbers of students with these wide-ranging learning characteristics and needs across multiple classes. We will return to ways of supporting educators later in the chapter.

Accessing Academic Content

DLLsSEN continue to benefit from ESL/bilingual pedagogy that is integrated and coordinated with special educational programming, as discussed in Chapter 2. For example, DLLsSEN can access the curriculum when educators implement strategies to make content area material comprehensible (Echevarria & Short, 2010). Providing **sheltered instruction** in content area classes makes abstract and complex content more understandable and accessible to students who are continuing to learn the language of instruction. Language and content is made comprehensible through the use of visual and linguistic scaffolds such as photographs, video clips, graphic organizers, sentence frames, and mathematics manipulatives. Providing a variety of readings on a particular topic of instruction and previewing instruction through the home language also serve to improve comprehensibility for DLLs. Content area instruction for DLLsSEN needs to incorporate supplementary materials and concrete examples, such as pictures, diagrams, video clips, or movement, to help students visualize the main concepts or big idea of lessons (Echevarria & Short, 2010).

In addition to implementing sheltered instruction, teachers can look for potential barriers to understanding that can cause their students to disengage or lose motivation (García & Tyler, 2010). Examples of obstacles to learning include complex linguistic demands of classroom instruction and interactions; advanced reading levels of texts in both the home language and the target language; and cultural irrelevance or potential bias in the way people are portrayed in the classroom materials or context (Artiles, 2003; Klingner et al., 2014). Anticipating potential barriers allows teachers to incorporate necessary supports and replace or augment materials to individualize instruction for the unique needs of DLLsSEN (Klingner et al., 2014). When educators who support DLLsSEN come together, they can systematically review upcoming lessons, units of study, and instructional approaches to identify and plan for the linguistic and cognitive demands of the instruction.

Classroom Snapshot 4.1 is an example of a content area lesson that incorporated aspects of the approaches described thus far in this chapter. This lesson occurred in a seventh-grade sheltered language arts class of DLLs who spoke various languages and included three students who had special educational needs. The teacher wanted to take a more conceptual approach to writing than she had in the past. Previously in this unit of study on descriptive writing, she had used a more bottom-up approach, starting by introducing her students to the topic of adjectives. After reviewing and discussing adjectives, she indicated that these were the types of words the students would need to write descriptive essays. Together they developed a bank of adjectives they could all use as a resource during writing. When students began sharing their writing with her during writing conferences, she found that the students' essays were similar to previous pieces they had written. She also noticed that the students had scattered various adjectives throughout their paragraphs but not always in meaningful ways.

This time, the teacher wanted to introduce descriptive writing conceptually, to support the students in understanding the impact of using adjectives. Her goal was to promote more effective and meaningful use of adjectives in their writing. She met with a district literacy specialist and an instructional coach to plan the unit. Classroom Snapshot 4.1 provides an account of the revised descriptive writing lesson.

Classroom Snapshot 4.1

The teacher started the lesson by sorting images into two columns, pausing between each pair of images to give students time to discuss what they noticed about the images in each column. The images in the first column were simple line drawings of a baby, trees, and a house, and the second column had real-life colorful photographs of an infant, a lush forest, and a house with a thatched roof in a mountainous valley. After seeing a few examples, students conversed with their partners using their home languages and English about the attributes of each category of images. All the students were partnered with same-language peers. The teacher ensured that DLLsSEN were each paired with a socially compatible peer and supported by the classroom assistant. The teacher went on to show another image and asked students to decide if it belonged in the first or second column. Students demonstrated their choices by raising one or two fingers, and then turned to their partners to explain their reasoning. This continued until both columns were filled with images.

The teacher then projected a simple black-and-white line drawing of a tree from the opening activity. She asked the students to talk with one another and then tell her what words they would use to describe the tree. Scaffolds were provided whenever needed to support the discussion among the pairs that included

DLLsSEN. After talking together, students offered words such as 'tree', 'branches', 'tall', 'trunk', and 'leaves'. The teacher wrote these words on the whiteboard where the tree image was projected. She then asked the students to use the words from the brainstorm and any other words or phrases to come up with a sentence or statement about the line drawing of the tree, which they would use to write a story. The students first discussed their ideas with their partners, then offered their sentences to the whole class. The teacher wrote down the 'story' and then the students and teacher read the story aloud:

This is a tree. It is tall.

It has a trunk and many branches.

The branches have leaves.

Next, the teacher projected a photograph of a forest of trees. The students followed the same procedure: generating words and phrases with their partners and then dictating a sentence for the teacher to write down on large chart paper. To support the activities, scaffolds were provided in the form of word banks that students generated as a group, partner discussions, rehearsal, and use of the home language. Working collaboratively provided students, including DLLsSEN, with opportunities to practice with their peers before sharing their ideas with the entire class. Then the students and teacher read the new story together:

This is a forest full of trees. It is cool, misty and quiet. It is mysterious and green with dew. I would like to sit in the branches of the trees and read all day long.

The teacher thanked the students and the following discussion ensued:

Teacher: If these were stories in a book, which one would you rather read?
Students: The second one! That one! [pointing at the photograph of the forest of trees]
Teacher: Why the second one?
Student A: It's more interesting.
Teacher: How is it more interesting?
Student B: You can feel like you are there.
Student C: You can imagine being in the forest. The first one wasn't good.
Teacher: Wasn't good?
Student C: Boring. Just words. You don't feel anything.
Teacher: Which story was more descriptive?
Students: The second one! Yeah. More descriptive. Cool!

For the final component of the lesson, the teacher distributed a selection of beautiful, evocative images for partners to use as a springboard to writing a descriptive paragraph together. The classroom was full of conversation in many languages. After a few minutes, the teacher walked around and looked at the students' work to see how they had understood the concept of descriptive writing. DLLsSEN were situated throughout the class, working with their DLL partners, and the teacher moved through the groups to check on how they were doing. All the paragraphs were interesting and creative, but one stood out. The teacher showcased this example by sharing it with the whole group. Two girls had started a story about a family that lived in the house with a thatched roof in their picture. The family in the story helped all the people in the village during the war, bringing them food and helping them after their houses had been bombed. The teacher told the students that they had the beginning of a very good story and congratulated them on how descriptive and interesting it was. She wanted to know how the picture had helped them to generate their ideas. The students pointed to the grass that was growing on the roof of the little cottage. They said that when the planes flew over the village, this house was camouflaged so the family's house was not bombed.

The teacher was impressed by how engaged the students were and by how interesting their written products were when she changed her instructional approach. When she began instruction by building conceptual knowledge through a shared experience, the students helped one another, used their linguistic and cultural knowledge, and produced much more complex and interesting writing (Sánchez-López, 2013). ■

Reflecting on Classroom Snapshot 4.1, we can see that many of the practices used in this lesson connect to elements outlined in Figure 2.1 that are essential in instruction for DLLsSEN. Students were engaged in *oral language practice* and *listening comprehension*, supported through partner conversations. The lesson emphasized *conceptual understanding* by providing the students with the opportunity to discover what it means to be descriptive. Skill work—in this case, the study of adjectives—was conducted in the purposeful and meaningful context of a lesson on descriptive writing. It was *culturally and linguistically responsive* in that instruction was built around students' strengths—which included *peer interaction*, creative thought, life experiences, and *home languages*—and used their *oral language* to access new content. The students could focus on *comprehension* because all the reading in this lesson was within their language proficiency level, as it was based on texts that emerged from their oral language. Similarly, background knowledge was established for oral instruction and reading comprehension as both were based on their initial shared experience (Klingner et al., 2014).

Supporting Teachers

Key to developing culturally and linguistically supportive inclusive learning environments for adolescent DLLsSEN is providing high-quality, consistent, and ongoing support to teachers. We began this volume by discussing the challenges involved in effectively addressing the complex needs of DLLsSEN, and in this chapter, we have described the particular challenges that teachers face in middle and secondary school settings. We recommend professional learning experiences that help teachers understand the linguistic, literacy, ethnic, and socioeconomic diversity among the student population they serve. In our work with DLLsSEN, we must also identify and remove multiple and intersecting barriers that limit opportunities to learn. Professional development needs to be designed to provide educators and other practitioners with opportunities to learn about these barriers. Our collaborative practice can leverage human and material resources to enable DLLsSEN to gain full access to learning and participate meaningfully in their classrooms and schools (Waitoller & Artiles, 2013).

Sustaining changes in practice and school culture also requires the support and leadership of school administrators. Administrators can schedule protected time for teachers to participate in ongoing coaching, modeling, and reflection (Klingner et al., 2001; Klingner, 2004) in order to fully implement instructional approaches with DLLsSEN. Teachers benefit from taking part in continuing professional learning exchanges where they reflect on and discuss successes and challenges with implementation and thus refine their practice over time (Vaughn, Klingner, & Bryant, 2001).

Klingner (2004) reviewed the work of researchers who had had success in implementing professional development as demonstrated by teachers who sustained the use of evidence-based instructional strategies for students with SEN. Professional learning activities that led teachers to improve their practices and to produce positive outcomes for students occurred when researchers worked closely with school districts. Teachers expressed their response to the learning activities by identifying what was important to them (Klingner, 2004):

- The strategies and approaches aligned closely with the school's curriculum.
- Student outcome data showing that the practice was effective was provided to all stakeholders.
- Teachers had support from their administration.
- Long-term support was provided for teachers, including demonstrations and coaching.
- Teachers took ownership of the practices and responsibility for mentoring their peers.

In the following sections, we will outline ways that schools can support teachers in providing effective inclusive instruction for all students, including DLLsSEN.

Professional Development

The first example comes from a study conducted during a year-long implementation of Collaborative Strategic Reading (CSR) in middle school classrooms. This research provides insight into the degree and nature of teacher support that can result in significant improvement in reading comprehension for students. Boardman et al. (2015) studied the frequency of implementation of CSR with sixth- to seventh-grade students in an urban school district. The student population included 59 percent Latino, 20 percent Caucasian, and 15 percent African American, with the remaining students representing various other ethnicities. The district reported that 72 percent of students were considered low-income, and 35 percent were DLLs who were receiving language services. In each participating school, teachers implemented CSR in middle school social studies and science classrooms that included DLLs, struggling readers, and students with LD— most of whom were reading below grade level. The researchers wanted to know if supporting teachers in their implementation of CSR in both science and social studies classrooms resulted in improved reading comprehension for culturally and linguistically diverse middle school students with a range of achievement levels.

The teachers received two days of professional development pertaining to strategy instruction and cooperative grouping techniques. Along with classroom observations, individual coaching and in-class support was provided by researchers who modeled, sometimes co-instructed, debriefed, and planned with all of the teachers. Additional coaching was offered based on teacher receptivity. Researchers collaborated closely with the teachers as well as with school administrators and district curriculum personnel over the school year to provide intensive and ongoing support for these middle school content teachers.

Results revealed that the students who made the greatest gains received CSR once a week in science and once a week in social studies throughout the school year. These students demonstrated significant improvement on standardized measures of reading comprehension (MacGinitie & MacGinitie, 1989) compared to students who did not receive the strategy instruction or received it only once weekly due to scheduling difficulties.

While CSR is a general reading comprehension strategy, the researchers (Boardman et al., 2015) sought to support middle school teachers as they implemented it in highly diverse inclusive classrooms that included DLLs and DLLsSEN. By using CSR in different content area classrooms, all students, including DLLsSEN, benefited from coordinated, cohesive, and comprehensive instructional approaches that enhanced access to the curriculum. Providing more frequent opportunities for students with SEN to practice the strategies using a variety of materials can also promote consolidation of strategy use while reading across content areas.

Technology

Another way to assist educators is to integrate technology into instructional approaches. Kim et al. (2006) developed a computer program to support teachers during initial strategy instruction of CSR. The goal was to reduce teacher time while actively engaging students in improving reading comprehension as they learned content. The researchers created and implemented Computer-Assisted Collaborative Strategic Reading (CACSR) with sixth-, seventh-, and eighth-grade students with SEN. CACSR was employed in 50-minute instructional sessions twice per week over 10 to 12 weeks for 16 students. Some of these students were also DLLs.

Teachers received two hours of training in implementing CACSR that focused on four of the CSR comprehension strategies: 'preview', 'click and clunk', 'get the gist', and 'wrap up'. Research assistants collaborated with educators to instruct the students on the use of the computer program. The students learned how to use CACSR through modeling and through guided and independent practice of the strategies. Students worked with partners to read a passage, discuss and answer questions, and then enter their responses on the computer. The partners took turns to read and type on alternate days. The computer program was designed to prompt next steps and provide feedback by supplying answers for comparison. Performance was recorded so that the teachers could review and refine the use of strategies with the students at the beginning of the following lesson. After learning about the different strategies, students applied CACSR to content learning. While the students read expository text passages, they completed an online learning log together. Computer supports included a 'clunk expert', a dictionary, and quick reports that offered opportunities for the students to compare their responses to model answers.

Using CACSR, all the students with SEN, including those who were DLLs, demonstrated substantial growth in comprehending text. Compared to initial testing, they improved significantly on researcher-developed assessments of strategy use and standardized measures of overall comprehension and decoding. Student interviews revealed positive experiences and interest in continuing to use the program. Teachers also expressed interest in ongoing use of CACSR, based on students' improvements in vocabulary development and reading comprehension. In this study, teachers were supported with professional development over ten weeks. They were given time to plan and use technology to implement CSR with students in their content subjects.

Collaborative Practice

Starling, Munro, Togher, and Arciuli (2012) followed a speech-language pathologist (SLP) who collaborated with eighth-grade teachers in adapting their oral and written language practices to facilitate learning for students with language impairment. Difficulties in understanding and using oral and written language can manifest themselves in poor academic progress, disengagement, and increased risk for social, emotional, and behavioral problems (Leonard, 1991; Johnson et al., 1999). Although these language-related challenges often persist into adolescence, some models of service delivery focus primarily on providing language and literacy services to younger students in the earlier grades. In the later grades, SLPs may have fewer opportunities to work directly with students or collaborate with their teachers. It becomes challenging to offer individualized services to students and to consult with multiple teachers as students rotate through numerous classrooms following schedules that are filled with content subjects taught by different teachers.

Starling et al. (2012) worked with the SLP to design and implement sustained interactive collaborative professional development to support 13 teachers of 43 students with SLI in a high school setting in Australia. Of these students, 81 percent were from various ethnic backgrounds and 66 percent spoke more than one language. Only DLLs at advanced levels of English language development were included. The SLP took a systems-based view of communication and language impairment (Paul, 2007), in which communication breakdowns are attributed to problems in the interaction between communication partners. This is very different from a deficit perspective that assumes that the causes of problems are situated in the student.

The SLP led a series of 50-minute weekly meetings with general classroom teachers for ten weeks. She focused on explaining and modeling language modification techniques used in therapy and discussing how teachers could implement them in their classrooms. The techniques included:

- being very visible and explicit with steps or frameworks
- moderating the difficulty of the tasks for students
- highlighting procedures using graphic organizers, sequence charts, and lists
- being explicit about strategies for planning and executing work
- using focused vocabulary instruction to help students become independent in understanding the meanings of words.

Ongoing discussions with teachers addressed issues that arose and allowed teachers to collaborate, generate ideas, and modify their classroom resources. The SLP observed the teachers and supported them with implementation of the strategies in their classrooms. The interactive forums led to the development of a community of practice where teachers sought and provided help to each other throughout the project. As Klingner (2004) has noted, empowering educators can facilitate long-term changes in practice.

The SLP worked with the teachers to adapt the strategies that were appropriate to their content areas and instructional approaches. For example, the physical education teacher developed written resources and review sheets for all students to complement her oral and physical instruction. The visual arts teacher modified written text assignments and tests to increase access to print information by including graphics. The SLP supported the history teacher in drawing interactive mind maps on the board to help students organize ideas while discussing the connections in dense text passages. As they used these strategies, all the teachers noted increased student engagement.

Providing teachers with sufficient flexibility and opportunities to tailor techniques to their needs and those of their students contributed to sustained changes in practice. Information from ethnographic interviews indicated that the seven teachers who participated in this collaborative professional learning with the SLP significantly increased their use of language modification strategies compared to six comparison teachers at a different school. During follow-up visits, observers reported that teachers had maintained these practices.

Overall, the students demonstrated significant improvements on two of four subtests on a standardized measure of achievement (Wechsler, 2007). Listening comprehension and written language were targeted explicitly through the techniques and showed the greatest growth. Gains made in these aspects of language remained evident on later assessment, suggesting that students maintained the progress they had made. This study provides a promising example of collaborative practice promoting language facilitation strategies that can be employed daily in general education classrooms to support DLLs and those with SLI as they are learning subject area content.

Developing Culturally Relevant Instruction

The departmentalized nature of many middle and high schools makes collaboration among educators who serve DLLsSEN challenging. Yet finding time to coordinate culturally and linguistically relevant instruction that supports students' linguistic, literacy, academic, and special needs is essential.

In Classroom Snapshot 1.1 (see page 10), we presented a conversation between two sixth-grade teachers who collaborated to better address the needs of all their students, especially their DLLsSEN. Classroom Snapshot 4.2 features educators on the same team who worked together to create a unit of study that was culturally relevant to the Latino students in their classroom. These sixth-grade teachers shared their specialized knowledge in ESL pedagogy, bilingual education, and special educational needs, as well as in specific content areas. When planning their year-long social studies curriculum, the teachers examined the content and realized that they addressed the evolution of civilization from the same perspective every year, always focusing on Mesopotamia, Egypt, Rome, and Greece. The team wanted to make social studies more engaging and relevant to their immigrant, refugee, and language minority students. They discussed the idea of looking across the globe at other civilizations to more closely reflect the backgrounds of the students in their classrooms whose families come from Asia and Latin America, as illustrated in Classroom Snapshot 4.2.

Classroom Snapshot 4.2

This team of teachers decided to incorporate the study of Mesoamerica as part of their curriculum to reflect the identities and ancestry of the students from Latin America as well as build appreciation and a more global lens for all students. The students learned about how geography, climate, culture, and economics interacted to bring about the rise of the ancient Olmec, Mayan, and Aztec civilizations more than 4,000 years ago.

All the students enjoyed hypothesizing about how the early people arrived in North and South America while examining maps and reading a variety of multileveled texts. When learning about the domestication of plants in Mesoamerica, students were fascinated to see that many of the crops that were staples of their ancestors' diets were things that they ate at home: corn, peppers, tomatoes, and squash. They also recognized contemporary versions of some of the early stone tools, such as the *metate*, which was used to grind corn, and the *molcajete*, a type of mortar and pestle. Students expressed pride in knowing that mathematicians, astronomers, engineers, farmers, and artisans played significant roles in these ancient civilizations (Sánchez-López, 1999). ∎

The social studies curriculum was brought to life and made relevant for the students from Latin American backgrounds. The same occurred with students from other cultural backgrounds as the curriculum expanded to include Ancient Persia, Ancient China, and the Incan civilizations.

While some topics involved in social studies or history units of study are globally oriented, many others focus on regional and even local concerns, issues, relationships, conflicts, and geography. It is important for teachers to find meaningful connections in order to make content topics relevant to the students in their classrooms. Developing background knowledge, making connections, and using multiple-level reading materials all support DLLsSEN. Lessons centered on single textbooks, without sufficient development of academic language to make meaning from complex text, reduces access to middle school and secondary level content for DLLsSEN (Taboada Barber et al., 2015).

Activity 4.3

Think about a unit of study in your content area.

1 Brainstorm strategies, activities, or experiences that you could use to build content-specific background knowledge with your students.
2 Talk with a colleague about how you could provide a global perspective to unit topics that would engage DLLsSEN. Consider ways to create opportunities for students to look at the topic from multiple perspectives.
3 Describe some ways in which students could share their thinking and work in multiple languages.

Affirming Multilingualism and Multiculturalism

As we saw in Chapter 2, students with SEN are not disadvantaged by speaking and understanding more than one language. As teachers and practitioners, it is imperative to support all assets that students bring to school. Some students may come to school already confident about using their home language, proud of their home culture, and willing to contribute, especially when their teachers include their languages and cultures in lessons. Others, however, may feel less confident about their multilingual skills, or they may feel embarrassed about anything that makes them stand out as different from their peers. Seeing the teacher's positive attitude toward their linguistic and cultural background will help these students to recognize and utilize their full range of linguistic resources.

Classroom Snapshot 4.3

A ninth-grade English teacher in southern Ontario was instructing a unit of study on writing from different perspectives. She had invited a professional political cartoonist to teach her students how to present their point of view about an issue through drawing. The guest cartoonist and teacher talked about how this would help her multilingual students, who were at different stages of learning English, to show what they were thinking. In this inclusive classroom, DLLs and DLLsSEN were asked to work with a partner or in a small group to brainstorm ideas and causes that they felt were important. They were encouraged to talk in any language they liked, and then 'take notes' through writing and drawing.

The teacher and cartoonist put up all the students' ideas and asked everyone to walk around the room to see what others were thinking about. Once the students had finished reviewing all the ideas and images and had asked any clarifying questions, they returned to their small groups or partners to have another conversation about the new ideas and causes they had seen. Next, they were asked to choose the idea and point of view they wanted to represent in their cartoon. The cartoonist then took students through the stages of developing a political cartoon that reflected their point of view.

The students worked on their cartoons for a couple of classes. Once they had completed them, the teacher asked the students to write a short passage that explained their cartoons and what point of view they were taking on the issue or cause. They would display the cartoons at a Curriculum Night. The multilingual students—there were many languages represented in the classroom—were invited to write their paragraphs in their home languages and then in English. The teacher knew that some of the students were newcomers and she did not want to pressure them, but she encouraged them to write first in the language they felt most comfortable using and then in the other language. The students had varying proficiencies in their home languages and English, and they helped one another write and translate their work into two languages.

On the evening when the parents visited the school, this teacher was overwhelmed by the response of the multilingual families. Many of the parents could not speak English but clearly wanted to express their appreciation of what she was teaching their children. Some mothers had tears in their eyes; some held the teacher's hand and smiled; other parents used their developing English to say thank you. It was clear that her students had been talking to their families at home about what they were learning at school. What seemed like a small gesture to the teacher—inviting students' languages into the classroom—changed the climate of her classroom and enhanced the relationship she had with her students' families (Sánchez-López, 2008). ■

Classroom Snapshot 4.3 shows how one teacher changed the sociocultural context of her classroom by inviting her students' languages into a ninth-grade general English class. Some of the DLLs were newcomers and others had come through the school system from elementary grades. While the teacher did not speak any of her students' home languages, she thought it was important to provide them with as many avenues as possible for sharing their thinking, learning, and creativity. This classroom example illustrates essential elements of inclusive education for DLLsSEN. Like all DLLs, those with SEN are well served by teachers who create supportive learning environments and embed culturally and linguistically responsive instruction and research-based interventions into lessons. The teacher in this example engaged students' home languages and cultures to create just such an environment. Special education approaches that are grounded in sociocultural theory take into account learners' strengths and characteristics, including their proficiency in multiple languages and their cultural and life experiences (Klingner et al., 2014).

Adolescent DLLsSEN require ESL/bilingual pedagogy that explicitly teaches the academic language and literacy they need to access content area material. Additionally, DLLsSEN benefit from concentrated support that focuses on their set of specific needs. For adolescent DLLs with LD, SLI, and reading disabilities, this can include instruction of oral language, auditory comprehension, and reading that is more intensive and of longer duration than that provided for typically developing DLLs. Adolescents are particularly responsive to approaches that integrate regular peer interaction in meaningful and relevant ways. Studies that focused on discipline-specific vocabulary development and reading comprehension exemplify effective practices that can be embedded into content area instruction. Adolescent students with disabilities benefit from inclusive environments where they have access to grade-appropriate curriculum through strategic use of supports, adaptations, and modifications particularly suited to their learning profile of strengths and challenges (Klingner et al., 2014).

Summary

In Chapter 4, we have focused on research that addresses effective instruction for adolescent DLLsSEN. The discussion of unique characteristics of adolescent learners and their learning environment provides insights into planning and instructing students in middle and high school settings. Studies specific to adolescent DLLs provide important guidance for aspects of instruction that may be overlooked for DLLs once they are diagnosed with SEN. It is important for professionals to take a sociocultural perspective when collaborating to integrate the effective features of ESL/bilingual and special education instructional practices.

Central to developing effective instruction for DLLsSEN is providing relevant in-depth professional development for teachers and practitioners. The instructional approaches used with DLLsSEN are necessarily multifaceted so that they address students' linguistic, literacy, academic, cultural, social-emotional, and special educational needs. This requires that schools provide sustained support and enriched opportunities for educators to meet together to discuss, implement, practice, and maintain effective approaches and strategies across content areas and grade levels.

5

Special Educational Needs:
What We Know Now

Preview

In this chapter, we will return to the statements in Activity 1.1 about dual language learners with special educational needs and respond to each statement on the basis of the theory, research, and examples that we have reviewed in this volume.

Activity 5.1: Review your opinions

In Activity 1.1, you responded to statements about the education of DLLsSEN. Before you continue reading this chapter, complete the questionnaire again. Compare the responses you provide now to those you gave previously. How have your views changed after having read Chapters 1–4 of this volume? Have your opinions been confirmed? If some responses are different, what has changed?

Reflecting on Ideas about DLLsSEN

1 It is important to start with the students' strengths in planning and implementing instruction and intervention for DLLsSEN.

In culturally and linguistically responsive learning environments, DLLs' strengths, abilities, interests, hobbies, talents, and gifts are explored, acknowledged, and employed in learning. In this context, educators and practitioners invest in learning about their students' languages, life experiences, and family stories. Incorporating these elements into instruction creates a supportive learning environment, affirms students' multicultural and multilingual identities, and engages DLLs in learning that is relevant and meaningful to them.

Creating culturally and linguistically responsive inclusive learning environments is especially important for DLLsSEN. In addition to understanding the nature of students' challenges, we also need to learn about their linguistic and cultural resources. By understanding what DLLsSEN know and can do in all their languages, both socially and academically, educators can leverage students' assets in addressing their learning needs. Research consistently demonstrates that speaking two languages does not disadvantage bilingual learners with disabilities. For DLLsSEN, continuing to develop their home languages supports learning and extends the number of potential communication partners with whom they can interact. Sociocultural theory of learning affirms that home languages and cultural experiences are important components of the background knowledge which students bring to acquiring new skills and curriculum content.

In contrast to the deficit perspectives that have historically framed the conceptualization of disability and special education approaches, the field of positive psychology advocates for starting with student strengths. Implemented along with the asset-oriented practices advanced in the field of ESL/bilingual education, this progressive approach to special education takes an ability perspective in all our interactions with DLLsSEN. By starting with and building on students' strengths, educators and practitioners can embrace the uniqueness and diversity of DLLsSEN while viewing them as capable learners as their needs are addressed.

2 Once a DLL has been diagnosed with a SEN, it would be better to focus on learning one language.

Despite the prevalence of this common misunderstanding, accumulating research consistently demonstrates that DLLsSEN are not disadvantaged by speaking two languages. DLLs with a variety of disabilities, including language impairment, Down syndrome, and autism spectrum disorder, demonstrate the same types and range of language challenges as their monolingual peers with the same conditions. Importantly, DLLsSEN have been found to benefit when their home languages have been incorporated into instruction and intervention. For example, use of home language has facilitated vocabulary learning for DLLs with SLI. DLLs with significant disabilities have improved their expressive abilities when both languages have been used in classroom instruction. Approaches that build on the knowledge and verbal skills of DLLsSEN in their home languages facilitate reading comprehension in both languages and English literacy development. Accessing students' linguistic resources in instruction has fostered engagement in learning and improved language and literacy outcomes.

Continuing to develop students' home languages facilitates parental engagement as well as extending the number of potential communication partners who can support DLLsSEN throughout their lives. In this volume, we have provided examples of ways educators and practitioners have created multilingual learning environments and intervention approaches that incorporate their students' home languages into learning, even when the teachers do not speak the students' home languages. All DLLs benefit when their languages are valued and supported in school settings.

3 DLLsSEN benefit from instruction and intervention that build on their cultural backgrounds as resources.

Affirming students' multicultural identities is a central component of developing culturally and linguistically responsive instruction. Students benefit from seeing themselves reflected in the curriculum, materials, languages, and perspectives employed in their learning environment. According to sociocultural theory, learning is most effective when instruction builds on students' life experiences. For example, when teachers connect classroom discussions and the use of books directly to the learners' cultural experiences and knowledge, DLLsSEN engage in extended conversations.

Culturally and linguistically responsive educators learn about the lives, experiences, and funds of knowledge of the students and families they serve. They also find ways to incorporate these resources into instruction and intervention which support student engagement in learning. By starting with students' cultural and linguistic resources in instructional planning and implementation, educators demonstrate that they are interested in and value DLLsSEN.

4 If DLLs are experiencing academic challenges, then special education is the most direct avenue to addressing their needs.

There has been an unfortunate history of inappropriately placing DLLs in special education. Too often, educators and practitioners have not had experience or training that prepares them to determine whether DLLs' challenges are due to learning disabilities, gaps in previous education, or inadequate opportunities to learn during the process of acquiring a new language. It is essential to first consider the learning environment as the potential source of difficulties rather than moving too quickly to the conclusion that DLLs require special educational services. Making changes to improve and enrich instruction based on ESL/bilingual pedagogy that matches their current level of language proficiency allows DLLs to show their full learning potential. This provides vital diagnostic information when addressing the source of DLLs' learning challenges in the classroom. At the same time, it is important to systematically gather information on students' progress by comparing them to peers with similar cultural and linguistic backgrounds and experiences rather than to monolingual students from the majority-language culture.

Establishing a culturally and linguistically responsive Multi-Tiered System of Supports enables schools and school systems to address students' specific learning needs before considering a referral for special education. The key is to ensure that the changes made in the instruction are solidly grounded in ESL/bilingual pedagogy to address this component of their learning profile. In this way, it is not assumed from the outset that any learning challenges are related to inherent disabilities. In the past, interpreting students' difficulties as an inability to learn rather than as a lack of opportunity to learn has too often prompted inappropriate referrals to special education. Disabilities occur with the same frequency among DLLs as among monolingual speakers. If it is established that students' learning needs as DLLs have been met and they continue to experience academic challenges compared to other DLLs with similar linguistic and cultural backgrounds and experiences, then a referral to special education can be warranted. Adding special educational programming to DLL pedagogy requires collaboration and coordination among educators and practitioners to ensure that students receive comprehensive services that address all their needs as DLLsSEN.

5 Instruction and interventions developed for monolingual students are effective for DLLsSEN.

We cannot assume that what works instructionally for monolingual students with special needs will be effective and sufficient for DLLsSEN. While some strategies and approaches developed for monolingual learners can be helpful for DLLsSEN, certain characteristics must be in place to ensure that they are effective for these learners who have SEN and who are also in the process of learning an additional language. Approaches must address the unique learning profile of DLLsSEN while simultaneously differentiating instruction to meet the students' linguistic, literacy, and academic strengths and needs in their multiple languages.

The research and classroom examples in this volume have illustrated key characteristics that make instruction and intervention effective for DLLsSEN. As summarized in the framework in Figure 2.1, these characteristics include systematically providing opportunities for students to develop oral language in their home language and in the language of instruction. Oral expression in all their languages is a resource for DLLs' literacy development and reading comprehension. Additionally, developing bilingual or multilingual oral proficiency is a life skill that can be an advantage beyond the classroom and beyond their years as students. Bilingualism affords DLLsSEN access to a greater number of communication partners in social, educational, and work contexts. Incorporating students' linguistic and cultural resources and funds of knowledge into instruction is key to removing barriers and facilitating access to the curriculum. Whole-to-part approaches integrate academic language and literacy development into content area instruction, and support comprehension and conceptual development for DLLs. In addition to using instruction that is optimal for DLLs, it is also imperative to address each student's individual learning characteristics related to their disability in culturally and linguistically responsive ways. Understanding that disabilities manifest uniquely for each student, educators can collaboratively develop, modify, and adjust instructional approaches that support DLLsSEN. Rather than assume that approaches developed for monolingual students with SEN will be effective for DLLsSEN, we propose the opposite. Given what we now know, it is clear that comprehensive instruction and intervention that draws upon a sociocultural perspective can benefit all students with SEN.

6 Instructional approaches that focus primarily on mastering discrete skills are optimal for DLLsSEN.

Like all learners, DLLsSEN can benefit from instruction that develops specific knowledge and skills to facilitate language, literacy, and academic progress. However, instruction that focuses primarily on decontextualized skill-building makes it difficult for DLLs to apply these skills. Classroom experience and research have demonstrated that skills that are taught within meaningful contexts facilitate learning for DLLs and DLLsSEN. Making meaningful connections among concepts and skills during instruction supports comprehension for all learners. Therefore, from a sociocultural perspective, all learners, including those with SEN, benefit from starting with what they know to make connections and build schemata as they learn new information and deepen their knowledge. This contrasts with reductionist approaches that require students to work on component skills outside of a meaningful context, with the goal of mastering individual elements before applying them to classroom content. While DLLsSEN work with the learning challenges related to their disability, they are also in the process of developing academic language, literacy, and content knowledge in a new language and in sometimes unfamiliar cultural contexts. Therefore, situating instruction and intervention within meaningful contexts to facilitate making connections and applying new learning is of even greater importance for DLLsSEN.

7 The development of oral language is integral to learning for DLLsSEN.

As we naturally seek to make meaning from all that is around us, language is inextricably linked to how we develop thinking. When we explore ideas and concepts, we learn and use words to encode and organize our evolving understanding into schemata. A sociocultural perspective posits that it is through our interactions with other speakers and with elements of our environments that we extend and refine our spoken language as knowledge is constructed. As our conceptual system grows, our language system develops to accommodate new learning.

Monolingual majority-language children typically enter school with age-level proficiency in the language they have been exposed to and have been using with their family and community. For these students, literacy instruction is naturally designed to match their oral language proficiency. When DLLs have started learning to read in a new language at school, their oral language development has often been overlooked. For both simultaneous and sequential bilingual learners, it is vital that oral language instruction be integrated into literacy instruction, with ample opportunities for practice. For DLLs, oral language development in both languages supports literacy achievement.

As DLLs continue developing the language of instruction while learning academic content throughout the grades, they benefit from ongoing opportunities to practice oral language in meaningful and purposeful ways for optimal learning. With DLLsSEN, learning and language development will also be influenced by the nature of their disability. If oral language is an area of particular need, they will require additional attention and time to develop specific receptive and/or expressive language skills, in both home and school languages. In this volume, Spotlight Studies and Classroom Snapshots have exemplified how to incorporate oral language practice into instruction and intervention from preschool to high school.

8 Emphasizing comprehension during reading instruction beginning in the early grades benefits DLLsSEN.

With DLLs and DLLsSEN who are learning to read in their L2, focusing on comprehension from the outset of instruction is fundamental. Because DLLs and DLLsSEN are often learning to read in a language that is different from their home language, their ability to understand what they read cannot be taken for granted. While strategies that explicitly teach decoding skills are beneficial for DLLsSEN, it is important that these occur in meaningful contexts as part of a comprehensive approach to reading instruction. This helps students develop understanding of what they are reading rather than just focusing on word identification. For example, reading instruction that is based on content area themes, big ideas, or topics provides meaningful contexts and purposes for decoding.

For native speakers of English, decoding words will more directly lead to comprehension, as they will frequently recognize and understand the words they are learning to read. They are building on comprehension of a language in which they already have oral proficiency. In contrast, DLLs are in the process of developing their oral proficiency in the language of instruction and may not yet know the meaning of the words they are decoding. Ensuring that DLLs are making meaningful connections to and understanding the words they are learning to decode is imperative. This is especially crucial for those whose SEN involve difficulties with language in general or reading in particular.

In addition to embedding decoding and other component skills into meaningful contexts, a critical element of reading comprehension for DLLsSEN is developing conceptual understanding of words. This contrasts with vocabulary instruction that relies on superficial memorization of words as unrelated terms or labels. Approaches that build students' comprehension of concepts and academic vocabulary from the early grades lay the groundwork for comprehending and using academic language across the grades as the linguistic level and complexity of academic content increase.

Frequently, DLLsSEN with reading disabilities experience difficulties with understanding and using oral language. Therefore, they benefit especially from approaches that strengthen their oral comprehension and expression. On the other hand, some students with reading disabilities may have relatively strong oral language skills that can be used to leverage their understanding of print. Systematically integrating vocabulary, oral language, and reading comprehension into subject and thematic content area instruction provides meaningful contexts for promoting overall comprehension. A focus on comprehension is imperative if DLLsSEN are to access the curriculum from early on and continue to develop their language and content knowledge through the grades.

9 Educators and practitioners can support the home languages of DLLsSEN, even when they do not speak these languages.

While we are not likely to be proficient in all the languages that our students speak, there are many steps we can take to validate bilingualism and multilingualism. We can invest in their languages and demonstrate interest in their linguistic resources. When educators promote learning of all the languages spoken by students in their classrooms, everyone can benefit. For example, educators can gather key words and exhibit curiosity about students' languages and how they use them. Asking about, searching for, and taking the risk of pronouncing words in languages with different sound systems are daily experiences for DLLs. Teachers and practitioners can join students by regularly venturing to pronounce words and use phrases in students' languages. In this way, they create an atmosphere that models how to take risks and learn from errors as a natural part of learning.

Inviting students' many languages into the classroom and providing time for students to think, speak, read, and write in their home languages is instrumental in maintaining and promoting home languages as valuable assets for DLLsSEN. Creation of dual-language identity texts by students and families has shown promise for DLLs across age and grade levels. These identity projects affirm students' lived experiences and enable them to see themselves reflected directly in the curriculum. In the classroom, students can access online and digital multilingual resources, translation technology, and bilingual glossaries or dictionaries. These tools can also be used to preview content with family members, bilingual paraprofessionals/teachers, and peers to facilitate understanding of the content of lessons in English or another instructional language. When students are systematically provided with the means to use all their linguistic resources and encouraged to do so on a regular basis, they can show more of what they know and think.

For DLLsSEN who have specific challenges with language learning, these approaches that strategically and systematically promote home language development are even more fundamental to their progress. These students may often develop language at slower rates than their bilingual peers and are at greater risk of losing language abilities that are not used regularly. Research reviewed in this volume clearly validates that even with language and learning impairments, DLLs are capable of developing bilingualism. Working with colleagues and families to access and develop all the linguistic resources that DLLsSEN bring to school fosters their growth holistically and can have lifelong effects.

10 DLLsSEN benefit from instruction provided by educators who understand DLL pedagogy and have knowledge of special educational practices.

The unique learning profiles of DLLsSEN require teachers to provide instruction that responds to students' strengths and challenges as language learners as well as to learning characteristics related to their disabilities. In serving DLLsSEN, educators must endeavor to address their students' language learning and special educational needs in each lesson and unit of study. In an ideal learning environment, each person who supports DLLsSEN would have knowledge of how to develop and deliver content-specific instruction in a comprehensible manner. They would also know how to explicitly teach the academic language and literacy objectives associated with each content area lesson. Additionally, they would have specialized knowledge of the specific language or learning needs of each DLLSEN. With all of this knowledge and experience, they would be able to adjust instruction and mediate learning in a variety of ways for individual students. Unfortunately, few educators have had the opportunity to develop such a range of specialized pedagogical skills. For this reason, it is often necessary to draw on the expertise of several different professionals. As illustrated in the Spotlight Studies and Classroom Snapshots in this volume, educators can collaborate to combine their different expertise to effectively optimize learning for DLLsSEN.

In addition to classroom teachers and paraprofessionals, educators and allied practitioners with special education expertise—for example, counselors, social workers, SLPs, school psychologists, and physical and occupational therapists—can support DLLsSEN. Like educators, related practitioners are called upon to become knowledgeable about L2 acquisition and ESL/bilingual pedagogy, and to learn about and integrate their students' funds of knowledge and multilingual resources. We can all draw on our knowledge of the pedagogy and practices found to be effective for DLLsSEN, tailoring them to each student's IEP goals through our professional lens.

Given that the educational experience for DLLsSEN is complex and multifaceted, we all can benefit from collaboration among the educators and practitioners involved with these students. When professionals with various specializations learn with and from one another in a collaborative spirit, they can leverage the range and depth of the knowledge, skills, and experience they bring to educate DLLsSEN. Teams can come together to build comprehensive, coordinated, and cohesive instruction and interventions across the multiple learning environments in our schools. We suggest that professionals advocate for collaborative time to serve their DLLsSEN in schools where formal arrangements for teamwork are not in place. Educators benefit from seeking out others informally to initiate collaborative conversations, explore print and online resources, and consider coursework to support their own learning. Moreover, we advocate combining all our knowledge, skills, experience, and resources to ensure that wherever DLLsSEN receive instruction, their learning is optimized throughout their school day.

Conclusion

In this book, we have reviewed research and theory to create a framework for culturally and linguistically responsive inclusive learning environments for DLLsSEN. Positioning the learner at the center, the framework outlines key elements of effective learning environments for DLLsSEN. Surrounding the DLLsSEN—meaning-makers who bring creativity and learning potential—is instruction that is embedded in meaningful and relevant contexts. Instruction for DLLsSEN which addresses their wide-ranging strengths and needs promotes conceptual understanding and oral communication. Additionally, DLLsSEN require instruction that addresses them as language learners by specifically incorporating academic language and literacy objectives while making academic content material comprehensible. Within culturally and linguistically responsive learning environments, the multilingual and multicultural identities of DLLsSEN are affirmed so that they see themselves reflected in the curriculum topics, points of view, images, and languages used in their classrooms and throughout their schools. For DLLs who also have SEN, it is particularly important that they see the knowledge and skills they already have as assets they bring to their learning. It is imperative that DLLsSEN experience themselves as capable learners as they make progress with their individual goals at their own pace.

Educators must view the language learning process of DLLsSEN as a work in progress rather than as a problem that cannot be addressed until students have reached proficiency in the language of instruction. The ability of DLLsSEN to understand and use more than one language for learning is an asset academically and in their lives beyond school. Making space for students to use all their languages in our classrooms validates these linguistic resources as powerful tools that promote multilingualism and affirm the value of their multicultural experiences.

DLLsSEN require special educational strategies and interventions to make progress and to experience success in school. When educators and practitioners work with DLLsSEN, they come to understand the nature of students' particular learning difficulties and how these manifest in the classroom. Starting with ESL/bilingual pedagogy, educators and practitioners need to create and adapt materials and tailor strategies and scaffolds for students. School administrators need to provide support for educators as they work collaboratively to implement focused instruction and interventions with sufficient intensity for DLLsSEN to experience success as learners. Special education approaches that are built upon sociocultural theoretical perspectives of learning and take a strengths-based approach facilitate learning experiences for students with SEN. These perspectives align with culturally and linguistically responsive pedagogy that provides the essential foundation for enriching instruction for all DLLs. Educators and practitioners optimize learning for DLLsSEN by building on a solid foundation of culturally and linguistically responsive instructional practice that is infused with special educational interventions grounded in sociocultural theory from an asset orientation.

When DLLsSEN enter our schools, culturally and linguistically responsive practitioners come together to learn about the students and share their perspectives to plan collaboratively. While focusing on individual students or groups of students, professionals combine their specialized knowledge, experience, and resources to develop and coordinate programming that builds comprehensive learning environments. By working together to understand the student as a whole learner, they can integrate practices from the fields of ESL/bilingual and special education to create cohesive instruction and intervention for DLLsSEN throughout the school day. Educators and practitioners who instruct DLLsSEN benefit from continued opportunities to learn about ESL/bilingual and special education pedagogy through intensive ongoing professional development that includes modeling, coaching, and opportunities to practice new approaches. Educators are able to provide culturally and linguistically responsive inclusive instruction for DLLsSEN when schools and school districts make a commitment to promoting collaboration among professionals in order to blend the expertise and practices of DLL and special education and thus enrich learning for DLLsSEN.

Suggestions for Further Reading

The following publications provide further background on enhancing the learning environment for language learners with SEN.

Delaney, M. (2016). *Special educational needs.* Oxford: Oxford University Press.

This book takes a pedagogical approach, offering teachers practical guidelines and strategies for helping SEN students to succeed in mainstream language classrooms. Part One provides an overview of SEN and outlines general pedagogical practices for working with SEN students in primary and secondary classrooms. Part Two discusses SEN students' needs and techniques to promote inclusion in the classroom. Part Three focuses on different types of SEN and successful teaching approaches to address them.

Kalyanpur, M., & Harry, B. (2012). *Cultural reciprocity in special education: Building family–professional relationships, second edition.* Baltimore, MD: Brookes Publishing.

Kalyanpur and Harry explore how our cultural values as practitioners influence our professional practices, addressing multiple features of diversity and the reciprocal nature of our interactions with families. They discuss diversity in terms of cultural, linguistic, and socioeconomic factors that impact learning and our conception and implementation of special educational services, providing insights that can enhance our communication with families. They expand on the nature and relevance of culture within the culturally and linguistically responsive inclusive framework presented in this book.

Klingner, J. K., & Eppolito, A. M. (2014). *English language learners: Differentiating between language acquisition and learning disabilities.* Arlington, VA: Council for Exceptional Children.

The authors provide a framework for understanding and addressing the needs of ELLs who are experiencing difficulties with reading. They challenge school problem-solving teams to look closely at ecological and environmental factors that impact ELLs' progress in reading before considering more intrinsic explanations for students' difficulties. They describe what professionals need to know in order to support the language and literacy development and academic learning of ELL students with reading difficulties and reading disabilities.

Kormos, J., & Smith, A. M. (2012). *Teaching languages to students with specific learning differences.* Bristol: Multilingual Matters.

This book seeks to help language teachers work effectively with students who have specific learning differences. It begins by reviewing the history of learning differences, including dyslexia, SLI, and ADHD, and research on associated learning processes. It goes on to focus on supporting students who struggle with learning in language classrooms. It includes information about the teaching of specific domains, such as vocabulary, reading, and speaking, as well as assessment, transition, and progression.

Miramontes, O. B., Nadeau, A., & Commins, N. L. (2011). *Restructuring schools for linguistic diversity: Linking decision making to effective programs, second edition.* New York, NY: Teachers College Press.

This volume provides educators and administrators with a framework for organizing their schools to address student diversity from the outset. This new edition offers insights from schools that have implemented this framework successfully, illustrating how applying these principles across the curriculum can benefit all language learners. It includes study questions and interactive activities for use in school-based book studies, with leadership teams, in professional learning communities, and on university courses.

Paradis, J., Genesee, F., & Crago, M. (2011). *Dual language development and disorders, second edition.* Baltimore, MD: Brookes Publishing.

This volume synthesizes research on young children and school-age students who are in the process of learning two languages and may also be experiencing language impairments, reading disabilities, and developmental delays. Essential for SLPs, psychologists, and educators, this accessible volume addresses dual language and immersion programs and internationally adopted children. The volume augments the professional knowledge base on which to build our culturally and linguistically responsive inclusive practices.

Appendices

Appendix 1: Elements of the Instructional Conversation

Instructional elements

1 *Thematic focus.* The teacher selects a theme or idea to serve as a starting point for focusing the discussion and has a general plan for how the theme will unfold, including how to 'chunk' the text to permit optimal exploration of the theme.

2 *Activation and use of background and relevant schemata.* The teacher either 'hooks into' or provides students with pertinent background knowledge and relevant schemata necessary for understanding a text. Background knowledge and schemata are then woven into the discussion that follows.

3 *Direct teaching.* When necessary, the teacher provides direct teaching of a skill or concept.

4 *Promotion of more complex language and expression.* The teacher elicits more extended student contributions by using a variety of elicitation techniques– invitations to expand (e.g. 'tell me more about that'), questions (e.g. 'What do you mean?'), restatements (e.g. 'in other words,—'), and pauses.

5 *Elicitation of bases for statements or positions.* The teacher promotes students' use of text, pictures, and reasoning to support an argument or position. Without overwhelming students, the teacher probes for the bases of students' statements—e.g. 'How do you know?' 'What makes you think that?' 'Show us where it says _____.'

Conversational elements

6 *Fewer 'known-answer' questions.* Much of the discussion centers on questions and answers for which there might be more than one correct answer.

7 *Responsivity to student contributions.* While having an initial plan and maintaining the focus and coherence of the discussion, the teacher is also responsive to students' statements and the opportunities they provide.

8 *Connected discourse.* The discussion is characterized by multiple, interactive, connected turns; succeeding utterances build upon and extend previous ones.

9 *A challenging but non-threatening atmosphere.* The teacher creates a 'zone of proximal development,' where a challenging atmosphere is balanced by a positive affective climate. The teacher is more collaborator than evaluator and creates an atmosphere that challenges students and allows them to negotiate and construct the meaning of the text.

10 *General participation, including self-selected turns.* The teacher encourages general participation among students. The teacher does not hold exclusive right to determine who talks, and students are encouraged to volunteer, or otherwise influence the selection of speaking turns.

(Goldenberg, 1992/1993, p. 319)

Appendix 2: Modified Guided Reading (MGR) Lesson-Planning Framework (for DLLs)

Planning the lesson(s)

1   Determine objectives of lesson(s) based upon instructional needs (English-language learning and literacy learning).
   a   Determine the main idea or essential message from text and supporting information.
   b   Read for information to use in performing a task and learning a new task.
   c   Identify words and construct meaning from the text.
2   Group students by name/oral L2 level–instructional reading level.
3   Select guided-reading books based upon objectives and students' instructional reading levels.
4   Analyze the text and identify literacy challenges based upon your knowledge of the students.
   a   Semantics
      i   Vocabulary
         1   Focus on common English morphemes (e.g. affixes) or orthographic patterns
         2   Identify two to three words for receptive vocabulary and five to nine words for productive vocabulary
         3   Understand the meaning of the story whenever possible
      ii Figurative language
      iii Homophones (words that sound the same, different meanings)
         1   Homographs (words that are spelled the same but have different meanings and origins)
   b   Grammar (complex syntax, punctuation)
   c   Text structure (narrative, expository)
   d   Content or concept (cultural relevance)
   e   Strategy instruction (if needed, identify good places to insert strategy instruction during shared reading [e.g. think-alouds, elicitation of predictions, word solving])

Extending the lesson(s)

Word work:
Writing:
Possible mini lessons:

Note: As ELLs become more proficient [in both oral and written language], they will need less support. This framework should be adjusted to reflect more student responsibility as the teacher facilitates learning and guides when necessary.

(Avalos, Plasencia, Chavez, & Rascón, 2008, p. 322)

Appendix 3: Sample CSR Lesson Design

The following outline has been adapted from Bremer, Vaughn, Clapper, and Kim (2002), and describes the steps that teachers can follow in order to implement Collaborative Strategic Reading (CSR) in their classrooms.

Preview

Purpose: activate prior knowledge; encourage prediction; build interest in the topic
Activities: brainstorm ideas; make predictions

1   The teacher introduces the topic of the passage.
2   Students write down everything they already know about the topic in the 'Preview' section of their learning log, under the heading 'What I already know about the topic'.
3   In pairs, students share their responses with each other.
4   Students skim the passage, using textual features—headings, pictures, graphs, etc.—to predict what they might learn as they read. They write down these predictions in the 'Preview' section of their learning log, under the heading 'What I think I will learn'.
5   Students share their best ideas with the class.

Click and Clunk

Purpose: identify known and unknown vocabulary; use strategies to understand unknown words
Activities: monitor understanding of word meanings during reading; identify unfamiliar vocabulary; use fix-up strategies to understand the text

In the click and clunk strategy, the words that students instantaneously understand are called 'clicks'. The words that make no sense to them and so interfere with comprehension are known as 'clunks'. Clunks are analogous to potholes in a road that impede the process of smooth driving.

1   The teacher demonstrates the difference between a click and a clunk.
2   The teacher reinforces this distinction by reading or asking the class to read a short section of text and then having students report any clunks they may have encountered.

3   Students who encounter a clunk must apply one or more of four
     fix-up strategies:
     • Re-read the sentence as though the clunk was a blank space and try to
       guess another word that might be appropriate in place of the clunk.
       There is a good chance that the clunk is a synonym.
     • Re-read the sentence containing the clunk and the sentences before or
       after it to look for clues, i.e. other words or phrases that may partially
       indicate the meaning of the clunk.
     • Look for a prefix or suffix in the clunk that may help to define
       its meaning.
     • If possible, break the clunk into smaller, more familiar words that may
       indicate its meaning.

Get the Gist

Purpose: recognize and understand the main ideas during reading, thereby
increasing the likelihood of understanding the text
Activities: identify main idea; restate main idea in ten words or fewer

1   The teacher explains how to restate the most important point of a section
     of text in one's own words. The teacher then assigns a passage for the
     students to read.
2   Students distinguish the most important idea in a section of text by using
     the following steps:
     • Identify whether the paragraph is primarily about a person, a place,
       or a thing.
     • Identify which person, place, or thing is being discussed.
     • Identify what is being said about the person, place, or thing that the
       paragraph is principally about—i.e. identify the basic argument, angle,
       spin, or perspective that the section adopts regarding its topic.
     • Restate the essence of the paragraph in a sentence containing ten words
       or fewer.

Wrap Up

After they have finished the passage, students are ready to implement the wrap up
strategy.
Purpose: understand and remember what has been learned
Activities: generate questions; review important ideas

1   Teachers start by asking students to imagine that they are teachers trying to
     write test questions based on the content of the text.
2   Students then generate and answer questions from the text by using the
     following steps:
     • Brainstorm a number of possible questions and write them in the 'Wrap
       Up' section of their learning logs, under the heading 'Questions about the
       important ideas in the passage'.

- Arrange the questions according to a question hierarchy that reflects lower- to higher-order thinking.
- Try to answer the questions. A question that cannot be answered might not be a good question or might require clarification.

3   Next, students review what was learned by using the following steps:

- Write down the most important ideas from the day's reading in the 'Wrap Up' section of their learning logs, under the heading 'What I learned'. This requires students to mentally organize the information and to focus on comprehending the text as a whole.
- Take turns sharing with the rest of the class what they consider to be their best ideas.

(Bremer, Vaughn, Clapper, & Kim, 2002)

Glossary

additive: describes an environment in which L1 development and use is honored and encouraged. Contrasts with *subtractive*.

asset orientation: describes an educational approach grounded in the view that all students have assets, or strengths, that can facilitate learning.

attention deficit hyperactivity disorder (ADHD): a chronic neurodevelopmental disorder characterized by developmentally inappropriate levels of inattention, impulsivity, and hyperactivity.

authentic: describes learning based on meaningful, relevant, and interesting real-life activities. Contrasts with *reductionist*.

autism spectrum disorder (ASD): a neurodevelopmental disorder diagnosed by medical practitioners. Also referred to as 'autism spectrum condition' (ASC).

code-mixing: use of at least two languages, especially in speaking. Also referred to as 'code-switching'.

cognitive theories: models of 'thinking' conceptualized as mental processes, such as attention, memory, and the development of mental connections or *schemata*.

comprehensible: describes input that a reader/listener can understand. Krashen (1982) hypothesized that L2 acquisition occurs when learners are exposed to language that they can understand and that contains a small amount of new language.

critical literacy: actively reading in a manner that promotes understanding of socially constructed concepts such as power, inequality, and injustice in human relationships.

culturally and linguistically responsive: describes pedagogy or practices that recognize the importance of including and valuing students' cultural experiences, perspectives, and references, together with all their linguistic resources, in learning.

differentiate: take students' diverse learning characteristics into account when planning and implementing instruction.

DLLsSEN: the acronym used in this book for *dual language learners* (DLLs) with *special educational needs* (SEN).

Down syndrome: occurs when an individual has a full or partial extra copy of chromosome 21 that alters the course of development.

dual language learners (DLLs): children and school-age students who are in the process of developing two or more languages, either simultaneously or sequentially.

dyslexia: often characterized as difficulties with accurate and/or fluent word recognition, spelling, and decoding resulting from a deficit in the phonological component of language. It is sometimes used interchangeably with *reading disability* and *reading impairment*.

English as a second language (ESL): the speaking or learning of English by students who are already speakers of another language.

English language learner (ELL): a student who is in the process of learning English and already speaks another language. The term is also used in US schools to identify students who have not yet fully developed language proficiency goals as determined by standardized tests. Also referred to as an 'English learner' (EL).

exceptional learner: a student who learns at a different rate and/or in a different way from those viewed as 'typical'.

first language (L1): the initial language that children are exposed to and learn to understand and speak.

funds of knowledge: cultural practices and knowledge that are embedded in the daily practices and routines of families and communities.

heritage speaker: an individual studying or exposed to a language spoken in that individual's family and/or community.

home language(s): the language or languages used in the home by students and their families. See also *first language*.

identity texts: literacy and content area projects—written, recorded, or dramatized—that incorporate students' languages, cultures, experiences, and perspectives.

inclusion: the removal of barriers to learning, such as discrimination or unequal access to resources. For students with SEN, it typically means instruction in a general education classroom with age peers that includes supports and scaffolds to address their individual learning needs.

Individual Education Plan (IEP): a written document developed by school teams together with parents for a student who has been deemed eligible for special educational services. Also referred to as an *Individualized Educational Program*.

Individualized Educational Program (IEP): see *Individual Education Plan*.

L1: see *first language* and *home language*.

L2: see *second language*.

language impairment: a disorder or delay characterized by persistent language learning difficulties. It affects the development of oral language and often impacts literacy development. It can present as part of other disabilities, such as hearing loss, cleft palate, and Down syndrome, and thus contrasts with *specific language impairment* or *primary language impairment*, in which language is the predominant area of functioning affected.

language proficiency: a learner's current level of skills in listening, speaking, reading, and writing in a given language at a particular time.

learning disability (LD): a disability characterized by significant challenges in learning across one or more ways that a person takes in, stores, or uses information. See also *specific learning disability*.

learning environment: the physical environment and cultural and social-emotional climate in which instruction is delivered, together with the methods and strategies used.

majority language: the language spoken by most people in a society and/or by those whose views carry influence or power. Contrasts with *minority language*.

mediation: the use of language facilitation or learning strategies in authentic communication contexts for real purposes by a more competent speaker, reader, or writer to guide the development of a less experienced learner. Strategies include modeling and scaffolding.

minority language: a language spoken by a small group of people in a society. Contrasts with *majority language*.

morphology: the study of morphemes, the smallest structural units that have meaning in words.

Multi-Tiered System of Supports (MTSS): a systemic continuous improvement framework in which data-based problem-solving and decision-making are practiced across all levels of the educational system for educating the diverse range of learners.

opportunity to learn: access to the content, language, skills, and higher-order thinking embedded in school curricula.

part-to-whole: describes instruction that begins with component skills (for example, phonics) before focusing on making meaning from text. Contrasts with *whole-to-part*.

phonology: the system of relationships among the speech sounds that constitute the fundamental components of a language.

pragmatics: how language is used relative to the context of use, including implicit culturally derived expectations.

primary language impairment (PLI): pronounced and persistent challenges in acquiring oral language in the typical way and at a typical rate, in the absence of sensory and physical causation. See also *specific language impairment* and *language impairment*.

reading disability: persistent difficulties with decoding and/or text comprehension. From a sociolinguistic perspective, it is viewed as an individual's difficulty with the use and coordination of strategies to make meaning from text. See *dyslexia* and *reading impairment*.

reading impairment: see *dyslexia* and *reading disability*.

recurrency: the practice of revisiting elements of a unit of study, such as vocabulary, concepts, structures, or strategies, in a new context.

reductionist: describes learning that reduces complex learning tasks to their smallest—considered simplest—components for controlled practice. See also *part-to-whole*.

Response to Instruction and Intervention (RTI): a systematic data-based assessment and intervention framework used by school systems to promote academic progress and prevent behavioral challenges for all students through evidenced-based instruction, early intervention, and frequent assessment of students' progress. See *Multi-Tiered System of Supports*.

scaffold: a form of mediation that aids the communicative and/or academic efforts of a learner.

schema (plural: **schemata**): knowledge organized into networks of associations or interconnected maps that change and grow with new experiences and information.

second language (L2): an additional or subsequent language that an individual learns.

semantics: the aspect of language that pertains to the meanings of words, phrases, sentences, and discourse.

sequential bilingual: an individual learning an additional language after learning the first language. Contrasts with *simultaneous bilingual*.

sheltered instruction: a pedagogical approach that makes instructional input more comprehensible for students and integrates the teaching of academic language and academic content.

simultaneous bilingual: an individual exposed to two languages before the age of three years. Contrasts with *sequential bilingual*.

special educational needs (SEN): learning needs that require special educational services and resources. Also referred to as 'special needs'.

specific language impairment (SLI): pronounced and persistent challenges in acquiring oral language in the typical way and at a typical rate in the absence of sensory, physical, or cognitive deficits. See also *language impairment* and *primary language impairment*.

specific learning difference (SpLD): a term used in the UK to acknowledge students that are different from the majority in their general approach to learning without viewing them as disabled or deficient.

specific learning disability (SLD): significant difficulty in understanding or using spoken and/or written language. SLD may manifest in persistent difficulties in listening, thinking, speaking, reading, writing, spelling, or doing mathematical calculations.

strengths-based orientation: see *asset orientation*.

subtractive: describes an environment in which the L1 is not used and may even be discouraged. Contrasts with *additive*.

syntax: the arrangement of words or phrases in grammatical sentences.

translanguaging: the fluid use by bilingual or multilingual speakers of all their linguistic repertoire in a dynamic and integrated manner.

whole-to-part: describes instruction that begins with conceptual understanding and embeds skills instruction into meaningful contexts. Contrasts with *part-to-whole*.

zone of proximal development (ZPD): the difference between what learners do independently and what they can do with assistance (Vygotsky, 1978).

References

American Psychiatric Association. (2013). *Diagnostic and statistical manual of mental disorders, fifth edition*. Washington, DC: American Psychiatric Association.

Artiles, A. (2003). Special education's changing identity: Paradoxes and dilemmas in views of culture and space. *Harvard Educational Review, 73,* 164–202.

Artiles, A. J., & Ortiz, A. A. (2002). *English language learners with special education needs: Identification, assessment and instruction*. McHenry, IL: Delta Systems.

Artiles, A. J., Trent, S. C., & Palmer, J. (2004). Culturally diverse students in special education: Legacies and prospects. In J. A. Banks & C. M. Banks (Eds.), *Handbook of research on multicultural education, second edition* (pp. 716–35). San Francisco, CA: Jossey Bass.

August, D., & Shanahan, T. (Eds.). (2006). *Developing literacy in second language learners: A report of the national literacy panel on language minority children and youth, Executive Summary, Center for Applied Linguistics*. Mahwah, NJ: Lawrence Erlbaum. Retrieved November 17 2017 from http://www.cal.org/projects/archive/nlpreports/Executive_Summary.pdf

Avalos, M. A., Plasencia, A., Chavez, C., & Rascón, J. (2008). Modified guided reading: Gateway to English as a second language and literacy learning. *The Reading Teacher, 61,* 318–29.

Baca, L., Baca, E., & de Valenzuela, J. S. (2004). Development of bilingual special education interface. In L. M. Baca & H. T. Cervantes (Eds.), *The bilingual special education interface, fourth edition* (pp. 100–23). Upper Saddle River, NJ: Pearson Prentice Hall.

Baca, L. M., & Cervantes, H. T. (2004). *The bilingual special education interface, fourth edition*. Upper Saddle River, NJ: Pearson Prentice Hall.

Bailey, A. L. (Ed.). (2007). *The language demands of school: Putting academic English to the test*. New Haven, CT: Yale University Press.

Baker, S., Lesaux, N., Jayanthi, M., Dimino, J., Proctor, C. P., Morris, J., & Newman-Gonchar, R. (2014). *Teaching academic content and literacy to English learners in elementary and middle school. NCEE 2014-4012*. Washington, DC: National Center for Education Evaluation and Regional Assistance.

Balu, R., Zhu, P., Doolittle, F., Schiller, E., Jenkins, J., & Gersten, R. (2015). *Evaluation of response to intervention practices for elementary school reading. NCEE 2016-4000*. Washington, DC: National Center for Education Evaluation and Regional Assistance.

Banks, J. (2005). *Cultural diversity and education: Foundations, curriculum, and teaching, fifth edition*. Boston, MA: Pearson.

Bernhard, J. K., Cummins, J., Campoy, F. I., Ada, A. F., Winsler, A., & Bleiker, C. (2006). Identity texts and literacy development among preschool English language learners: Enhancing learning opportunities for children at risk for learning disabilities. *Teachers College Record, 108,* 2380–405.

Bialystok, E. (2001). *Bilingualism in development: Language, literacy and cognition*. Cambridge: Cambridge University Press.

Bialystok, E. (2011). Reshaping the mind: The benefits of bilingualism. *Canadian Journal of Experimental Psychology/Revue Canadienne de Psychologie Experimentale, 65,* 229–35.

Bialystok, E., Craik, F. I. M., & Freedman, M. (2007). Bilingualism as a protection against the onset of symptoms of dementia. *Neuropsychologia, 45,* 459–64.

Bialystok, E., & Hakuta, K. (1994). *In other words: The science and psychology of second-language acquisition*. New York. NY: Basic Books.

Biancarosa, G., & Snow, C. E. (2006). *Reading next: A vision for action and research in middle and high school literacy: A report to Carnegie Corporation of New York, second edition.* Washington, DC: Alliance for Excellent Education.

Bloodstein. O., & Bernstein-Ratner, N. (2008). *A handbook on stuttering, sixth edition.* Clifton Park, NY: Delmar Learning.

Boardman, A., & Blake, D. (2014, May). *CCSS, ELs, and CSR.* Presentation at International Reading Association Conference, New Orleans, LA.

Boardman, A. G., Klingner, J. K., Buckley, P., Annamma, S., & Lasser, C. J. (2015). The efficacy of Collaborative Strategic Reading in middle school science and social studies classes. *Reading and Writing, 28*, 1257–83.

Bransford, J. D., Brown, A. L., & Cocking, R. R. (2000). *How people learn: Brain, mind, experience, and school, expanded edition.* Washington, DC: National Academy Press.

Bremer, C. D., Vaughn, S., Clapper, A. T., & Kim, A.-H. (2002). Collaborative Strategic Reading (CSR): Improving secondary students' reading comprehension skills. *Improving Secondary Education and Transition Services through Research, 1.* Retrieved November 17 2017 from http://www.ncset.org/publications/researchtopractice/NCSETResearchBrief_1.2.pdf

Brice, A., & Roseberry-McKibbin, C. (2001). Choice of languages in instruction: One language or two? *Teaching Exceptional Children, 33*, 10–16.

Burningham, J. (1990). *Mr Gumpy's outing.* New York, NY: Henry Holt.

Carroll, J. B. (1993). *Human cognitive abilities.* Cambridge: Cambridge University Press.

Cazden, C., Cope, B., Fairclough, N., & Gee, J. (1996). A pedagogy of multiliteracies: Designing social futures. *Harvard Educational Review, 66*, 60–92.

Cheatham, G. A., Santos, R. M., & Kerkutluoglu, A. (2012). Review of comparison studies investigating bilingualism and bilingual instruction for students with disabilities. *Focus on Exceptional Children, 45*, 1–12.

Cheng. L., Klinger, D., & Zheng, Y. (2009). Examining students' after-school literacy activities and their literacy performance on the Ontario Secondary School Literacy Test. *Canadian Journal of Education, 32*, 116–48.

Chow, P., & Cummins, J. (2003). Valuing multilingual and multicultural approaches to learning. In S. R. Schecter & J. Cummins (Eds.), *Multilingual education in practice: Using diversity as a resource* (pp. 32–61). Portsmouth, NH: Heinemann.

Chumak-Horbatsch, R. (2012). *Linguistically appropriate practice: A guide for working with young immigrant children.* Toronto: University of Toronto Press.

Cisco, B. K., & Padrón, Y. (2012). Investigating vocabulary and reading strategies with middle grades English language learners: A research synthesis. *RMLE Online, 36*, 1–23.

Clark, C., & St. John, K. (1995). Using bilingual literature with students who have severe disabilities. *Multiple Voices for Ethnically Diverse Exceptional Learner, 1*, 47–9.

Cloud, N., Genesee, F., & Hamayan, E. (2009). *Literacy instruction for English language learners: A teacher's guide to research-based practices.* Portsmouth, NH: Heinemann.

Cloud, N., Lakin, J., Leininger, E., & Maxwell, L. (2010). *Teaching adolescent English language learners: Essential strategies for middle and high school.* Philadelphia, PA: Caslon.

Commins, N. L. (2011). Meaning is everything: Comprehension work with second language learners. In H. Daniels, H. (Ed.), *Comprehension going forward: Where we are and what's next?* (pp. 192–214). Portsmouth NH: Heinemann.

Commins, N. L., & Miramontes, O. B. (2006). Addressing linguistic diversity from the outset. *Journal of Teacher Education, 57*, 240–6.

Cook, H. G., Boals, T., & Lundberg, T. (2011). Academic achievement for English learners: What can we reasonably expect? *Phi Delta Kappan, 93*, 66–9.

Cook, H. G., Wilmes, C., Boals, T., & Santos, M. (2008). *Issues in the development of annual measurable achievement objectives for WIDA Consortium states. WCER Working Paper no. 2008-2.* Madison, WI: Wisconsin Center for Education Research.

Corbett, J. (1992). *Bad-mouthing: The language of special needs.* London: The Falmer Press.

Cummins, J. (1981). Age on arrival and immigrant second language learning in Canada: A reassessment. *Applied Linguistics, 2*, 132–49.

Cummins, J. (1984). *Bilingual education and special education: Issues in assessment and pedagogy.* San Diego, CA: College-Hill Press.

Cummins, J. (1991). Language development and academic learning. In L. Malave & G. Duquette (Eds.), *Language, culture and cognition* (pp. 161–75). Clevedon: Multilingual Matters.

Cummins, J. (1994). Knowledge, power, and identity in teaching English as a second language. In F. Genesee (Ed.), *Educating second language children: The whole child, the whole curriculum, the whole community* (pp. 103–25). Cambridge: Cambridge University Press.

Cummins, J. (2007). Pedagogies for the poor? Realigning reading instruction for low-income students with scientifically based reading research. *Educational Researcher, 36,* 564–72.

Cummins, J. (2008). BICS and CALP: Empirical and theoretical status of the distinction. In B. Street & N. H. Hornberger (Eds.), *Encyclopedia of language and education, Volume 2: literacy, second edition* (pp. 71–83). New York, NY: Springer Science & Business.

Cummins, J. (2009). Multilingualism in the English-language classroom: Pedagogical considerations. *TESOL Quarterly, 43,* 317–21.

Cummins, J. (2017, March). *Evidence-based literacy instruction: The central role of literacy engagement.* Paper presented at the ECIS ESLMT Conference, Copenhagen.

Cummins, J., & Early, M. (2011). *Identity texts: The collaborative creation of power in multilingual schools.* Stoke-on-Trent: Trentham.

Cummins, J., & Persad, R. (2014). Teaching through a multilingual lens: The evolution of EAL policy and practice in Canada. *Education Matters, 2,* 3–40.

Cummins, J., Bismilla, V., Chow, P., Cohen, S., Giampapa, F., Leoni, L., Sandu, P., & Sastri, P. (2005). Affirming identity in multilingual classrooms. *Educational Leadership, 63,* 38–43.

Cummins, J., Mirza, R., & Stille, S. (2012). English language learners in Canadian schools: Emerging directions for school-based policies. *TESL Canada Journal/Revue TESL du Canada, 29,* 25–48.

Damico, J. S., & Ball, M. J. (2010). Prolegomenon: Addressing the tyranny of old ideas. *Journal of Interactional Research in Communicative Disorders, 1,* 1–30.

Damico, J. S., & Damico, S. K. (1993). Mapping a course over different roads: Language teaching with special populations. In J. W. Oller, Jr. (Ed.), *Methods that work: A smorgasbord of language teaching ideas, second edition* (pp. 320–31). New York, NY: Newbury House.

Damico, J. S., & Nelson, R. L. (2005). Interpreting problematic behavior: Systematic compensatory adaptations as emergent phenomena in autism. *Clinical Linguistics and Phonetics, 19,* 405–18.

Damico, J. S., & Nelson, R. L. (2010). Reading and reading impairments. In J. S. Damico, N. Müller, & M. J. Ball (Eds.), *The handbook of language and speech disorders* (pp. 267–95). Oxford: Blackwell.

Delaney, M. (2016). *Special educational needs.* Oxford: Oxford University Press.

Delgado, R. (2010). Poco a poquito se van apagando: Teachers' experiences educating Latino ELLs with disabilities. *Journal of Latinos and Educators, 9,* 150–7.

DeCasper, A. J., & Spence, M. J. (1986). Prenatal maternal speech influences newborns' perception of speech sounds. *Infant Behavior and Development, 9,* 133–50.

Delpit, L. (1995). *Other people's children.* New York, NY: The New Press.

de Oliveira, Ê. (2015). A literature review on bilingualism among children diagnosed with autism spectrum disorders. *Revista Chilena de Fonoaudiología, 14,* 33–44.

de Oliveira, L. C., & Schleppegrell, M. J. (2015). *Focus on grammar and meaning.* Oxford: Oxford University Press.

Doherty, R. W., & Hilberg, R. S. (2007). Standards for effective pedagogy, classroom organization, English proficiency, and student achievement. *The Journal of Educational Research, 101,* 24–35.

Donovan, M. S., & Bransford, J. (Eds.). (2005). *How students learn history, mathematics, and science in the classroom.* Washington, DC: National Academy Press.

Donovan, M. S., & Cross, C. T. (Eds.). (2002). *Minority students in special and gifted education.* Washington, DC: National Academy Press.

Drysdale, H., van der Meer, L., & Kagohara, D. (2015). Children with autism spectrum disorder from bilingual families: A systematic review. *Review Journal of Autism and Developmental Disorders, 2,* 26–38.

Ebert, K. D., Kohnert, K., Pham, G., Disher, J. R., and Payesteh, B. (2014). Three treatments for bilingual children with primary language impairment: Examining cross-linguistic and cross-domain effects. *Journal of Speech, Language, and Hearing Research, 57,* 172–86.

Echevarria, J., & McDonough, R. (1995). An alternative reading approach: Instructional Conversation (IC) in a bilingual special education setting. *Learning Disabilities Research & Practice, 10,* 108–19.

Echevarria, J., & Short, D. (2010). Programs and practices for effective sheltered content instruction. In California Department of Education (Ed.), *Improving education for English learners: Research-based approaches* (pp. 250–321). Sacramento, CA: CDE Press.

Echevarria, J., Vogt, M. E., & Short, D. (2004). *Making content comprehensible to English learners: The SIOP model, second edition.* Boston, MA: Pearson/Allyn & Bacon.

Ellis, N. (2002). Frequency effects in language processing: A review with implications for theories of implicit and explicit language education. *Studies in Second Language Acquisition, 24,* 143–88.

Enguidanos, T., & Ruiz, N. T. (2008). Shared reading for older emergent readers in bilingual classrooms. *Focus on Exceptional Children, 40,* 4–16.

Feltmate, K., & Kay-Raining Bird, E. (2008). Language learning in four bilingual children with Down syndrome: A detailed analysis of vocabulary and morphosyntax. *Canadian Journal of Speech-Language Pathology and Audiology, 32,* 6–20.

Fletcher, T. V., Bos, C. S., & Johnson, L. M. (1999). Accommodating English language learners with language and learning disabilities in bilingual education classrooms. *Learning Disabilities Research & Practice, 14,* 80–91.

Fountas, I. C., & Pinnell, G. S. (1996). *Guided reading: Good first teaching for all children.* Portsmouth, NH: Heinemann.

Francis, D., Lesaux, N., & August, D. (2006). Language of instruction. In D. L. August & T. Shanahan (Eds.), *Developing literacy in second-language learners* (pp. 365–413). New York, NY: Routledge.

Fu, D., & Matoush, M. M. (2015). *Focus on literacy.* Oxford: Oxford University Press.

Fuchs, D., Fuchs, L. S., & Burish, P. (2000). Peer-Assisted Learning Strategies: An empirically-supported practice to promote reading achievement. *Learning Disabilities Research and Practice, 15,* 85–91.

Fuchs, D., Mock, D., Morgan, P. L., & Young, C. L. (2003). Responsiveness-to-intervention: Definitions, evidence, and implications for the learning disabilities construct. *Learning Disabilities Research & Practice, 18,* 157–71.

Gándara, P., & Rumberger, R. W. (2009). Immigration, language, and education: How does language policy structure opportunity? *Teachers College Record, 111,* 750–82.

García, O. (2009). Emergent bilinguals and TESOL: What's in a name? *TESOL Quarterly, 43,* 322–6.

García, O., & Kleifgen, J. (2010). *Educating emergent bilinguals: Policies, programs and practices for English language learners.* New York, NY: Teachers College Press.

García, O., & Wei, L. (2014). *Translanguaging: Language, bilingualism and education.* New York, NY: Palgrave Macmillan.

García, S. B., & Ortiz, A. A. (2006). Preventing disproportionate representation: Culturally and linguistically responsive pre-referral interventions. *Teaching Exceptional Children, 38,* 64–8.

García, S. B., & Ortiz, A. A. (2008). A framework for culturally and linguistically responsive design of response-to-intervention models. *Multiple Voices for Ethnically Diverse Exceptional Learners, 11,* 24–41.

García, S. B., & Tyler, B. (2010). Meeting the needs of English language learners with learning disabilities in the general curriculum. *Theory into Practice, 49,* 113–20.

Gardner, H. (2011). *The unschooled mind: How children think and how schools should teach, second edition.* New York, NY: Basic Books.

Gay, G. (2000). *Culturally responsive teaching: Theory, research, and practice.* New York, NY: Teachers College Press.

Gee, J. P. (2008). Sociocultural perspective on opportunity to learn. In P. Moss (Ed.), *Assessment, equity and opportunity to learn* (pp. 76–108). New York, NY: Cambridge University Press. Retrieved November 17 2017 from http://www.jamespaulgee.com/publications

Genesee, F. (2009). Early childhood bilingualism: Perils and possibilities. *Journal of Applied Research on Learning, 2 (Special Issue), Article 2,* 1–21.

Genesee, F., Lindholm-Leary, K., Saunders, W., & Christian, D. (2005). English language learners in US schools: An overview of research findings. *Journal for Education for Students Placed at Risk, 10,* 365–85.

Genesee, F., Lindholm-Leary, K., Saunders, W., & Christian, D. (2006). *Educating English language learners: A synthesis of research evidence.* New York, NY: Cambridge University Press.

Genesee, F., & Riches, C. (2006). Literacy: Instructional issues. In F. Genesee, K. Lindholm-Leary, W. Saunders, & D. Christian (Eds.), *Educating English language learners: A synthesis of research evidence* (pp. 109–75). New York, NY: Cambridge University Press.

Gersten, R., & Woodward, J. (1994). The language-minority student and special education: Issues, trends, and paradoxes. *Exceptional Children, 60,* 310–22.

Geurts, H. M., & Embrechts, M. J. (2008). Language profiles in ASD, SLI, and ADHD. *Journal of Autism and Developmental Disorders, 38,* 1931–43.

Girolametto, L., Verbey, M., & Tannock, R. (1994). Improving joint engagement in parent–child interaction: An intervention study. *Journal of Early Intervention, 18,* 155–67.

Goldenberg, C. (1992/1993). Instructional conversation: Promoting comprehension through discussion. *The Reading Teacher, 46,* 316–26.

Goldstein, B. (1995). Critical pedagogy in a bilingual special education classroom. *Journal of Learning Disabilities, 28,* 463–75.

Goldstein, H. (2006). Clinical issues: Language intervention considerations for children with mental retardation and developmental disabilities. *Perspectives on Language Learning and Education, 13,* 21–6.

González, N., Moll, L. C., & Amanti, C. (Eds.). (2006). *Funds of knowledge: Theorizing practices in households, communities, and classrooms.* London: Routledge.

González, T., & Artiles, A. J. (2015). Reframing venerable standpoints about language and learning differences: The need for research on the literate lives of Latina/o language minority students. *Journal of Multilingual Education Research, 6,* 9–34.

Gottlieb, M., & Sánchez-López, C. (2008). Assessing English language learners: A perplexing puzzle. Perspectives on school-based issues. *ASHA Perspectives, 9,* 41–83.

Grandin, T. (2012). *Different … not less: Inspiring stories of achievement and successful employment from adults with autism, Asperger's and ADHD.* Arlington, TX: Future Horizons, Inc.

Gutiérrez, K. D., & Rogoff, B. (2003). Cultural ways of learning: Individual traits or repertoires of practice. *Educational Researcher, 32,* 19–25.

Gutiérrez-Clellen, V. F., Simon-Cereijido, G., & Leone, A. E. (2009). Codeswitching in bilingual children with specific language impairment. *The International Journal of Bilingualism: Cross-Disciplinary, Cross-Linguistic Studies of Language Behavior, 13,* 91–109.

Gutiérrez-Clellen, V. F., Simon-Cereijido, G., & Sweet, M. (2012). Predictors of second language acquisition in Latino children with specific language impairment. *American Journal of Speech-Language Pathology, 21,* 64–77.

Gutiérrez-Clellen, V. F., Simon-Cereijido, G., & Wagner. C. (2008). Bilingual children with language impairment: A comparison with monolinguals and second language learners. *Applied Psycholinguistics, 29,* 3–19.

Hakuta, K., Butler, Y. G., & Witt, D. (2000). *How long does it take English learners to attain proficiency?* Policy report. The University of California Linguistic Minority Research Institute, Stanford University.

Hamayan, E. V., & Damico, J. S. (Eds.). (1991). *Limiting bias in the assessment of bilingual students.* Austin, TX: Pro-Ed.

Hamayan, E., Marler, B., Sánchez-López, C., & Damico, J. (2013). *Special education considerations for English language learners (ELLs): Delivering a continuum of services, second edition*. Philadelphia, PA: Caslon Publishing.

Hambly, C., & Fombonne, E. (2012). The impact of bilingual environments on language development in children with autism spectrum disorders. *Journal of Autism and Developmental Disorders, 42,* 1342–52.

Harry, B. (2014). The disproportionate placement of ethnic minorities in special education. In L. Florian (Ed.), *Handbook of special education research, second edition* (pp. 74–95). London: Sage.

Harry, B., & Klingner, J. (2006). *Why are so many minority students in special education? Understanding race and disability in schools*. New York, NY: Teachers College Press.

Harry, B., & Klingner, J. (2007). Discarding the deficit model: Ambiguity and subjectivity contribute to disproportionate placement of minorities in special education. *Educational Leadership, 64,* 16–21.

Helman, A. L., Calhoon, M. B., & Kern, L. (2015). Improving science vocabulary of high school English language learners with reading disabilities. *Learning Disability Quarterly, 38,* 40–52.

Herrera, S., Perez, D., & Escamilla, K. (2010). *Teaching reading to English language learners: Differentiated literacies*. Boston, MA: Pearson.

Hickman, M. J. (2004). *Sociocultural dimensions of White principal leadership in multicultural elementary schools*. (Unpublished PhD thesis). University of Texas at Austin.

Hill, J. D., & Miller, K. B. (2013). *Classroom instruction that works with English language learners, second edition*. Alexandria, VA: ASCD.

Hock, M. F., Brasseur, I. F., Deshler, D. D., Catts, H. W., Marquis, J. G., Mark, C. A., & Stribling, J. W. (2009). What is the reading component skill profile of adolescent struggling readers in urban schools? *Learning Disability Quarterly, 32,* 21–38.

Holland, A. L., & Nelson, R. L. (2018). *Counseling in communication disorders: A wellness perspective, third edition*. San Diego, CA: Plural Publishing.

Honigsfeld, A., & Dove, M. G. (2010). *Collaboration and co-teaching strategies for English learners*. Thousand Oaks, CA: Corwin.

Hoover, J. J., & Baca, L. (2008). *State of the States in implementing RTI*. Washington, DC: National Association of State Directors for Special Education.

Hoover, J. J., Eppolito, A., Klingner, J. K., & Baca, L. (2012). Collaborative decision-making in multicultural contexts. In J. B. Crockett, B. S. Billingsley, & M. L. Boscardin (Eds.), *Handbook of leadership and administration for special education* (pp. 191–208). New York, NY: Routledge.

Hunt, P., Hirose-Hatae, A., Doering, K., Karasoff, P., & Goetz, L. (2000). 'Community' is what I think everyone is talking about. *Remedial and Special Education, 21,* 137–42.

Ijalba, E. (2015). Effectiveness of a parent-implemented language and literacy intervention in the home language. *Child Language Teaching and Therapy, 31,* 207–20.

Individuals with Disabilities Education Improvement Act (IDEIA), H.R. 1350, 108th Congress (2004).

Jang, E. E. (2014). *Focus on assessment*. Oxford: Oxford University Press.

Jiménez, R. T. (1997). The strategic reading abilities and potential of five low-literacy Latina/o readers in middle school. *Reading Research Quarterly, 32,* 224–43.

Jiménez, R. T., García, G. E., & Pearson, P. D. (1996). The reading strategies of bilingual Latina/o students who are successful English readers: Opportunities and obstacles. *Reading Research Quarterly, 31,* 90–112.

Johnson, C. J., Beitchman, J. H., Young, A., Escobar, M., Atkinson, L., Wilson, B., Brownlie, E. B., Douglas, L., Taback, N., Lam, I., & Wang, M. (1999). Fourteen-year follow-up of children with and without speech/language impairments: Speech/language stability and outcomes. *Journal of Speech, Language, and Hearing Research, 42,* 744–60.

Johnson, D. W., & Johnson, R. T. (1989). Cooperative learning: What special educators need to know. *The Pointer, 33,* 5–10.

Kalyanpur, M., & Harry, B. (2012). *Cultural reciprocity in special education: Building family-professional relationships, second edition*. Baltimore, MA: Brookes.

Kay-Raining Bird, E., Cleave, P., Trudeau, N., Thordardottir, E., & Thorpe, A. (2005). The language abilities of bilingual children with Down syndrome. *American Journal of Speech Language Pathology, 14*, 187–99.

Kay-Raining Bird, E., Genesee, F., & Verhoeven, L. (2016). Bilingualism in children with developmental disorders: A narrative review. *Journal of Communication Disorders, 63*, 1–14.

Kay-Raining Bird, E., Lamond, E., & Holden, J. (2012). Survey on bilingualism in autism spectrum disorders. *International Journal of Language & Communication Disorders, 47*, 2–64.

Kim, A. H., Vaughn, S., Klingner, J. K., Woodruff, A. L., Klein Reutebuch, C., & Kouzekanani, K. (2006). Improving the reading comprehension of middle school students with disabilities through computer-assisted collaborative strategic reading. *Remedial and Special Education, 27*, 235–49.

Kim, W., Linan-Thompson, S., & Misquitta, R. (2012). Critical factors in reading comprehension instruction for students with learning disabilities: A research synthesis. *Learning Disabilities Research & Practice, 27*, 66–78.

Klingner, J. K. (2004). The science of professional development. *Journal of Learning Disabilities, 37*, 248–55.

Klingner, J. K., Arguelles, M. E., Hughes, M. T., & Vaughn, S. (2001). Examining the schoolwide 'spread' of research-based practices. *Learning Disability Quarterly, 24*, 221–34.

Klingner, J. K., Artiles, A. J., Kozleski, E., Harry, B., Zion, S., Tate, W., Durán, G. Z., & Riley, D. (2005). Addressing the disproportionate representation of culturally and linguistically diverse students in special education through culturally responsive educational systems. *Education Policy Analysis Archives, 13*(38), 1–39.

Klingner, J. K., Artiles, A. J., & Méndez Barletta, L. (2006). English language learners who struggle with reading: Language acquisition or learning disabilities? *Journal of Learning Disabilities, 39*, 108–28.

Klingner, J. K., Boelé, A., Linan-Thompson, S., & Rodriguez, D. (2014). Essential components of special education for English language learners with learning disabilities: Position statement of the Division for Learning Disabilities of the Council for Exceptional Children. *Learning Disabilities Research & Practice, 29*, 93–6.

Klingner, J. K., & Edwards, P. (2006). Cultural considerations with response to intervention models. *Reading Research Quarterly, 41*, 108–17.

Klingner, J., & Eppolito, A. (2014). *English language learners: Differentiating between language acquisition and learning disabilities.* Arlington, VA: Council for Exceptional Children.

Klingner, J. K., Hoover, J. J., & Baca, L. M. (2008). *Why do English language learners struggle with reading? Distinguishing language acquisition from learning disabilities.* Thousand Oaks, CA: Corwin Press.

Klingner, J., & Soltero-Gon   zález, L. (2009). Culturally and linguistically responsive literacy instruction for English language learners with learning disabilities. *Multiple Voices for Ethnically Diverse Exceptional Learners, 12*, 4–20.

Klingner, J. K., & Vaughn, S. (1996). Reciprocal teaching of reading comprehension strategies for students with learning disabilities who use English as a second language. *The Elementary School Journal, 96*, 275–93.

Klingner, J. K., & Vaughn, S. (1998). Using collaborative strategic reading. *Teaching Exceptional Children, 30*, 32–7.

Klingner, J. K., & Vaughn, S. (1999). Promoting reading comprehension, content learning, and English acquisition through Collaborative Strategic Reading (CSR). *The Reading Teacher, 52*, 738–47.

Klingner, J. K., & Vaughn, S. (2000). The helping behaviors of fifth graders while using collaborative strategic reading during ESL content classes. *TESOL Quarterly, 34*, 69–98.

Klingner, J. K., Vaughn, S., Arguelles, M. E., Tejero Hughes, M., & Ahwee Leftwich, S. (2004). Collaborative Strategic Reading: 'Real-world' lessons from classroom teachers. *Remedial and Special Education. 25*, 291–302.

Klingner J. K., Vaughn, S., & Schumm, J. S. (1998). Collaborative strategic reading during social studies in heterogeneous fourth-grade classrooms. *The Elementary School Journal, 99*, 3–22.

Kohnert, K. (2002). Picture naming in early sequential bilinguals: A 1-year follow-up. *Journal of Speech, Language, and Hearing Research, 45,* 759–71.

Kohnert, K. (2010). Bilingual children with primary language impairment: Issues, evidence and implications for clinical actions. *Journal of Communication Disorders, 43,* 456–73.

Kohnert, K. (2013). *Language disorders in bilingual children and adults, second edition.* San Diego, CA: Plural Publishing.

Kohnert, K., & Ebert, K. D. (2010). Beyond morphosyntax in developing bilinguals and 'specific' language impairment. *Applied Psycholinguistics, 31,* 303–10.

Kohnert, K., Yim, D., Nett, K., Kan, P. F., & Duran, L. (2005). Language intervention with linguistically diverse preschool children: A focus on developing home language(s). *Speech and Hearing Services in Schools, 36,* 251–64.

Kormos, J., & Smith, A. M. (2012). *Teaching languages to students with specific learning differences.* Clevedon: Multilingual Matters.

Krashen, S. (1982). *Principles and practice in second language acquisition.* New York, NY: Prentice-Hall International.

Krashen, S. D. (1985). *The Input Hypothesis: Issues and implications.* New York, NY: Longman.

Kuehn, D. P., & Moller, K. T. (2000). Speech and language issues in the cleft palate population: The state of the art. *The Cleft Palate-Craniofacial Journal, 37,* 348–83.

Kuhl, P. K. (2011, February) *Patricia Kuhl: The linguistic genius of babies.* [Video file]. Retrieved 17 November 2017 from https://www.ted.com/talks/patricia_kuhl_the_linguistic_genius_of_babies

Ladson-Billings, G. (1995). Toward a theory of culturally relevant pedagogy. *American Educational Research Journal, 32,* 465–91.

Ladson-Billings, G. (2006). It's not the culture of poverty, it's the poverty of culture: The problem with teacher education. *Anthropology and Education Quarterly, 37,* 104–9.

Leonard, L. (1991). Specific language impairment as a clinical category. *Language, Speech, and Hearing Services in Schools, 22,* 66–8.

Leonard, L. (1998). *Children with specific language impairment.* Cambridge, MA: MIT Press.

Leonard, L., Weismer, S. E., Miller, C. A., Francis, D. J., Tomblin, J. B., & Kail, R. V. (2007). Speed of processing, working memory, and language impairment in children. *Journal of Speech, Language, and Hearing Research, 50,* 408–28.

Lerner, R. M., & Steinberg, L. (Eds.). (2009). *Handbook of adolescent psychology, Volume 1: Individual bases of adolescent development.* New York, NY: Wiley.

Lesaux, N. K., Kieffer, M. J., Faller, S. E., & Kelley, J. G. (2010). The effectiveness and ease of implementation of an academic vocabulary intervention for linguistically diverse students in urban middle schools. *Reading Research Quarterly, 45,* 196–228.

Lieven, E., & Tomasello, M. (2008). Children's first language acquisition from a usage based perspective. In P. Robinson & N. C. Ellis (Eds.), *Handbook of cognitive linguistics and second language acquisition* (pp. 168–96). London: Routledge.

Lightbown, P. M., & Spada, N. (2013). *How languages are learned, fourth edition.* Oxford: Oxford University Press.

Linan-Thompson, S. (2010). Response to instruction, English language learners and disproportionate representation: The role of assessment. *Psicothema, 22,* 970–4.

Lindholm-Leary, K., & Borsato, G. (2006). Academic achievement. In F. Genesee, K. Lindholm-Leary, W. Saunders, & D. Christian (Eds.), *Educating English language learners: A synthesis of research evidence* (pp. 176–222). New York, NY: Cambridge University Press.

Lipson, M. Y., & Wixson, K. K. (2013). *Assessment of reading and writing difficulties: An interactive approach, fifth edition.* Boston, MA: Pearson.

Lopez-Reyna, N. A. (1996). The importance of meaningful contexts in bilingual special education: Moving to whole language. *Learning Disabilities Research and Practice, 11,* 120–31.

MacGinitie, W. H., & MacGinitie, R. K. (1989). *Gates-MacGinitie Reading Tests.* Chicago, IL: Riverside.

Maldonado, J. A. (1994). Bilingual special education: Specific learning disabilities in language and reading. *Journal of Education Issues of Language Minority Students, 14,* 127–47.

Massey, D. D., & Heafner, T. L. (2004). Promoting reading comprehension in social studies. *Journal of Adolescent & Adult Literacy, 48,* 26–40.

McArthur, G., Hogben, J., Edwards, V., Heath, S., & Mengler, E. (2000). On the 'specifics' of specific reading disability and specific language impairment. *The Journal of Child Psychology and Psychiatry and Allied Disciplines, 4,* 869–74.

McIntosh, A. S., Graves, A., & Gersten, R. (2007). The effects of response to intervention on literacy development in multiple-language settings. *Learning Disability Quarterly, 30,* 197–212.

Miramontes, O. B., & Commins, N. L. (2014). Redefining literacy and literacy contexts: Discovering a community of learners. In E. H. Hiebert (Ed.), *Literacy for a diverse society: Perspectives, practices, and policies* (pp. 79–85). New York, NY: Teacher's College Press.

Miramontes, O. B., Nadeau, A., & Commins, N. L. (2011). *Restructuring schools for linguistic diversity: Linking decision making to effective programs, second edition.* New York, NY: Teachers College Press.

Moll, L., Amanti, C., Neff, D., & González, N. (1992). Funds of knowledge for teaching: Using a qualitative approach to connect homes and classrooms. *Theory into Practice, 31,* 132–41.

Myers, M. (2009). *Achievement of children identified with special needs in two-way Spanish immersion programs.* (Unpublished PhD thesis). Graduate School of Education and Human Development, George Washington University, Washington, DC.

Nagy, W. E., García, G. E., Durgunoğlu, A. Y., & Hancin-Bhatt, B. (1993). Spanish-English bilingual students' use of cognates in English reading. *Journal of Reading Behavior, 25,* 241–59.

Nagy, W. E. (2007). Metalinguistic awareness and the vocabulary-comprehension connection. In R. K. Wagner, A. E. Muse, & K. R. Tannenbaum (Eds.), *Vocabulary acquisition: Implications for reading comprehension* (pp. 52–77). New York, NY: Guilford Press.

National Academies of Sciences, Engineering, and Medicine. (2017). *Promoting the educational success of children and youth learning English: Promising futures.* Washington, DC: The National Academies Press.

National Center on Response to Intervention. (2010). Essential components of RtI–A closer look at RtI. Retrieved November 17 2017 from: http://www.rti4success.org/sites/default/files/rtiessentialcomponents_042710.pdf

Nieto, S. (1996). *Affirming diversity: The sociopolitical context of multicultural education, second edition.* New York, NY: Longman.

Nieto, S. (1999). *The light in their eyes: Creating multicultural learning communities.* New York, NY: Teachers College Press.

Nieto, S. (2003). *What keeps teachers going?* New York, NY: Teachers College Press.

Noddings, N. (1999). Response: Two concepts of caring. *Philosophy of Education Archive,* 36–9.

Ntelioglou. B. Y., Fannin, J., Montanera, M., & Cummins, J. (2014). A multilingual and multimodal approach to literacy teaching and learning in urban education: A collaborative inquiry project in an inner city elementary school. *Frontiers in Psychology, 5*(533), 1–10.

OECD. (2004). *Messages from PISA 2000.* Paris: Organisation for Economic Co-operation and Development.

OECD. (2010). *PISA 2009 results: Learning to learn–student engagement, strategies and practices, Volume III.* Paris: Organisation for Economic Co-operation and Development. Retrieved November 17 2017 from http://www.oecd.org/dataoecd/11/17/48852630.pdf

Ohashi, J. K., Mirenda, P., Marinova-Todd, S., Hambly, C., Fombonne, E., Szatmari, P., Bryson, S., Roberts, W., Smith, I., Vaillancourt, T., Volden, J., Waddell, C., Zwaigenbaum, L., Georgiades, S., Duku, E., Thompson, A., & the Pathways in ASD Study Team. (2012). Comparing early language development in monolingual- and bilingual-exposed young children with autism spectrum disorders. *Research in Autism Spectrum Disorders, 6,* 890–7.

Oliver, R., & Philp, J. (2014). *Focus on oral interaction.* Oxford: Oxford University Press.

Orosco, M. J. (2010). A sociocultural examination of response to intervention with Latino English language learners. *Theory into Practice, 49,* 265–72.

Orosco, M. J., & Klingner, J. (2010). One school's implementation of RTI with English language learners: 'Referring into RTI'. *Journal of Learning Disabilities, 43,* 269–88.

Orosco, M. J., & O'Connor, R. (2014). Culturally responsive instruction for English language learners with learning disabilities. *Journal of Learning Disabilities, 47*, 515–31.

Ortiz, A. A. (2001). *English language learners with special needs: Effective instructional strategies.* Washington, DC: ERIC Clearinghouse on Languages and Linguistics.

Ortiz, A. A., Robertson, P. M., Wilkinson, C. Y., Liu, Y., McGhee, B. D., & Kushner, M. I. (2011). The role of bilingual education teachers in preventing inappropriate referrals of ELLs to special education: Implications for Response to Intervention. *Bilingual Research Journal, 34*, 316–33.

Ortiz, A. A., & Wilkinson, C. Y. (1991). Assessment and intervention model for the bilingual exceptional student (AIM for the BESt). *Teacher Education and Special Education, 14*, 35–42.

Palincsar, A. S., & Brown, A. L. (1984). Reciprocal teaching of comprehension-fostering and comprehension-monitoring activities. *Cognition and Instruction, 1*, 117–75.

Paneque, O. M., & Rodriguez, D. (2009). Language use by bilingual special educators of English language learners with disabilities. *International Journal of Special Education, 24*, 63–9.

Paradis, J. (2010). Keynote article: The interface between bilingual development and specific language impairment. *Applied Psycholinguistics, 31*, 3–28.

Paradis, J., Crago, M., & Genesee, F. (2005/2006). Domain-general versus domain-specific accounts of specific language impairment: Evidence from bilingual children's acquisition of object pronouns. *Language Acquisition, 13*, 33–62.

Paradis, J., Crago, M., Genesee, F., & Rice, M. (2003). French-English bilingual children with SLI: How do they compare with their monolingual peers? *Journal of Speech, Language, and Hearing Research, 46*, 113–127. (Erratum: *Journal of Speech, Language, and Hearing Research, 46*, 404.)

Paradis, J., Genesee, F., & Crago, M. (2011). *Dual language development and disorders, second edition.* Baltimore, MD: Brookes Publishing.

Partanen, E., Kujala, T., Näätänen, R., Liitola, A., Sambeth, A., & Huotilainen, M. (2013). Learning-induced neural plasticity of speech processing before birth. *Proceedings National Academy Science, USA, 110*, 15145–50.

Pathways in Autism Spectrum Disorder. (n.d.). Retrieved November 17 2017 from http://www.asdpathways.ca/

Paul, R. (2007). *Language disorders from infancy to adolescence.* St. Louis, MO: Mosby Elsevier.

Perkins, M. R. (2005). Pragmatic ability and disability as emergent phenomena. *Clinical Linguistics and Phonetics, 19*, 367–78.

Perozzi, J. A., & Sánchez, M. L. C. (1992). The effect of instruction in L1 on receptive acquisition of L2 for bilingual children. *Language, Speech, and Hearing in Schools, 23*, 348–52.

Pesco, D., MacLeod, A. A., Kay-Raining Bird, E., Cleave, P., Trudeau, N., de Valenzuela, J. S., Cain, K., Marinova-Todd, S. H., Colozzo, P., Stahl, H., Segers, E., & Verhoeven, L. (2016). A multi-site review of policies affecting opportunities for children with developmental disabilities to become bilingual. *Journal of Communication Disorders, 63*, 15–31.

Petersen, J. M., Marinova-Todd, S. H., & Mirenda, P. (2012). Brief report: An exploratory study of lexical skills in bilingual children with autism spectrum disorder. *Journal of Autism and Developmental Disorders, 42*, 1499–503.

Peterson, C., & Seligman, M. E. P. (2004). *Character strengths and virtues: A handbook and classification.* Oxford: Oxford University Press.

Pham, G., & Kohnert, K. (2014). A longitudinal study of lexical development in children learning Vietnamese and English. *Child Development, 85*, 767–82.

Piaget, J. (1951). *The child's conception of the world (No. 213).* London: Routledge & Kegan Paul.

Pinnell, G. S., & Fountas, I. C. (2011). *Literacy beginnings: A prekindergarten handbook.* Portsmouth, NH: Heinemann.

Poulin-Dubois, D., Blaye, A., Coutya, J., & Bialystok, E. (2011). The effects of bilingualism on toddlers' executive functioning. *Journal of Experimental Child Psychology, 108*, 567–79.

Prelock, P. A., Hutchins, T., & Glascoe, F. P. (2008). Speech-language impairment: How to identify the most common and least diagnosed disability of childhood. *The Medscape Journal of Medicine, 10*, 136.

Prizant, B. M., & Fields-Meyer, T. (2015). *Uniquely human: A different way of seeing autism.* New York, NY: Simon & Schuster.

Restrepo, M. A., Morgan, G. P., & Thompson, M. S. (2013). The efficacy of a vocabulary intervention for dual-language learners with language impairment. *Journal of Speech, Language, and Hearing Research, 56,* 748–65.

Richards-Tutor, C., Baker, D. L., Gersten, R., Baker, S. K., & Smith, J. M. (2016). The effectiveness of reading interventions for English learners: A research synthesis. *Exceptional Children, 82,* 144–69.

Rolstad, K., Mahoney, K., & Glass, G. V. (2005). The big picture: A meta-analysis of program effectiveness research on English language learners. *Educational Policy, 19,* 572–94.

Rowe, M. B. (1986). Wait time: Slowing down may be a way of speeding up! *Journal of Teacher Education, 37,* 43–50.

Ruiz, N. T. (1995). The social construction of ability and disability: II. Optimal and at-risk lessons in a bilingual special education classroom. *Journal of Learning Disabilities, 28,* 491–502.

Ruiz, N. T. (2012). It's different with second language learners: Learning from 40 years of research. In C. Dudley-Marling & S. Michaels (Eds.), *High-expectation curricula: Helping all students succeed with powerful learning* (pp. 145–61). New York, NY: Teachers College Press.

Ruiz, N. T., García, E., & Figueroa, R. A. (1996). *The OLE curriculum guide.* Sacramento, CA: California State Bureau of Publications.

Ruiz, N. T., Vargas, E., & Beltrán, A. (2002). Becoming a reader and writer in a bilingual special education classroom. *Language Arts, 79,* 297–309.

Ruiz-de-Velasco, J., Fix, M., & Clewell, B. C. (2000). *Overlooked and underserved: Immigrant students in US secondary schools.* Washington, DC: The Urban Institute.

Sáenz, L. M., Fuchs, L. S., & Fuchs, D. (2005). Peer-assisted learning strategies for English language learners with learning disabilities. *Exceptional Children, 71,* 231–47.

Sánchez, B., Colón, Y., & Esparza, P. (2005). The role of sense of school belonging and gender in the academic adjustment of Latino adolescents. *Journal of Youth and Adolescence, 34,* 619–28.

Sánchez-López, C. (1999). Co-planning. (Unpublished data).

Sánchez-López, C. (2008). Classroom observation and teacher interview. (Unpublished data).

Sánchez-López, C. (2011). Teacher implementation and reflection. (Unpublished data).

Sánchez-López, C. (2013). Coaching session. (Unpublished data).

Sánchez-López, C., & Young, T. (2008, January). *Continuum of interventions for English language learners experiencing difficulties: An inquiry based problem solving framework.* Paper presented at Thirty-First Annual Statewide Conference for Teachers Serving Linguistically and Culturally Diverse Students, Oak Brook, IL.

Saunders, W., & Goldenberg, C. (1992, April). *Effects of instructional conversations on transitions students' concepts of 'friendship'. An experimental study.* Paper presented at the meeting of the American Education Research Association, San Francisco, CA.

Schecter, S. R., & Cummins, J. (2003). *Multilingual education in practice: Using diversity as a resource.* Portsmouth, NH: Heinemann.

Schleppegrell, M. (2004). *The language of schooling: A functional linguistics perspective.* Mahwah, NJ: Lawrence Erlbaum.

Schön, D. A. (1987). *Educating the reflective practitioner: Toward a new design for teaching and learning in the professions.* San Francisco, CA: Jossey-Bass.

Schonewise, E. A., & Klingner, J. K. (2012). Linguistic and cultural issues in developing disciplinary literacy for adolescent English language learners. *Topics in Language Disorders, 32,* 51–68.

Seligman, M. E. P. (2011). *Flourish: A visionary new understanding of happiness and well-being.* New York, NY: Free Press.

Seligman, M. E. P., Ernst, R. M., Gillham, J., Reivich, K., & Linkins, M. (2009). Positive education: Positive psychology and classroom interventions. *Oxford Review of Education, 35,* 293–311.

Seung, H., Diddiqi, S., & Elder, J. H. (2006). Intervention outcomes of a bilingual child with autism. *Journal of Medical Speech-Language Pathology, 14,* 53–63.

Sheng, L., Lu, Y., & Kan, P. F. (2011). Lexical development in Mandarin–English bilingual children. *Bilingualism: Language and Cognition, 14,* 579–87.

Short, D. J., & Fitzsimmons, S. (2007). *Double work. Challenges and solutions to acquiring language and academic literacy for adolescent English language learners. A report to Carnegie Corporation of New York.* New York, NY: Carnegie Corporation.

Shuell, T. J. (1986). Cognitive conceptions of learning. *Review of Educational Research, 56,* 411–36.

Silberman, S. (2015). *Neurotribes: The legacy of autism and the future of neurodiversity.* New York, NY: Penguin.

Simon-Cereijido, G., & Gutiérrez-Clellen, V. (2014). Bilingual education for all: Latino dual language learners with language disabilities. *International Journal of Bilingual Education and Bilingualism, 17,* 235–54.

Simon-Cereijido, G., Gutiérrez-Clellen, V. F., & Sweet, M. (2013). Predictors of growth or attrition of the first language in Latino children with specific language impairment. *Applied Psycholinguistics, 34,* 1219–43.

Slee, R. (2011). *The irregular school: Exclusion, schooling and inclusive education.* New York, NY: Taylor & Francis.

Smith, F. (1998). *The book of learning and forgetting.* New York, NY: Teachers College Press.

Snow, C. E., Burns, M. S., & Griffin, P. (Eds.). (1998). *Preventing reading difficulties in young children.* Washington, DC: National Academy Press.

Speidel, G. E. (1987). Language differences in the classroom: Two approaches for developing language skills in dialect-speaking children. In E. Oksaar (Ed.), *Sociocultural perspectives of language acquisition and multilingualism.* Tübingen: Gunter Narr.

Starling, J., Munro, N., Togher, L., & Arciuli, J. (2012). Training secondary school teachers in instructional language modification techniques to support adolescents with language impairment: A randomized controlled trial. *Language, Speech, and Hearing Services in Schools, 43,* 474–95.

Taboada Barber, A., Buehl, M. M., Kidd, J. K., Sturtevant, E. G., Richey Nuland, L., & Beck, J. (2015). Reading engagement in social studies: Exploring the role of a social studies literacy intervention on reading comprehension, reading self-efficacy, and engagement in middle school students with different language backgrounds. *Reading Psychology, 36,* 31–85.

Tharp, R. G. (1997). *From at-risk to excellence: Research, theory, and principles for practice, Research Report 1.* Berkeley, CA: University of California, Santa Cruz, The Center for Research on Education, Diversity and Excellence.

Tharp, R., & Gallimore, R. (1988). *Rousing minds to life: Teaching, learning, and schooling in social context.* Cambridge: Cambridge University Press.

Tharp, R., & Gallimore, R. (1991). *The instructional conversation: Teaching and learning in social activity, Research Report 2.* Santa Cruz, CA: The National Center for Research on Cultural Diversity and Second Language Learning, University of California.

Thomas, W. P., & Collier, V. P. (2002). *A national study of school effectiveness for language minority students' long-term academic achievement.* Center for Research on Education, Diversity, and Excellence. Retrieved November 17 2017 from http://www.crede.ucsc.edu/research/llaa/1.1_final.html

Thordardottir, E., Ellis Wesimer, S., & Smith, M. E. (1997). Vocabulary learning in bilingual and monolingual clinical intervention. *Child Language Teaching and Therapy, 13,* 215–27.

Toohey, K., Dagenais, D., & Schulze, E. (2012). Second language learners making videos in three contexts. *Language and Literacy, 14,* 75–96.

Trumbull, E., & Pacheco, M. (2005). *Leading with diversity: Cultural competencies for teacher preparation and professional development.* Providence, RI: The Education Alliance at Brown University.

Tsybina, I., & Eriks-Brophy, A. (2010). Bilingual dialogic book-reading intervention for preschoolers with slow expressive vocabulary development. *Journal of Communication Disorders. 43,* 538–56.

Uljarević, M., Katsos, N., Hudry, K., & Gibson, J. L. (2016). Practitioner review: Multilingualism and neurodevelopmental disorders–An overview of recent research and discussion of clinical implications. *Journal of Child Psychology and Psychiatry, 57,* 1205–17.

UNESCO. (1994). The Salamanca Statement and framework for action on special needs education. Paris: UNESCO.

Vacca, R. T., Vacca, J. A. L., & Mraz, M. E. (2005). *Content area reading: Literacy and learning across the curriculum.* Boston, MA: Allyn & Bacon.

Valencia, R. (2010). *Dismantling contemporary deficit thinking: Educational thought and practice.* New York, NY: Routledge.

Valicenti-McDermott, M., Tarshis, N., Schouls, M., Galdston, M., Hottinger, K., Seijo, R., Shulman, L., & Shinnar, S. (2012). Language differences between monolingual English and bilingual English–Spanish young children with autism spectrum disorders. *Journal of Child Neurology, 28*(7), 1–4.

Vaughn, S., Klingner, J. K., & Bryant, D. P. (2001). Collaborative strategic reading as a means to enhance peer-mediated instruction for reading comprehension and content-area learning. *Remedial and Special Education, 22,* 66–74.

Vaughn, S., Martinez, L. R., Linan-Thompson, S., Reutebuch, C. K., Carlson, C. D., & Francis, D. J. (2009). Enhancing social studies vocabulary and comprehension for seventh-grade English language learners: Findings from two experimental studies. *Journal of Research on Educational Effectiveness, 2,* 297–324.

Vygotsky, L. S. (1978). *Mind in society: The development of higher psychological processes.* Cambridge, MA: Harvard University Press.

Waitoller, F. R., & Artiles, A. J. (2013). A decade of professional development research for inclusive education: A critical review and notes for a research program. *Review of Educational Research, 83,* 319–56.

Waitoller, F. R., Artiles, A. J., & Cheney, D. A. (2010). The miner's canary: A review of overrepresentation research and explanations. *The Journal of Special Education, 44,* 29–49.

Weaver, C. (1998). Reconceptualizing reading and dyslexia. In C. Weaver (Ed.), *Practicing what we know. Informed reading instruction* (pp. 292–324). Urbana, IL: National Council of Teachers of English.

Wechsler, D. (2007). *Wechsler Individual Achievement Test, second edition, (WIAT–II). Australian standardised edition.* Marrickville: Harcourt.

Wells, G. (1986). *The meaning makers: Children learning language and using language to learn.* Portsmouth, NH: Heinemann.

Westby, C., & Watson, S. (2004). Perspectives on ADHD: Executive functions, working memory, and language disabilities. *Seminars in Speech & Language, 25,* 241–54.

Westernoff, F., Young, T., & Shimotakahara, J. (in press). The Kindergarten Early Language Intervention (KELI) program: Multiculturalism in action. *Journal of Interactional Research in Communication Disorders.*

Whitehurst, G. J., Falco, F. L., Lonigan, C. J., Fischel, J. E., DeBaryshe, B. D., & Valdez-Menchaca, M. C. (1988). Accelerating language development through picture book reading. *Developmental Psychology, 24,* 552–9.

WIDA Consortium. (2007). *WIDA English Language Proficiency Standards.* Madison, WI: Board of Regents of the University of Wisconsin System.

WIDA Consortium. (2012). *Amplification of the English language development standards, Kindergarten–Grade 12.* Madison, WI: Board of Regents of the University of Wisconsin System.

WIDA Consortium. (2013). *RtI²: Developing a culturally and linguistically responsive approach to response to instruction & intervention (RtI²) for English language learners.* Madison, WI: Board of Regents of the University of Wisconsin System.

Williams, D., Botting, N., & Boucher, J. (2008). Language in autism and specific language impairment: Where are the links? *Psychological Bulletin, 134,* 944–63.

Wong-Fillmore, L. (1991). When learning a second language means losing the first. *Early Childhood Research Quarterly, 6,* 323–46.

Wong-Fillmore, L. (2000). Loss of family languages: Should educators be concerned? *Theory into Practice, 39,* 203–10.

Wong-Fillmore, L., & Snow, C. E. (2000). *What teachers need to know about language.* Washington, DC: Center for Applied Linguistics.

World Health Organization. (2001). *ICF: International classification of functioning, disability and health.* Geneva: World Health Organization.

Ylvisaker, M., Hanks, R., & Johnson-Greene, D. (2002). Perspectives on rehabilitation of individuals with cognitive impairment after brain injury: Rationale for reconsideration of theoretical paradigms. *The Journal of Head Trauma Rehabilitation, 17,* 191–209.

Young, T. (2005). Classroom co-instruction. (Unpublished data).

Young, T. (2010). Classroom demonstration. (Unpublished data).

Young, T., & Sánchez-López, C. (2017). *An inquiry-based solution-seeking process to support English language learners within a Multi-Tiered System of Supports (MTSS): Collaborative practice.* Presentation at the Illinois Resource Center, Arlington Height, IL.

Young, T., & Westernoff, F. (1996). Overcoming barriers to effective parental partnerships: Implications for professionals in an educational setting. *The Journal of Educational Issues of Language Minority Concerns, 16,* 193–206.

Zehler, A. M., Fleischman, H. L., Hopstock, P. J., Pendzick, M. L., & Stephenson, T. G. (2003). *Descriptive study of services to LEP students and LEP students with disabilities: Findings on special education LEP students.* Washington, DC: US Department of Education, Office of English Language Acquisition.

Zetlin, A., Beltrán, D., Salcido, P., González, T., & Reyes, T. (2011). Building a pathway of optimal support for English language learners in special education. *Teacher Education and Special Education, 34,* 59–70.

Zheng, Y. (2005). *Exploring factors associated with ESL/ELD students' performance on the Ontario secondary school literacy test.* (Unpublished M.Ed. thesis). Queen's University, Kingston, Ontario.

Index

Page numbers annotated with 'g' refer to glossary entries.